CISTERCIAN STUDIES SERIES: NUMBER ONE HUNDRED TWENTY-SIX

Brian Patrick McGuire

The Difficult Saint

BERNARD OF CLAIRVAUX AND HIS TRADITION

CISTERCIAN STUDIES SERIES: NUMBER ONE HUNDRED TWENTY-SIX

The Difficult Saint

BERNARD OF CLAIRVAUX AND HIS TRADITION

by

Brian Patrick McGuire

Cistercian Publications
Kalamazoo, Michigan
1991

© Copyright, Brian Patrick McGuire, 1991
The work of Cistercian Publications is made possible in part
by support from Western Michigan University to
The Institute of Cistercian Studies

Available in Britain and Europe from Cassell/Mowbray plc
Villiers House   41/47 Strand   London   WC2N 5JE

Available in Canada through Meakin & Associates
Unit 17   81 Auriga Drive   Nepean, Ontairo   K2E 7Y5

Available elsewhere from
Cistercian Publications (Distribution)
St Joseph's Abbey   Spencer, MA 01562

Library of Congress Cataloguing in Publication Data

McGuire, Brian Patrick.
    The difficult saint   :   Bernard of Clairvaux and his tradition / by Brian
Patrick McGuire.
        p.   cm. — (Cistercian studies series)
        ISBN 0-87907-626-7 (hard). — ISBN 0-87907-726-3 (pbk.)
    1. Bernard, of Clairvaux, Saint, 1090 or 91-1153.   I. Title.   II. Series.
BX4700.B5M254   1991
    271' . 1202—dc20
[B]   91-12727
                                                                                                         CIP

Printed in the United States of America

To Sir Richard Southern

Table of Contents

Preface

This book is a collection of studies rather than a full-scale biography. To a large extent it reflects the unique combination of medieval and monastic studies found at Western Michigan University. In the winter and spring of 1989, I spent a delightful four and a half months at Kalamazoo as a visiting scholar at the Medieval Institute and the Institute of Cistercian Studies. In Michigan, after several years during which I had dedicated myself primarily to helping political asylum applicants in Denmark, I realized a long-standing desire to return to primary research on medieval topics.

With the resources of the Obrecht collection in the Institute of Cistercian Studies Library at my disposal, it was only natural for me to turn to the manner in which Bernard of Clairvaux was interpreted and used in the later Middle Ages. Once I had begun to consider fifteenth-century uses of Saint Bernard, however, I contemplated the possibility of a book on this most controversial and provocative of saints. Years before, in Oxford, my D.Phil. supervisor, Sir Richard Southern, had suggested to me that I write a biography of Bernard.

I had immediately rejected the idea, for I felt I could not write about someone whom I so intensely disliked.

In the course of the 1980s, however, I kept returning to Bernard and found his style, his actions, his heritage more and more attractive—or at least understandable. After I began attending the Medieval Congresses and Cistercian Conferences at Kalamazoo, it became almost inevitable that some of my research came to centre on Bernard.

This movement towards Bernard accelerated when I began to do research for my book on friendship and community in the monastic experience. Here, however, I found that I could best describe Bernard by keeping at a distance from him, by tracing the impact of his personality and activities in terms of other people, and the network of friends which became visible in the 1130s and 1140s. At Kalamazoo, and afterwards in Copenhagen, I continued to maintain this distance to Bernard by considering him in terms of the manner in which the image of Bernard changed in the later Middle Ages.

My point of departure has been the problem I had as a student, as a young researcher, and as a university teacher in appreciating the phenomenon of Bernard. I have assumed that the reader also approaches Bernard with some scepticism and reservations. It is only after many years of reading Latin that I can begin to trust that I understand something of Bernard's writings and at times feel at ease with them. It is only after years of fighting for what I consider to be a just cause, that of refugees from the Middle East in Denmark, that I can begin to understand why Bernard sometimes seemed one-sided and fanatical in his defence of causes. And it is only after getting to know modern cistercian men and women and talking with them about twelfth-century life and spirituality that I have begun to realize the value of Bernard's contribution to the ongoing history of christian institutions.

I cannot impose my own personal development on my readers, but I want to suggest that Bernard becomes more understandable as one grows older and gains more life experience. Bernard's life indicates that the process of aging does not necessarily bring with it disillusionment or cynicism, for in the context of a pragmatic and loving community, the individual can continue to grow and change. The romantic myth of limitless youth and disappointed old age has nothing to do with the man who after his political defeats of the 1140s withdrew to the monastery and lived, apparently happily, with his monks until his undramatic death in 1153.

The book begins with a general essay that is intended to provide the reader with an introduction to Bernard's life. I provide no chronological reviews, for these are already legion, as can be seen by the bibliographical note at the end of this first chapter. From there I approach Bernard in various ways as a friend and member of a community. In the fifth chapter, I turn to what I consider to be one of the most important and overlooked contributions of Bernard to christian spirituality and emotional life: his interpretation of the so-called 'grace of tears'.

The second half of the book leaves behind Bernard in his lifetime and considers the way Bernard—or the image of Bernard—grew after his death. These studies start with a revision of an article from *Cistercian Studies* that was written with modern Cistercians in mind and which tries to show how a more intimate view of Bernard becomes visible for us at Clairvaux in the 1170s. A further development in Bernard's *Nachleben* I have recently described at a Bernard conference held in October 1990 at the Herzog August Bibliothek in Wolfenbüttel: Bernard in James of Voragine's *Legenda Aurea*. The Wolfenbüttel congress showed the vitality of Bernard's writings and ideas in late medieval and early modern history.

I have added an epilogue on foundation myths, comparing the myth of origins at Cîteaux, to which Bernard contributed, with the myth of american origins, seen especially in a comparison with John Winthrop and Ronald Reagan. This highly untraditional ending to a book on a medieval topic may very well put the reader on guard and create the feeling that I am using Saint Bernard as a point of departure for my own political views. I cannot help indicating these, but the purpose of the epilogue is not *conversio* to any modern truth, but awareness of the way myths have fashioned not only our medieval brethren but also ourselves. The continuing debate about cistercian origins and ideals is paralleled by a much larger—and for the world at large, more important—debate about american origins and ideals.Almost all the chapters in this book were originally lectures that were given to cistercian audiences at monasteries across the United States. I am grateful to the monks and nuns of the american province of the Cistercians of the Strict Observance for all their responses, both favourable and critical. These have made it easier for me as an historian to include considerations about the modern situation of Cistercians and Americans.

Like so many other cistercian authors, I am greatly indebted to Dr. E. Rozanne Elder at the Cistercian Institute for all her advice—both scholarly and editorial—in my preparation of this book. For anyone who has worked with Cistercian Publications, Dr. Elder's blue pencil must be famous and notorious. Her comments are precise and clear. In my case she has rescued many an obscure passage and pointed out many a weak or unjustified assertion. Rozanne Elder took a collection of disparate articles and insisted on my making a coherent book out of them. She coaxed me into rewriting drastically several articles. I am grateful for the time and trouble she has spent on me and my versions of Saint Bernard.

In one area, however, Dr. Elder has allowed me to maintain a peculiarity: my use of british orthography. This I first developed in writing my D.Phil. thesis in Oxford, and although I now publish in America, I hope this audience will forgive me for not changing my custom.

The list of other friends at Kalamazoo is too long to include here, but I will name a few of those who helped along the process of creation: Beatrice Beech, the competent and ever-available librarian at the Institute of Cistercian Studies, who guided me through the Obrecht Collection; her husband George Beech, professor of history, whose home-grown wine in modest amounts inspired many an illuminating lunchtime conversation about our field; Otto Gründler, Director of the Medieval Institute, who helped in both practical and academic matters in making it possible for me and my family to come to Kalamazoo—and who provided needed guidance in the spirituality of the *Devotio Moderna*. Many of the Kalamazoo faculty opened their homes to me and my family and provided us with evenings of good food and rich conversation, convincing me that Kalamazoo is one of american academe's best-kept secrets: Clifford and Audrey Davidson, Bill and Marie Combs receive special thanks. Karen Jayazeri and Alice Duthie-Clark at Cistercian Publications also deserve mention, as well as my graduate student and first computer teacher Dan Le Corte, as well as other students at the Medieval Institute, especially Ulrike Strasser; the chair at the Department of History, Ernst Breisach; his successor, Ronald Davis; and the President of Western Michigan University, Diether Haenicke.

While at Kalamazoo, I was kindly received at the Medieval Institute at Notre Dame University. Here the Director, John Van Engen, gave me the privilege of working in an outstanding library. I am especially grateful to Professor Kent Emery for his guidance in approaching late medieval authors and their uses of Saint Bernard.

My ever-faithful guide in cistercian studies during the past years has been Father Chrysogonus Waddell at Gethsemani Abbey in Kentucky. His letters and conversations have been a source of inspiration, enlightenment and joy. Practically every article in this collection owes something to Father Chrysogonus, whose warmth, humour, care and insight have been invaluable to me and to numberless other scholars.

At the same time I owe a debt to my own University, Copenhagen, to its Institute of Greek and Latin Medieval Philology, to the Danish Research Council for the Humanities, and to the Fulbright Commission, for making it possible for me to be absent from Copenhagen for a semester, and to do research at Western Michigan University. I have had the perhaps unique privilege of being an american Fulbright scholar in Oxford in 1968–70 and then of returning to America in 1989 as a danish researcher with a Fulbright travel grant.

In looking back over the past twenty years and more, I realize how much I owe to Sir Richard Southern, who was the *primus motor* of this book. In the year of confusion, 1968, Sir Richard gave me the encouragement I needed to keep to the study of history. To Sir Richard, for all that he has been and continues to be, I dedicate this book.

B.P. McG.

The Medieval Centre, Copenhagen University
The Feast of All Souls, 1990

Abbreviations

AC   *Analecta Sacri Ordinis Cisterciensis* (Rome 1945–64). Since 1964, *Analecta Cisterciensia.*

CC CM   *Corpus Christianorum. Continuatio Mediaevalis.* Turnhout, 1971–.

CF   Cistercian Fathers series, Cistercian Publications 1969–.

CS   Cistercian Studies series, Cistercian Publications, 1969-. Not to be confused with the journal *Cistercian Studies*, edited at Gethsemani Abbey, Kentucky until 1990, now at New Clairvaux Abbey, Vina, California.

Cîteaux   *Commentarii Cistercienses*, formerly *Cîteaux in de Nederlanden*, Westmalle, then Achel, Belgium, now Cîteaux, France, since 1950.

Csi   Bernard of Clairvaux, *De Consideratione*

DM   *Dialogus Miraculorum*, ed. Joseph Strange 1–2. Cologne, 1851, reprinted Ridgewood, New Jersey, 1966.

15

EM   *Exordium Magnum Cisterciense*, ed. Bruno Griesser. Series Scriptorum Sacri Ordinis Cisterciensis 2. Rome, 1961.

Friendship *Friendship and Community: The Monastic Experience 350–1250*, CS 95, 1988.

James   Bruno Scott James, *The Letters of St. Bernard of Clairvaux*. London, Burns Oates, 1953.

KLNM   *Kulturhistorisk Leksikon for Nordisk Middelalder* 1–17. Copenhagen: Rosenkilde og Bagger, 1956–72.

LM   *Liber Miraculorum* of Herbert of Clairvaux, PL 185:1273–1384.

LVM   *Liber Visionum et Miraculorum*, ascribed to Prior John of Clairvaux, in MS Troyes 946.

PL   *Patrologia Latina*, ed. J. P. Migne. Paris 1844–.

R Ben.   *Revue Bénédictine*. Maredsous, Belgium, 1884–.

SBOp   *Sancti Bernardi Opera* 1–8 in 9 volumes, ed. Jean Leclercq, Henri Rochais, C.H. Talbot. Editiones Cistercienses. Rome, 1957–77.

SC   *Sources Chrétiennes*, Paris, 1942–.

V Mal   Bernard of Clairvaux. The Life of Malachy (*Vita Malachiae*).

VP   *Vita Prima*, the first Life of Bernard, compiled by Geoffrey of Auxerre, William of Saint Thierry, and Arnold of Bonnevaux, in PL 185:225–368.

1. The Difficult Saint

Bernard as a Person

Bernard of Clairvaux is not an easy person with whom to deal. We all know he dominated the second quarter of the twelfth century. Few modern historians have liked him. Bernard's dynamism and aggressiveness have repelled many observers, who will probably never entirely forgive him for the way he treated Peter Abelard. For those who take the trouble to read him, even in modern translation, Bernard is not easily approachable. His highly rhetorical style and his delight in echoing Scripture in almost every line make it difficult for us to concentrate on what the man is really saying. One can easily end up with two Bernards, the abbot who is forever lost to us in the silence of the cloister, and the ecclesiastical politician whose voice is almost too strident.

A nineteenth-century biography by the french historian Elphège Vacandard remains the best introduction to Bernard as a complete person, while the british historian Watkin Williams in the 1930s never quite succeeded in getting beyond a careful record of Bernard's movements through Europe. Recently the dutch historian Adriaan Bredero has given us a useful review of the past century's debates about

Bernard, and he has provided his own interpretation by pointing out that wherever Bernard went in the 1130s and 1140s, new monasteries were sure to appear. Bredero claims that the key to understanding Bernard's actions is his enthusiasm for spreading the Cistercian Order. Bernard's involvement in church politics must be seen in terms of his desire to found new houses. This explanation can take us a long way in interpreting Bernard's actions, but Bernard in his life as a whole manifested more than this drive for expansion. He did not always act in his own best interests and could confuse contemporary observers. We need to admit inner contradictions and inconsistencies in order to see Bernard as a very human person who came to be regarded as a saint.

Saints are not made in heaven. They participate in the same earthly limitations and frustrations familiar to anyone aware of self and society. As recently as the mid–1970s a good friend and mentor suggested I might write a biography of Bernard. I refused, because, as I immediately replied, 'I can't stand the man.' Since then, the privilege of growing older and of getting involved in the fates of other human beings has made Bernard much more understandable to me. When it came to defending the people whom he loved and wanted to protect, Bernard's lack of restraint may have been a necessary human reaction.

Bernard as a Complete Human Being

Many of us are wounded people, carrying around inside our deepest layers of consciousness unresolved childhood traumas. As we get older we sense ever more keenly an inability to heal these wounds. It is hard to imagine a person somehow growing up with no traumas. Yet this seems to have been the case for Bernard in the years between 1090 and 1113. Born into a family of the lower nobility, Bernard from the very start knew his place and opportunities. Even though William of Saint Thierry in the first book of Bernard's twelfth-century biography, the so-called *Vita Prima*, gives us

only fragments about Bernard's childhood, there is enough
material to indicate that his youth brought no great crises.

By William's account, as well as by everything else we can
glean about Bernard's early years, he loved both his father
and his mother dearly. They loved him and let him do what he
wanted and needed to do. He went to school and chose not
to become a soldier (VP I.3 = PL 185:228). There is no indication that he was revolted by war. When Bernard convinced
his warrior brothers and other fighters to become monks, he
did not condemn military life itself. In many ways he seems
to have approved of a class which was dedicated to war and
not to have distanced himself from it.

Bernard's identification with an aggressive class in an ex-
pansive era of western history may make it difficult for us, after a century of wars, which still continue in the Third World,
to sympathize with his social background and its values. It
would perhaps be more satisfying to discern in him a paci-
fist who hated war and ran away from his family to join the
monastery. But instead of criticizing the martial arts, Bernard
translated them into another context. He eventually brought
every member of his family with him into the monastery,
for he felt that the monastic life was so attractive that he
wanted to share it with family and friends. Here we find a per-
suasiveness that impressed contemporary observers. Bernard
could convince people because he was very sure of himself. He believed in himself and trusted his own impulses.
This self-confidence inspired confidence in the people who
knew him. They wanted to be with him, and he with them.
Bernard would chase friends all over the landscape in order to bring them back to the monastery with him. Bernard's
pursuit of Hugh of Vitry, probably a school companion, as
told in William, is probably only one of many manhunts in
Bernard's cistercian life (VP I.14 = PL 185:235).

In recent years historians have preferred to look at interesting disturbed personalities of the twelfth century rather
than at solid types like Bernard. In the 1970s, thanks to the
pioneering work of the american medievalist John Benton,

the best-known type of the medieval cleric was Guibert of Nogent. Benton retranslated Guibert's autobiography and did his best to psychoanalyse him. John Benton would have been among the first to acknowledge that his results were only preliminary and had to be limited by the literary pretensions of his sources. But Benton's work, indirectly given the great monastic historian Jean Leclercq's blessing in an important article in *Speculum*, made it easier for other medievalists, such as Lester Little in dealing with Peter Damian, to deal with personality. Clerical figures have been seen in terms of problems they may have had with their parents and traumas they suffered in acknowledging and coming to terms with their sexuality. In the decade of sexual liberation, it was natural to look at medieval church figures as sexually repressed and to ask what consequences this factor had on their behaviour.

But Bernard has been spared such conclusions. When in the 1970s Jean Leclercq at Rome analysed Bernard's writings with a battery of psychiatric experts, he concluded that distortions in Bernard's personality evident in the *Vita Prima* were not Bernard's at all. They were projections made by Bernard's first biographer, William of Saint Thierry, and pointed to William's aggressivity and psychic imbalance.

I find Dom Leclercq's conclusion misleading, for William in his very devotion and openness about his own feelings for Bernard lets us get close to the abbot of Clairvaux in a way other, more respectful biographers do not allow. But I would agree with Leclercq in seeing Bernard as a person who was in inner balance and harmony. This was in some degree due to the fact that he did not have to break away from home and family to become what he wanted to be, a monk in a contemplative community.

With Bernard we depart from what is often thought to be the model of a medieval saint's *Bildungsgeschichte*: a painful childhood, a growing awareness of sin, especially of the sexual kind, and then a process of conversion culminating in some religious awakening that changes one's life completely. This type of development is deeply rooted in descriptions of medieval saints because their biographers were usually aware of Saint Augustine's *Confessions*, which they read as a true autobiography and not as the extended prayer and sermon for friends that it actually is. Because Augustine had to go through hell to find God and cling to him, medieval writers, and their modern successors, have looked for similar stages in their subjects. Even Guibert of Nogent tried to pattern his autobiography on the *Confessions*. In our own time, Erik Erikson's *Young Man Luther*, written in 1958 and influential in the university upheavals of the 1960s in America, basically follows the augustinian pattern in discovering Luther.

Thanks to 'psycho-historians' such as Erik Erikson, the relatively new concept of the teenager and an overwhelming awareness of human sexual drives have strengthened the augustinian developmental model. It is expected that a young man or woman in finding a viable identity will go through a period of self-doubt and even agonizing search until the call comes which integrates his or her life and enables the self to love.

By no means would I question that such a process took place in the High Middle Ages or today. This model seems to describe the development experienced by Saint Anselm (1033–1109), who after the death of his mother broke with his father, left home and never returned. Such a pattern, however, has no apparent relevance to Bernard. His biography contains hagiographical clichés about how he avoided sexual temptations from eager women enamoured by his appearance (VP I.7 = PL 185:230–31), tales one can dismiss either as literary imitation of similar anecdotes about earlier saints or as confirmation that Bernard was attractive to women. Bernard's pointed refusals, however, do not indicate a turning point in his life but merely confirm what by then was obvious: Bernard was meant not for war or for women but for the service of God in a community of dedicated young men. Perhaps an industrious scholar will one day find sizeable skeletons in Bernard's closet, but I see none, only the tale of a boy who grew up in family surroundings where he was loved and could love in return.

Bernard as Spiritual Knight and Bard

Before Bernard arrived at Cîteaux with some thirty relatives and friends in 1113, he had lived together with them for a period of trial and testing at the family home (VP I.15 = PL 185:235). This first experiment with a common life indicates Bernard's special talent: he loved to be with his friends, and so it was only natural for him to see if a more durable community would work. The friendship group was casting about for a lasting commitment, and feelers were probably put out to several religious communities before Cîteaux was chosen.

Only a few years earlier, when Bernard was still a boy, members of his social class had departed on the First Crusade and had ended up conquering Jerusalem and founding a new if fragile christian state in Palestine. Bernard would have grown up with stories about these exploits, and there may have been a time in his life when he wanted to become a crusading knight. In choosing to become a monk, he did not give up fighting. The physical battle against Christ's enemies simply became a spiritual one.

The image of war with the devil is deeply engrained in early medieval christian thought. After our own century of hideous wars, however, it is essential for us to realize that the medieval knight looked upon fighting as a praiseworthy activity. Bernard and his contemporaries did not apologize to each other or to posterity for what they were. They were on God's side, fighting the good fight, and few had second thoughts about it. At the same time, however, some of these youths did not want to go around killing people, even if it was in a 'good cause'. They asked for something different in their lives, a fight that would enable them to band together permanently, a crusade that would continue in their own hearts and minds. As Bernard himself wrote concerning monks who left their monasteries to go on crusade, 'Why do they sew the sign of the cross on their clothes, when they always carry it on their hearts so long as they cherish their religious way life?' (Ep 544; SBOp 8:511).

How could so many young nobles feel attracted to such a spiritual ideal when they had such aggressive class instincts? Perhaps the answer lies in their schooling. Its exact content remains forever hidden to us, but youths trained in latin grammar and rhetoric would have been excited with the prospect of translating the impulses of their hearts into writing. It is hard for us, with our modern computers that perhaps too effortlessly convey every thought, to imagine what it must have been like to scratch out onto wax tablets in an acquired language the vocabulary of another world. Latin was the gateway to a world of fathomless riches, where physical delight and spiritual heights could meet.

According to one of his opponents, Bernard as a young scholar wrote erotic poetry. When we think of the intensity of his *Commentary on the Song of Songs*, in which Bernard used erotic images to convey spiritual meaning, this charge does not seem farfetched. Bernard in later life expressed much of his sensuality in a balanced latin style, and so it is conceivable that in youth he had put at least some of his energies into the praise of lovely girls. What emerges from his youth, however, is not the story of a frustrated poet who turned from Eve to Mary. So far as we can tell in the silences and in the hints that come from his later writings, Bernard turned easily from the praises of women to the celebration of a life in friendship seeking God. From his early twenties onwards, Bernard became a bard of friendship in monastic life.

This aspect of his personality needs more attention today. The political Bernard and the theological Bernard have become well-defined areas of study, independent of each other, while Bernard the bard of love integrated the areas of his life. Once monastic life in friendship became his central concern, Bernard would do practically anything to sing its praises or to negotiate for its success. To express this transition in psychological terms, Bernard replaced the drive of a young man for sexual union with an insistence that friendship within the cloister provided the surest route to the spiritual union he preferred.

A virtually unknown factor in this development is Bernard's relationship with the abbot at Cîteaux when Bernard arrived there in 1113, Stephen Harding. In recent years, especially in the work of Jean-Baptiste Auberger, the approaches of Stephen and of Bernard to the monastic life have been contrasted. Stephen wanted stricter adherence to the Rule of Saint Benedict, while Bernard sought perfection itself. I am aware of the careful review of the difficult and confusing early texts of Cîteaux which lies behind this view, but I would still point out that no matter what differences of nuance there may have been, the two men seem to have respected each other and to have made good use of each other. Stephen appreciated Bernard's talents sufficiently to send him out to form a daughter house at Clairvaux in 1115, less than three years after his entrance. Modern cistercians have sometimes suggested to me that Stephen sent Bernard away so quickly because he could not stand having him around! But Stephen treated Bernard in the same way as Bernard dealt with favoured and trusted monks at Clairvaux. The best ones he sent off to make new foundations, however painful it was to say goodbye to friends.

Bernard as a Sensible Abbot

Certain hagiographical anecdotes about Bernard keep appearing in modern treatments and make him look like a hardened fanatic. There is the story about how when he was in the novice quarters he never noticed the ceiling of the room (VP I.20 = PL 185:238). Despite regular visits to the church, he did not know whether its clerestory in the chancel had one or three windows. We also hear how, as abbot, he travelled along Lake Geneva for an entire day but never once realised he was going past a body of water (VP III.4 = PL 185:306). William of Saint Thierry was sufficiently aware of

Bernard's early fanaticism to point out how the abbot's body revolted at the treatment he gave it, and how his friends insisted that he take better care of himself. The description of Bernard's inability to keep food down indicates that in his youthful enthusiasm for the new cause he may have ruined his digestion. In any case, such anecdotes do not play well in the late-twentieth century, even with our understanding of 'holy anorexia'. Bernard can be seen here as a compulsive personality, locked into his own regime of asceticism.

But such a view distorts the fuller picture that William of Saint Thierry offers us. Bernard modified his regime of self-discipline and eventually accepted separate quarters and a milder diet (VP I.32 = PL 185:246). There are several hints that Bernard also softened the monks' routine because he felt it was too harsh (VP I.20 and 38 = PL 185:238,249). Bernard fought hard for his goals but also adjusted them when his efforts overstrained his own body or the lives of those whom he loved. There was a streak of fanaticism in Bernard, but one modified by an awareness of his own needs and those of his companions.

One area where Bernard would not compromise was that of friendship. He insisted on having his friends with him, often on his own conditions, as William found out when Bernard convinced him to visit Clairvaux during a bout of illness. When William decided he was better and could leave Clairvaux, Bernard managed to talk him into a relapse to get him to remain with him (VP I.59 = PL 185:259). Bernard's need for William was something William could accept. William himself was not always an easy friend to have. He insisted on becoming a cistercian against Bernard's advice and once complained to Bernard that the latter did not love him as much as he, William, loved Bernard (Ep 85; SBOp 7:220). But the abbot of Clairvaux was willing to put up with a lot from his friends. In turn he asked a lot from them.

Perhaps one of the best examples of Bernard's sensitivity to his friends is hinted at in a letter he wrote to Aelred of Rievaulx (Ep 523; SBOp 8:486–89). This letter, which the great historian of monastic spirituality André Wilmart in 1933 identified as Bernard's work, has now found its rightful place as a preface to Aelred's *Mirror of Charity*. Here Bernard encouraged Aelred to write a work on love and its manifestations in monastic life, despite Aelred's insistence that he was better at looking after kitchens than at composing theological treatises. Aelred's protest and Bernard's response recreate for us what may have transpired between them at Clairvaux in the 1130s when they first met, in connection with a mission Aelred had undertaken to Rome. Bernard recognized in Aelred a talented, articulate teacher who knew how to communicate personal experience to young monks in a way that spoke to them directly. He saw in Aelred a writer who would be able to craft a disciplined work in which he could convey the experience of love as lived in a monastic community. In the early decades of cistercian life, Bernard selected a younger colleague to express in theological language the content of this new form of monasticism.

By assigning Aelred to the task, Bernard encouraged a talented young man who might otherwise have been hesitant to write down his thoughts and teachings. Aelred's protests were, of course, also in accord with literary practice and medieval authors' insistence that they were incapable of carrying out the task set for them by their superior or friends. Yet Bernard's letter to Aelred shows that he knew Aelred in a way we today can recognize: as an able, solid writer who could convey his thoughts easily and directly to an audience versed in the language of monastic spirituality.

Bernard manifested the same ability to direct his friends' abilities and talents in dealing with Malachy, the archbishop of Armagh, whose biography (as we shall see in a later chapter) he wrote as a tribute to their bond. Bernard wrote little of his personal relationship with Malachy, but he cultivated the man in life and in death because he saw him as an exponent both of church reform and of cistercian monasticism in Ireland. Bernard listened to Malachy as a man after his own heart, a fighter who could make a difference in his surroundings.

At critical moments Bernard showed sensitivity to those around him. There is, for example, the story of how one day, when he was preaching to the monks in chapter, he realized that most of them were looking quite downcast and discouraged. He then gave them what is called a *magnificum verbum*, a wonderful saying, promising that if his monks remained in the Cistercian Order and died in its habit, they would all be saved. Even Judas, he assured them, if he had become a Cistercian, would have been able to gain salvation! (EM II.4)

Bernard's confidence in the cistercian way can seem chauvinistic, but when put into context, the anecdote points to Bernard's awareness of his monks. He preached penance and asceticism, but he knew he was dealing with people who could get depressed and feel everything was too difficult. Such a frank story, not surprisingly, was not included in the more public documents that made up the biography of Bernard used to further the process of canonization. The tale first appeared in the more internal literature of the monks at Clairvaux, for their own edification, before it was incorporated at the end of the twelfth century into the great record of early cistercian life, the *Exordium Magnum Cisterciense*.

Bernard as an Absent Abbot

Stories collected about Bernard of Clairvaux after his death and at the time of his canonization, but not included in the canonization dossier, indicate that his monks sometimes felt he had spent too much time away from them. From the early 1130s until the late 1140s, Bernard was more often away from Clairvaux than present. It may have been hard for the monks to accept all his travels. Bernard acknowledged such a sense of loss at Clairvaux by telling the monks in chapter a story (EM II.11). He had just returned from three years in Italy healing a papal schism. He assured the monks he had returned to the monastery in spirit once a year to inspect it and make sure that everything was being done properly. After making this annual visitation, his spirit returned to Italy. In another story, he was seen to have entered the novices' cell to comfort one of them who missed him greatly, probably his later secretary Geoffrey of Auxerre (EM II.12). No direct criticism comes out in such stories, only a hint that it was not easy for his monks to accept his long absences.

Another story that may indicate how Bernard communicated himself to the Clairvaux monks is one that has become familiar through the iconography of the Order. A monk of Clairvaux once saw Bernard alone in prayer in the church. The image of Jesus on the cross embraced the abbot (EM II.7). This moment of almost sensual union points to Bernard's emphasis on the humanity of Christ, an aspect of Bernard's message that became ever more important in the later Middle Ages. But the story also points to the Clairvaux monks' curiosity about Bernard's closeness to the Lord. In its voyeurism, the anecdote implies that it was important for the monks of Clairvaux to get hold of their abbot as he really was, rather than by hearing about him in terms of his exploits all over Europe. Bernard spoke of his interior life readily in his sermons to the monks in chapter, but the monks felt a need to grasp the Bernard for whom Christ had reached out.

Just as monks needed to see Bernard, they needed to know that he, in life as well as in death, was watching them. This concern explains for me a familiar monastic story of Bernard's vision at Clairvaux in which he saw angels going from one monk to another to write down the words they sang (EM II.3). Some of the monks sang so well that their words were recorded in golden letters. Others merited inscriptions in silver, while some who were sleepy and did not try very hard had their words copied in ink. Those who made no effort and even let sleep overcome them had their words written in water. Such an edificatory story or *exemplum* gained popularity in monastic circles, for it touched on the daily problem of keeping attentive in choir. But Bernard is at the centre of the story. He is seen as being at home with his monks at Clairvaux, watching them and witnessing the strains of their everyday lives. The monks needed to know that Bernard was there, that he cared, and that he provided an assurance of their prayers' efficacy.

In such stories we find at least a hint of how possessively the community at Clairvaux responded to Bernard. The monks knew that he had been offered many bishoprics but had refused them all (VP I.69 = PL 185:265). One of the reasons may, in fact, have been that the monks would not have let him go. Bernard may also have thought that as abbot of Clairvaux he could exercise more influence on the church than he could from a single see. At the same time, however, Bernard identified closely with his community and seems genuinely to have wanted to stay at Clairvaux.

Bernard would go anywhere and do practically anything to spread the word of the blessings of monastic life. This could be his ultimate defence for his many absences from Clairvaux. What was good for some men had to be good and available for others, and so he had to leave Clairvaux to make new Valleys of Light wherever his duties in the church took him.

Bernard can be seen as fulfilling the pauline formula concerning the follower of Christ who becomes all things to all persons in order to save all (I Cor 9:22). He would do practically anything to bring someone into the Cistercian Order, even convincing the Count of Champagne to cut down a thief about to be hung and have him turned over to Clairvaux in order to secure for the condemned man a far harsher punishment as a monk (EM II.15). One wonders who this thief was and if he came from an aristocratic background or if he was a peasant. Whatever his origins, Bernard wanted him and would become his father and prison warden in a punishment that would last much longer than that of hanging. Thereby the thief would be able to repent of his sins and gain salvation, so the death of the cloister, in the christian paradox, brought life to a man twice condemned to death.

Bernard's treatment of the thief sums up his passion for recruitment to the monastery. But Bernard's action would have been impossible had it not been for his friendship with Thibaut, count of Champagne, who commuted the sentence he was about to carry out only because he knew and trusted Bernard. Unorthodox behaviour in Bernard was acceptable to his contemporaries because he knew how to ally himself in friendships with both laymen and clerics who would back him up.

Bernard's absences from Clairvaux, however vexing for the monks, apparently did not create divisions at the monastery. Although we must concede that medieval cistercian chroniclers papered over their houses' embarrassments by selectivity with sources, it still looks as though Clairvaux experienced no reaction against Bernard after his death. The memory of Bernard of Clairvaux did not divide the monks into factions. There arose no dispute over which group laid claim to the correct interpretation of Bernard's life and teachings.

We are perhaps more familiar with saints like Francis of Assisi, who left behind a legacy of controversy. Clairvaux and the Cistercians of the twelfth and thirteenth centuries were fortunate that they experienced no disputes over what Bernard meant to them. However strident his voice became in the extra-claustral politics of his day, Bernard always returned to his beloved Clarevallians, as they are called in some of the sources of the later twelfth century. The Clairvaux line never separated itself from the rest of the Order, despite its spectacular success in founding new monasteries (VP V.15). Bernard in his life and after his death, despite his many absences from Clairvaux, remained a rallying point for monastic unity.

Bernard as a Friend of Men, not Women

Bernard loved having friends around him, especially in the monastery. Yet it could not have been easy to be Bernard's friend, as the monk Nicholas of Montièramey found when he became his secretary. He shared confidences with the master but also had a heavy workload that finally led to a dramatic parting of the ways. But before the break everything was sweet. When a letter would come from the abbot of Cluny and a mutual friend Peter the Venerable, Bernard delighted in going aside with Nicholas in the closest thing twelfth-century monasticism could offer to a moment of privacy in community. The two friends could not wait to share the letter from their mutual friend. Even though its contents soon would become public knowledge in the monastery, the letter was still primarily intended for Bernard and Nicholas.

Bernard needed his friends, not only so that they could take care of his practical needs, but also so that he could share his feelings with them. This helps explain why Bernard wept so bitterly at the death of his brother, who had been cellarer at Clairvaux (SC 26:3–14; SBOp 1:171–81). Bernard knew he would sorely miss a central administrator and handyman, but he also would miss the brother and friend with whom he had shared so much of himself.

In one area, however, I do not see Bernard as a friend: in his dealings with women. Like Anselm, Bernard could be courtly and even responsive to women. He knew that he had to pay attention to them if he was to get their sons into his monasteries, or if he was going to make new foundations. But there is little evidence for any affectionate bonds between Bernard and individual women. He saw to it that a house for women was established so that wives would have a place to go when their husbands joined Bernard's monastery (VP I.19 = PL 185:237). Only at the insistence of his brothers did Bernard go out to speak with his sister when she came to visit him (VP I.30 = PL 185:244). We find none of the moments of affection that characterized Bernard's involvements with men. Today Bernard is especially remembered for corresponding with Hildegard of Bingen, whose visions and learning attract ever more attention. But the correspondence between them is stiff and formal, hardly an indication of the warmth of spiritual friendship that later would become visible when cistercian life formally opened itself to women.

The versatile Jean Leclercq has given much-needed attention to the subject of Bernard and women. I can only assent to his view that Bernard was not anti-female. In his sermons and in some of his letters, Bernard showed an appreciation of women that indicates medieval churchmen were not necessarily misogynous. I would add, however, that though Bernard was not anti-woman, he was generally a-woman, for in his noble military world, as in the cloister, women were not important to him. Since his emotional bonds were with other men, Bernard had no room in himself for spiritual friendship with women.

We must imagine a culture where women were very subordinate, where men believed that they made all the important decisions (despite what the reality may have been), and where it seemed quite natural for men to live without women. In such a context, women were distant, either patrons (whether noblewomen or the Blessed Virgin) or threats (women who opposed new cistercian foundations on their lands or women who 'seduced' men from the monastery).

Without being homosexual, Bernard enjoyed living in an all-male world and found more than sufficient emotional sustenance in his bonds with other men. It would be fascinating if we had an account of a visit by Bernard to the home of some noble family in Champagne, so we could see how he treated the lady of the castle. But it is no accident that the descriptions of Bernard's life do not bother with such details: his meetings with representatives of secular culture were considered important only in so far as they enhanced his monastic way of life.

As a youth and later on, during his many journeys, Bernard probably heard the singing of the trouvères and recognized in their themes secular versions of his own spiritual theme of love. Recent work on the twelfth century, with Jean Leclercq again in the lead, has placed Bernard in the context of this lay world, in opposition to Etienne Gilson's contention that

Bernard and courtly love could have nothing to do with each other. I am inclined to follow Gilson in thinking that there were no direct connections between court singers and Bernard's *Commentary on the Song of Songs*. One can always assert that practically everyone who had a little learning in the period talked, wrote and even sang of love. But Bernard's loves were so circumscribed and so male-oriented that they eliminated even interest in what we call courtly love. In our search for total history and an interdisciplinary approach, it would be wrong to enmesh Bernard in the poetry of a world which in fact he wanted to transform according to his own vision with the monastery at its centre, a place where women had no role to play.

Bernard as a Follower of Friends

Bernard's attack on Abelard's and Gilbert of Poitiers' theology, as well as his preaching of the Second Crusade, are fair game for any biographer who wants to emphasize the man's divisiveness and aggressiveness. There is no reason to minimize the degree of Bernard's involvement here. Once Bernard made up his mind to pursue a course of action, he followed it with a determination that allowed no compromise. Bernard can rightly be seen as a spiritual knight riding out to meet the enemies of the church. It was his preaching which galvanized an uncertain opposition to Abelard and persuaded reluctant knights into taking the cross.

It was not always, however, Bernard himself who took the initiative. His friends often encouraged him to act. They knew that if Bernard involved himself, they would get results. It was William of Saint Thierry who warned Bernard about the threat to orthodox trinitarian theology in Abelard (Ep 327; SBOp 8:263). William, not Bernard, was *primus motor* in the campaign that followed. I intend by no means to 'exonerate' Bernard from his role in attacking new forms of theology. Solidly anchored as he was in the theology of scriptural exegesis, he must have had little sympathy with Abelard's more abstract classifications and comparisons of authorities on both sides of a question.

Bernard was not looking for a fight. He was not a church-man who sent agents everywhere to ferret out heresy. Nor was he an inquisitor *avant le mot*, ready to trap anyone who crossed his path. Bernard, like his much-maligned cister-cian successor in the fourteenth century, Jacques Fournier, had a firm belief in the necessity of doing his job correctly. Unlike Jacques, he was not very thorough, and the proceed-ings against Abelard were both superficial and summary. But the campaign was not Bernard's invention. In attack-ing Abelard, Bernard was being loyal to friends whom he respected.

Such an old boys' (or new boys') network is hardly sympa-thetic in a world which at least claims to believe in democra-tizing decision-making. But in the twelfth century the church was run through webs of personal contact. This was not ab-solutism, but a consensus which could shift gradually but could not make room for a teacher as brash and provocative as Abelard. Bernard pursued him not because he wanted his blood but because friends like William told him it was his duty to christian orthodoxy to bring Abelard to heel.

I am not trying to weaken my own description of an ag-gressive, energetic Bernard by claiming that he was a passive follower of other men's decisions for him. Bernard made his own choices and carried them out in his own manner. But he could be influenced by his friends precisely because they were friends, people for whom he cared and whom he re-spected. When they convinced Bernard to preach the Second Crusade, he put his reputation very much on the line. For the first time in his life, he got involved in a losing project. When he tried to explain the defeat in his treatise *On Con-sideration* to the cistercian pope, Eugenius, Bernard did not accuse his friends of misleading him (Csi II.2–3; SBOp 3:411–12). Bernard kept to the standard medieval explanation: the sins of the crusaders themselves that made it impossible for God to give them victory. Between the lines we can see his frustration, even his bitterness, but Bernard did not turn his regret or anger against those who had involved him.

Bernard's loyalty to his friends required loyalty in return. This attitude helps explain Bernard's 'orders' to Pope Eugenius, instructions which Eugenius often disregarded. Since the pope had been formed as a cistercian, Bernard could play with the father-son role and make the father pope into a cistercian son. Bernard would have been the first to point out that he was only the humble abbot of Clairvaux. But Eugenius was one of his friends, and Bernard expected him, as a friend, to take his views into consideration. One trusts one's friends for the advice they give. So it was appropriate for Bernard to give advice to a pope when the pope was his own cistercian friend. In spite of political upsets and disagreements, the bond between Bernard and Eugenius continued until their deaths in 1153.

Bernard as an Aristocrat for All People

Umberto Eco, the author of the skilful and popular medieval gothic novel of the 1980s, *The Name of the Rose*, apparently once conceded that his model for the scoundrel of his murder mystery was Bernard of Clairvaux. If this is true, Eco associated himself with those who still think of Bernard as some dark reactive force trying to turn back the clock and fighting new impulses of logic and rational thinking in twelfth-century theology. In my view Bernard has many faces, some of them congenial and even loving, some of them aggressive and even vindictive, but behind all these *personae* I find an aristocrat of social standing and spiritual bearing whose very security in his own identity made him enormously attractive to his contemporaries.

Descriptions of Bernard on the road in Germany in the 1140s, for example, provide several eyewitness accounts of his miracles. Here it is apparent that his reputation had reached the peasants and town dwellers who sought him out in order to obtain cures or witness miracles. Bernard was known as a potent man of God, whose *virtus* could be activated for their benefit. Almost every medieval saint could attract people who hoped for miracles, but Bernard, in the near-hysteria around him, expresses such power at its zenith.

After Bernard's death, pilgrims came to Clairvaux to get near the sacred relics. The monastery was besieged by spiritual 'fortune hunters' until the abbot of Cîteaux arrived and ordered Bernard from his new home in the next world to stop the miracles. According to the *Exordium Magnum* (II.20), the flow ceased at once, except for those cures beneficial to members of the Cistercian Order! Cistercian apartness from the world was preserved, but Bernard's special attractiveness to other men is also emphasized in this story. Despite his insistence on locating himself in an exclusively monastic world, Bernard became known and celebrated among lay people of all backgrounds.

How is it that Bernard could have been so attractive to his contemporaries, the same Bernard whom many observers in the last century have found difficult to accept? Bernard appealed to others as a man of noble blood who was close to his origins. His stratum of society was just coming into its own, and the members of the lower nobility had confidence in their rights and privileges. Bernard grew up on the land and stayed on the land. He took the land holdings of his father into the monastery and later expanded them greatly. He wanted to remain independent of material possessions and concerns, but he almost instinctively made sure that his new territory was protected by lands that the monks could cultivate and use to provide a material basis for their daily lives.

This natural ease with origins and acquisitiveness contrasts sharply with the situation of an earlier generation from another part of Europe. If R. W. Southern is right, Anselm of Aosta, later of Bec and Canterbury, grew up in a family from the lower aristocracy which was on its way down the social ladder. He abandoned this legacy after the death of his mother and after a long period of tension with his father. Anselm belonged to a privileged family which was in decline.

Later in life, he did his best to maintain a distance from his social and familial background. In Anselm a trauma led to a break, while in Bernard there was a transition that emphasized and asserted his identity. As an aristocrat secure in his own class, Bernard developed into a man of spiritual power. Anselm was terrified of losing a single cow or piece of land when he was archbishop of Canterbury and felt responsible to God for everything under him. Bernard accepted as a fact of life Clairvaux with its lands, cows and all, and he did not fret about them. He had been born into all this and rejoiced in transforming his rightful legacy into God's valley of light.

Bernard: An Approachable Saint?

I do not think it is possible, at least in our time, to make Bernard into an easy saint. His personality and life experience are too full of fire for us to draw close to him without hesitation. At the same time, however, Bernard cannot be dismissed as a stubborn and narrow-minded fanatic who had no room in himself for anything except his cause, whether this were doctrinal orthodoxy or the spread of the Cistercian Order.

Bernard belongs among the saints not because he was likeable but because he made a difference to his generation. Wherever we meet him, we find him upsetting people, even offending them, for he refused to accept the *status quo* and argued for something more perfect and more in harmony with what he saw as God's plan. In Peter the Venerable's letters to Bernard, one can see how the abbot of Cluny had to bend over backwards to appease and mollify this potential volcano of self-righteousness. Peter emerges as a consummate diplomat. We can ask why he bothered. Cluny did not need Cîteaux in order to flourish in the twelfth century. Peter wanted to win Bernard's friendship and sympathy not only because Bernard could be a political ally but also because he found in him a kindred spirit in the continuing reform of monastic life.

Peter the Venerable's attention to Bernard points out that Bernard was an exceptional personality, a man of God who had a sharp temper and an enormous capacity for loving. Bernard will have to remain for us what he probably also was for Peter: a mysterious combination of affection and hostility, a tireless ally, an unpredictable opponent. One can rightly ask whether Bernard's activities in God's name were anything more than Bernard's self-aggrandizement. It could be claimed that in spreading the Order he was simply magnifying his own ego. But the question returns: how could such a person have taken up so many causes in no way destined to contribute to the success of the Cistercian Order? How could he have written so many letters in which he expressed great affection, loyalty and concern for his friends?

The easiest explanation would be the cynical one that Bernard did it all for himself. But when we see him going aside with friends at Clairvaux, or preaching in the chapter room, or when we meet the disciplined, soaring passages of his prose, I can only conclude that none of us will ever finish with him. As with Anselm, Francis, or Jesus himself, Bernard remains an enigma, an object of love and a focus for hostility.

Bibliographical Note

Major studies on Bernard include Elphège Vacandard, Vie de Saint Bernard, Paris, 1895; Watkin Williams, Saint Bernard of Clairvaux, Manchester University Press, 1935, supplemented by New Monastic Studies, MUP, 1935; Jean Leclercq, Bernard of Clairvaux and the Cistercian Spirit, CS 16, Kalamazoo, 1976, a translation of Saint Bernard et l'esprit cistercien, Paris, 1966. Leclercq's fullest work on Bernard is contained in his Recueil d'études sur Saint Bernard et le texte de ses écrits 1–3, Editiones Cistercienses, Rome, 1953. His psycho-historical study of Saint Bernard, Nouveau visage de Bernard de Clairvaux, Paris, 1976, has been published as A Second Look at Saint Bernard, CS 105, 1990.

Still much used is Ailbe John Luddy OCSO, Life and Teaching of Saint Bernard, Dublin, 1950. Also Thomas Merton, The

Last of the Fathers. Saint Bernard of Clairvaux and the Encyclical Letter, 'Doctor Melifluus', New York, 1954. The australian cistercian Michael Casey's *Athirst for God: Spiritual Desire in Bernard of Clairvaux's Sermons on the Song of Songs*, CS 77, 1988, is not a biography but provides many fresh insights into this central work by Bernard. Michael Casey is working on a new biography of Bernard.

For Adriaan Bredero's work, two articles are invaluable, 'Saint Bernard and the Historians' and 'The Canonization of Bernard of Clairvaux', in *Saint Bernard of Clairvaux. Studies Commemorating the Eighth Centenary of his Canonization*, CS 28 ed. M. Basil Pennington, 1977, 27–62 and 63–101. Also 'The Conflicting Interpretations of the Relevance of Bernard of Clairvaux to the History of his own Time', *Cîteaux. Commentarii Cistercienses* 31 (1980) 53–81. In connection with the 900th anniversary of the birth of Bernard in 1990 Bredero presented new work on the tradition of the *Vita Prima* at congresses held at Himmerod, Lyon, Rome and Wolfenbüttel. The publications of these meetings will cast new light on the difficult saint. The proceedings of the Cistercian Conference at Kalamazoo in 1990, edited by John Sommerfeldt and forthcoming in Cistercian Publications, will also be of great interest.

The *Vita Prima* is available in a preliminary english translation from 1990 in two volumes by Martinus Cawley (Guadalupe Translations, PO Box 97, Lafayette, Oregon 97127). Otherwise it is best to turn to J.P. Migne, *Patrologia latina* vol. 185. It is in the early chapters of Book I of the VP that I find the most relevant information (col. 227–35). Bernard's writings are now available in the *Opera Sancti Bernardi* 1–8, edd. Jean Leclercq, Henri Rochais and C.H. Talbot, Editiones Cistercienses, Rome, 1957–77. The *Letters of Saint Bernard* were translated by Bruno Scott James, Chicago, 1953. I have used this edition in quoting from Bernard's letter on monks and crusading, p 469 in James. (See also James' attractive *Saint Bernard of Clairvaux: An Essay in Biography*, London, 1957). For english translations of Bernard's other writings, the Cistercian Fathers series from Kalamazoo is fairly complete.

Further studies on Bernard include: *The Chimaera of his Age. Studies on Bernard of Clairvaux*, CS 63, ed. E. Rozanne Elder, 1980 and, for the traditions surrounding the saint, Jacques Berlioz, *Saint Bernard en Bourgogne: Lieux et mémoire*, Les éditions du bien public, Paris, 1990. For Bernard and women, Jean Leclercq, *La femme et les femmes dans l'oeuvre de saint Bernard*, Paris, 1983, now available as *Women and Saint Bernard of Clairvaux*, CS 104, 1990. G.R. Evans, *The Mind of Saint Bernard of Clairvaux*, Cambridge, 1983, has not replaced the classic study by Etienne Gilson, *La théologie mystique de Saint Bernard*, trans. as *The Mystical Theology of Saint Bernard*, 1940 and 1990.

Bibliographies of work on Bernard are available as *Bibliographie bernardine* 1891–1957, ed. Jean de la Croix Bouton, Paris, 1958, and *Bibliographie bernardine* 1957–70, Documentation cistercienne 6, ed. Eugene Manning, Rochefort, 1972.

John Benton, *Self and Society in Medieval France: The Memoirs of Abbot Guibert of Nogent*, New York, 1970, was reissued in the Medieval Academy Reprints for Teaching, 15, University of Toronto Press, 1985. Leclercq's article, 'Modern Psychology and the Interpretation of Medieval Texts', is in *Speculum* 48 (1973) 476–90. Leclercq's work here should be seen in the context of his *Monks and Love in Twelfth-century France: Psycho-historical Essays*, Oxford: Clarendon Press, 1979. See also Lester Little, 'The Personal Development of Peter Damian', *Order and Innovation in the Middle Ages. Essays in Honor of Joseph R. Strayer*, ed. William C. Jordan *et alii*, Princeton, 1976, 317–41.

For my remarks on Augustine I am indebted to Peter Brown for his classic *Augustine of Hippo: A Biography*, London: Faber, 1967. See also his challenging new work, *The Body and Society: Men, Women and Sexual Renunciation in Early Christianity*, New York: Columbia, 1988. Erik H. Erikson, *Young Man Luther: A Study in Psychoanalysis and History*, New York: W. W. Norton and Co., first published in 1958, was reissued as a paperback in 1962 and has appeared often in recent years.

For Saint Anselm, R. W. Southern, *Saint Anselm and his Biographer*, Cambridge, 1966, which Sir Richard is revising for a new edition. See now also *The Letters of Saint Anselm of Canterbury* 1, trans. Walter Fröhlich, CS 96 (1990).

For Bernard's schooling and the contention that he wrote erotic poetry, see G. R. Evans, 'The Classical Education of Bernard of Clairvaux', *Cîteaux. Commentarii Cistercienses* 32 (1982) 121–34.

Many of my remarks about images and language in early Cîteaux's literature are ultimately drawn from the conclusions in Jean-Baptiste Auberger, *L'unanimité cistercienne primitive: Mythe ou realité?*, Cîteaux. Studia et Documenta 3. Achel, 1986, esp. pp 255–77.

For Bernard's obliviousness to his surroundings, see Michael Casey's excellent 'Bernard the Observer', *Goad and Nail. Studies in Medieval Cistercian History* X, CS 84, ed. E. Rozanne Elder, 1985, 1–20.

For Aelred's *Speculum caritatis*, see A. Hoste and C.H. Talbot, *Aelredi Rievallensis Opera Omnia* 1. *Opera Ascetica*, Corpus Christianorum. Continuatio Mediaevalis 1. Turnholt, 1971. Bernard's letter is on pp 3–4. The work is now available as in English as *The Mirror of Charity*, CF 17, 1990. Wilmart's pioneering article is in *Revue d'ascetique et de mystique* 14 (1933).

For the *Exordium Magnum Cisterciense*, ed. Bruno Griesser, Editiones Cistercienses, Rome, 1961, and its stories about Bernard, see below, "The First Cistercian Renewal. . . ".

'Clarevallians' are mentioned in Nicholas of Montiéramey, who, along with Peter the Venerable, is treated in terms of his relationship with Bernard in my *Friendship and Community: The Monastic Experience 350–1250*, CS 95, 1988, esp. pp 251–270 and 279–295. I am greatly indebted both to John Benton, who died all too soon in 1988, and to his friend, Giles Constable, for letters and conversations on this difficult question of the bonds among Peter, Nicholas, and Bernard.

For Hildegard of Bingen, Barbara Newman, *Sister of Wisdom: St. Hildegard's Theology of the Feminine*, Berkeley and Los Angeles: University of California, 1987, is excellent. See also my article "The Cistercians and the Transformation of Monastic Friendships", *Analecta Cisterciensia* 37 (1981) 1–63. For the position of women in medieval society, there are several good recent studies, including *Medieval Women*, ed. Derek Baker, Ecclesiastical History Society, Oxford: Blackwell, 1978. Gilson's views on Bernard and courtly love are contained in a famous appendix to his *Mystical Theology of Saint Bernard* (see above), pp 170–97.

There are several studies of Bernard and Abelard: Denis Meadows, *A Saint and a Half: A New Interpretation of Abelard and Saint Bernard of Clairvaux*, New York: Devin-Adair, 1963; Albert Victor Murray, *Abelard and Saint Bernard: A Study in Twelfth-century 'Modernism'*, Manchester University Press, 1967; Leif Grane, *Peter Abelard: Philosophy and Christianity in the Middle Ages*, New York: Harcourt, Brace and World, 1970.

Jacques Fournier has been made world-famous through Emmanuel Le Roy Ladurie's *Montaillou*, whose various editions in different languages have had many different subtitles. The original french edition in 1975, published in Paris by Gallimard, was called *Montaillou, village occitan de 1294 à 1324*. The Penguin edition, Harmondsworth, 1980, is *Montaillou: Cathars and Catholics in a French Village 1294–1324*.

A good presentation of the growth of church government in the Middle Ages is Colin Morris's very readable *The Papal Monarchy*, Oxford, 1989. R.W. Southern, *Western Society and the Church in the Middle Ages*, Pelican History of the Church, Harmondsworth, 1970, is still invaluable.

Umberto Eco's identification of his villain with Bernard of Clairvaux is based on hearsay, but Eco's awareness of Bernard's writings is evidenced by the fact that the young Adso's first sexual experience is described in language that comes directly or indirectly from Bernard's *Sermons on the Song of Songs*.

The account of Bernard's travels through Germany is contained in PL 185:370–94. It deserves more attention, as an indication of Bernard's effect on lay people.

2. Was Bernard a Friend?[1]

Bernard of Clairvaux might seem to be one of the least likely candidates in twelfth-century western Europe for the title of friend. Political organizer, theologian, founder of cistercian abbeys, even saint, he is so much larger than life that it is difficult to imagine him as a friend and companion to other men. Recent studies have tried either to emphasize the all-embracing sanctity of Bernard or else to show how one-sided and ungenerous he could be to other men. According to Jean Leclercq, one can either hate Bernard or love him: there is no middle ground. A hated Bernard can be seen as manipulating men for the purposes of his political and monastic programmes, while a loved Bernard can easily be reduced to a man who in nearly all situations acted as a man of God should act. Either extreme leaves little room for a human being with strengths and weaknesses of character, for contradictions in his words

[1]First published in *Goad and Nail*, Studies in Medieval Cistercian History X (Kalamazoo, CS 84. 1985). This new version contains some small changes in terms of content and style.

and actions, for moments of inspiration and regrettable acts.

It is my contention that by looking at Bernard in terms of the friendships he actually experienced in his life, we can find a middle way with him. So long as we see him in the context of the twelfth century and do not judge him as if he belonged to our own time, his words and actions can be understandable to us. In what follows I shall neither try to debunk the saint nor to praise the man to the skies. He was a human being as we all are human beings, and by looking at the content and language of his personal relations, we can touch upon an aspect of this humanity. I shall not deal directly with Bernard the saint here, but perhaps through a pedestrian portrait of the man, the saint will become more apparent. By looking at Bernard as a potential friend we can perhaps better grasp why the man engendered fierce loyalties and enmities.

A point of departure for any understanding of friendship is a definition of the phenomenon that was current in the Middle Ages and can still be conceived of in terms of modern life. Here we are much better off than with many other terms that are modern coinage about medieval life (as 'courtly love', 'feudalism', 'scholasticism'). *Amicitia* was a well-known concept among medieval intellectuals, and the first place they looked for a definition of the term was the treatise *Laelius de amicitia* of Cicero. 'Friendship is nothing other than an identity of all things divine and human in mutual goodwill and affection' (V.20: *Est enim amicitia nihil aliud nisi omnium divinarum humanarumque rerum cum benevolentia et caritate consensio.*) The central word here is *consensio*, which implies that the friends simultaneously experience or gain awareness of the same phenomena. But friendship in Cicero also implies good acts proceeding from goodwill, as well as a climate of affection, perhaps even bordering on tenderness.

Medieval intellectuals, who in the twelfth century were almost all clerics or monks, were not always satisfied with a definition of friendship that came from a non-christian writer.

It was natural for writers on friendship to include quotations or examples from the Bible. One of the phrases that frequently appears is taken from the Acts of the Apostles, where the community of early Christians is described as being of one heart and mind (Ac 4:32—*cor unum et anima una*). The passage has been used in recent times by socialist thinkers to emphasize the 'natural communism' of these men and women. Even in the Middle Ages, the passage was noticed as a description of life in common sharing of all goods. But in most cases the phrase was taken out of its immediate socio-religious context and seen as a description of harmony among human beings arising out of friendship, a friendship linked to Christ and the christian community.

It is this kind of friendship which we will look for in Bernard, one that is at one and the same time individualized and particularized and yet can be coordinated to the needs and requirements of community life. Could any monk, especially an abbot with all his obligations, ever be of one heart and mind with other members of his community and with people outside his monastery? Is there any room for friendships in a human living situation where the most important goal is to maintain harmony among the community's members?

Centuries earlier, John Cassian had shown great optimism about the possibility of friendships in the monastic and even in the eremitical life. If we look at his famous sixteenth conference on friendship, however, we find it is more concerned with stability and peace in the community as a whole rather than with individual friendships. For Cassian the one mind and soul encompassed the whole of the monastery and did not mean bonds between individual monks.

If Bernard had followed Cassian alone and ignored Cicero, it is likely he would have argued only for friendship of community and not among individuals. This does not seem to have been the case. A review of Bernard's writings suggests that he saw friendship as something natural in human affairs. In his sermons and letters he indicated that friendship is worth literary expression.

The fullest statement of this idea comes in the twenty-sixth sermon On the Song of Songs, preached in 1138:

> It is but human and necessary that we respond to our friends with feeling: that we be happy in their company, disappointed in their absence. Social intercourse, especially between friends, cannot be purposeless; the reluctance to part and the yearning for each other when separated, indicate how meaningful their mutual love must be when they are together.[2]

Non erit otiosa socialis conversatio, praesertim inter amicos: the words are so self-confident and matter-of-fact that it is easy to forget how significant they are in a monastic context. Bernard is telling his brethren that it is quite in order that they cultivate friendships with each other, and he is answering a long tradition gong back to the Fathers and insisting that separations are of no importance for real friendship. They would love each other no matter how far apart they were physically. Bernard accepts human desire for union and presence as something natural.

'For a long time now we have been united in the closest friendship', Bernard wrote in 1149 to Peter the Venerable, abbot of Cluny: '. . . an equal affection has rendered us equals'.[3] In earlier letters Bernard had emphasized his unworthiness to come up to the same level as Peter and to deserve his love. Bernard's expression of humility may have been more a literary pose than a genuine feeling, but here he said that because of friendship the two men became equals. His doctrine of equality in friendship, regardless of one's own status in the world, is derived ultimately from Cicero (De amicitia XX.71). Bernard could cast away the traditional apparatus of humility and speak to Peter directly and immediately about a misunderstanding that had arisen between them. One of his letters to Peter had apparently contained expressions that

[2] SC 26.10, trans. Kilian Walsh; CF 7:69.
[3] Ep 387, SBOp 8:355–6, trans. Bruno Scott James, The Letters of Bernard of Clairvaux (London, 1953) 378.

might have been offensive. Bernard insisted that his secretaries sometimes misunderstood his intentions when he had them write letters for him:

> Believe me who love you that nothing could have come from my heart or left my lips which would have offended your ears. My many occupations are to blame, because when my secretaries have not fully grasped my meaning they are apt to write too sharply, and I do not have time to read through what they have written. Forgive me this time, for whatever I may do with other letters, I shall in future look through my letters to you and trust no one's ears or eyes but my own.[4]

The passage has been noticed because it gives us insight into the process of composition at Clairvaux. Bernard had become so busy that he apparently had to assign a major responsibility to his secretaries in order to answer his correspondence. But just as significant as this glimpse of Bernard and his secretaries is his insistence on maintaining goodwill towards his friend Peter the Venerable. Bernard wanted to keep his friendship with Peter. This was a goal in itself, not subordinated to any other purpose.

A sceptical historian might reply that it was in Bernard's best interest to maintain good relations with Cluny and its powerful abbot. There is no doubt that Bernard was aware of the importance of such a bond. But in this letter he most of all wanted Peter to know that he loved him as the person he was, and to do so he drew on the tradition of classical and christian friendship, where friends want to share themselves completely with each other. As he began his apology, 'Would that I were able to express in this letter all that I feel towards you!'

Bernard, like many other twelfth-century writers, is difficult to catch making direct quotations from the Fathers or from classical literature. His language is always his own, with

[4] *Ibid.* The relationship was complicated by the fact that one of Bernard's secretaries, Nicholas of Montiéramey, was also close to Peter.

faint echoes of a thorough and intense training in latin grammar but without the mark of individual authors. In Bernard's boyhood, however, scholars in german and french schools, from Worms to Chartres, were making use of letter collections that dealt with the theme of friendship and relating it to classical models. The last half of the eleventh century is a golden age for the reformulation of the idea of friendship in classical and christian terms. It is likely that Bernard the eager young student, who preferred the schoolroom to the tournament, would have been affected by this new expression of friendship in clerical letters and life. Bernard's school training apparently encouraged him to accept friendship as something worth writing about. Classical ideals found a rich christian mould in Bernard's youth.

In entering the monastery of Cîteaux in 1113, the young Bernard, now in his early twenties, could easily have been convinced that the process of conversion meant he had to leave friends and friendship behind. After all, Christ himself had indicated more than once in the Gospels that in order to follow him, one must leave everything. The abandonment of material possessions was not enough: family and friends must also be left behind. The Eastern Fathers had understood this message and found great virtue in the men who refused to see their mothers or brothers once they had gone into the desert for good. But this eastern model, breaking all family bonds, was now replaced in the west by what could be called the bernardian model: in the process of conversion friendship is not abrogated. It is transformed into something even better, monastic friendship.

William of Saint Thierry's account of Bernard's conversion to the monastic life describes this process in such a natural and inevitable manner that one can fail to notice how original Bernard was in insisting on entering Cîteaux not alone but in the company of family members and good friends. If we look at the Vita Prima carefully, we can see that Bernard's decision to enter Cîteaux did not take place from one day to the next. First he decided on the monastic life. Then he went about convincing his brothers and near relations and friends to accompany him. The whole band settled down for a while on the family property and made themselves ready for the great move (VP I.15 = PL 185:235). Only then did Bernard and his brothers and friends come knocking on the door of Cîteaux. Abbot Stephen Harding was not confronted with a few individuals who had gotten together by chance in the last stages of their decision to become monks. He had to deal with a well-coordinated and determined group of men who had prepared themselves not just to enter a monastery but also to maintain their bonds to each other and yet to alter them radically within the context of monastic life. Stephen took on friends who intended to continue being each other's friends in more exciting ways than they ever could experience in the world of the school or of the castle.

The story of the conversion of Bernard's brothers in William of Saint Thierry deserves a certain amount of credence (VP I:9–12 = PL 185:231–4). The stories are not just miraculous accounts: they evidence the strength of Bernard's will. It was he who insisted on getting all his brothers, except the youngest, with him. He did not care if they were married, if they had duties as soldiers, or if they had economic commitments. Here, of course, are parallels to Christ's calling of the apostles. But these seem to have been disparate men, for the most part unrelated to each other. Bernard called his own brothers. For him the process of conversion was a family affair.

The most striking indication of the importance of bonds of friendship for the young Bernard and his insistence on converting them into bonds of monastic life in friendship is the story of how Bernard convinced Hugh of Vitry to come with him. The first narrator of the incident is Geoffrey of Auxerre, who in his rough draft for a Life of Saint Bernard included the incident and provided an emotional account of a man driven by a need to include his friend in the most momentous decision of his life:

He said one day to his brothers; 'I have a friend at Macon, Hugh of Vitry. We have to get hold of him so that
he also will become one of us'. This man was a cleric of
noble birth who had reached a mature age. He was well
off both in terms of lay and ecclesiastical possessions.[5]

Bernard was not to be stopped, even though 'those who knew
him began to accuse Bernard of being too rash'.

Hugh must have heard something about Bernard's decision to change his way of life, and he wanted to do whatever
he could to make sure that the brilliant young man instead
made his career in the secular church, as he himself intended
to do:

> When Hugh saw Bernard he wept and rushed to em-
> brace him, but the man of God paid no attention to his
> tears. After Hugh became calmer, Bernard revealed his
> intention to him, and so Hugh's sorrow returned and
> the fount of tears flowed all the more, so that during
> that entire day his eyes did not have rest.[6]

Bernard, who became well known for his tears here refused
to weep. He could not see any reason for sorrow in his decision to become a monk, and he intended to do everything
possible to see to it that Hugh joined him. This must be why
he decided to spend the night together with Hugh. They slept
'in a very narrow bed so that there was hardly room for one
of them'.[7] Hugh's sobs kept Bernard from falling asleep for
a long time. Geoffrey made no attempt to hide his master's
irritation with these superfluous tears:

> In the morning when Hugh again was weeping, Bernard
> was irritated and began to reproach him all the more

[5] 'Les fragmenta de *Vita et Miraculis S. Bernardi*', ed. Robert Lechat,
Analecta Bollandiana 50 (1932) 94–5 (my translation).

[6] *Ibid.*, p 94.

[7] *Ibid.*: Sequenti nocte pariter accubuerunt in angustissimo strato ita ut
vix capere alterum.

harshly. But he replied to Bernard: 'The reason why I
cry is not the same today as it was yesterday. Yesterday I wept for you, today I weep for myself. For I know
your way of life and am aware that a conversion to the
monastic life is more necessary for me than for you'.

Hugh had been convinced: a night of fitful and interrupted
sleep had paid off for Bernard! 'Weep', he said, 'as much as
you wish, for these tears are excellent. Don't stop'. The friend
would now follow Bernard into the monastic life, and so
Bernard could lavish on him all the outward signs of friendship. Bernard and Hugh 'walked about together in sharing
each other's joy, and did not leave each other for a moment'.
They were bosom friends again, to the anger and scandal of
the secular clerics who wanted to keep Hugh in the world.[8]
The story goes on to relate how the clerics did manage
to separate Hugh from Bernard for a while. They used their
bodies to keep Bernard at a distance from Hugh, but Bernard
made it possible to get into contact with Hugh by summon-
ing up a rainstorm on a field where Hugh's 'bodyguard' had
to head for cover. Once again Geoffrey makes use of intimate details: he describes how Bernard, when at first he
could not speak to Hugh still managed to get close enough
to him to shed tears down his friend's neck. We also hear
how the two friends, 'having confirmed a bond of spiritual
union . . . returned hand in hand'.[9]
Hugh's tears, his embrace of Bernard, the narrow bed,
Bernard's tears on Hugh's neck, and the final hand-in-hand
scene are all missing in William of Saint Thierry's version
of the episode. He concentrates the narrative on the way
Bernard succeeded in convincing Hugh to become a monk
(VP I.13–14 = PL 185:234–35). But even if the outward emotional signs of friendship are missing in William's account,
he makes the same point, that Bernard and Hugh shared a

[8] Ibid., p 95.
[9] Ibid.: Ibi confirmato ex integro sodalicio spirituali, redierunt manu sese
tenentes alterutrum. . . .

close friendship. He is even more specific about the nature of the relationships, which he calls *familiaris amicitia*.

William may have found Geoffrey's enthusiasm for Bernard's physical closeness to Hugh a distraction from the central content of the story. But like Geoffrey, William could see how Bernard was able to transform a close friendship outside the monastery into one that led into the monastery. The friendship in the world could become more permanent and true 'in a pace of new life', and William appropriately ended the passage with a reference to the key phrase from the Acts of the Apostles: 'they became far more worthily and truly of one heart and one mind in Christ than they had been in the world' (VP I.13 = PL 185:235). William, like his friend Bernard, did not deny the value of friendships outside the monastery. He saw them as a point of departure and inspiration for the much richer and deeper friendships of the cloister.

Perhaps the main problem with William of Saint Thierry's narration is that it is so smooth and literary that one is not jolted into a realization of what happened here in Bernard's experience of other people and influence on them. He did not just get them into the monastery because he saw the monastic way of life as the best one to salvation. He converted people because they were his friends. Friendship requires Cicero's *consensio*, and in Bernard's mind the best way to live in harmony is to live within the monastery, where all can be one in Christ. Thanks to Geoffrey of Auxerre's much less literary and more anecdotal description of winning over Hugh of Vitry, we can see how determined Bernard was to make sure that his friends did come with him. He could not imagine a community of monks without the inclusion of his friends and relatives. In Bernard's life and writings, friendship received an independent value with the christian and especially the monastic life. This is not just a process of friend first and then monk. It is the transformation of the friend in the world into the even stronger friend in the monastery. Bernard was satisfied with nothing less!

In Bernard the western monastic ambiguity about the value of friendship, going back to John Cassian and before him the Desert Fathers, was resolved. For Bernard this was probably not a question of choice but of inner necessity. He could not imagine life without friends. At the same time, however, Bernard did not lose sight of the place friendship had to take within the monastery. Despite its intrinsic value friendship had to be subordinated and coordinated to the goal of monastic community. Bernard in his treatises and letters intended to make visible those friends who contributed to such a goal. As Adriaan Bredero has pointed out, Bernard's actions can best be understood if they are seen as working towards the spread of the Cistercian Order. To go a step further than Bredero, one could claim that any person who helped Bernard towards this goal deserved to be qualified as his friend, whether or not Bernard knew this person well or not.

In a letter to Eskil, archbishop of Lund in Scandinavia, probably written in 1151, Bernard expressed the degree of his affection:

> I believe I owe you and you owe me all the favour and affection that absent friends can bestow on one another. . . . I cannot repay you for your affection, but I have one, whose mercy endures for ever, who will repay for me. I speak of the Lord in whom and for whom you love me with such devotion and bind me to you with such affection.[10]

Eskil had apparently written Bernard about his problems in opposing the power and influence of the archbishop of Hamburg-Bremen, and now Bernard showed his full sympathy. But Eskil had probably also informed Bernard of his own intention to found a cistercian monastery at Esrum in

---

[10] Ep 390; SBOp 8:358 (trans. James, note 3 above, p 493). See chapter 4 below, on Bernard and Eskil.

Northern Zealand. The bearer of the letter and Eskil's messenger, William, the first abbot of the new danish house,
would proceed to the pope in December 1151 to get a foundation document for Esrum. Eskil had already provided a gift
of property at the site, and Bernard could now look upon the
archbishop as a man who was contributing to the spread of
the Cistercians in the North.

Eskil may well have written Bernard an affectionate letter, but the latter seems mainly to have been responding to
the fact that the archbishop of Lund intended to champion
Bernard's Cistercians in Denmark. Because of such cooperation, Eskil became a friend, even though Bernard may never
yet have seen him. The two were united in a mutual affection stemming from the common effort. Because of this unity,
Bernard could turn to Eskil all the eloquence of his pen:

> Would that I had the power from on high to say all this
> to you and not write it, so that I might open my heart
> to you by word of mouth rather than by the written
> word. Certainly the living word is more welcome than
> the written word, and the tongue more eloquent than
> the pen; for the eyes of the speaker lend credence to his
> words, and the expression of the face conveys affection
> better than the pen. But, being absent from you, this is
> beyond my power and so I must satisfy myself with the
> second best alternative of a letter.[11]

The contrast between written and spoken word is perhaps
one of the oldest clichés in letter writing, but the words seem
to have had an effect on Eskil. Soon after receiving this letter,
he went to Clairvaux and met Bernard. Whatever the political
motives for his trip, it is hard to think he was not drawn by the
desire to see the man who could promise so much intensity
in human contact and friendship.

Another close friend to whom Bernard can be seen drawing near because of the friend's willingness to support the
spread of the Cistercian Order in his country is Malachy of

---

[11] *Ibid.*, James pp 493–4.

Ireland, the only person whose biography Bernard wrote. In what is called a 'letter of confraternity' to Malachy as papal legate in Ireland, dated to some time after 1145 and before Malachy's death in 1148, Bernard managed to combine both the devotion of friendship with his enthusiasm and gratefulness for the good work Malachy was doing. In the very salutation of the letter Bernard summarized this double relationship, for he called Malachy a 'great priest and his best friend' (*summo amico suo*). The first part of the letter starts out as a classical statement of friendship, which can exist even though friends are separated:

> Even though you are far away from us, you are still not far from our mind, since holy love admits to no inhibitions from time and place. Even if we are separated by the wide sea, we are still joined in charity.[12]

Such a sentiment could probably be traced back to the letters of Seneca to Lucilius, and on the way the idea can be found in the sixth-century poetry of Venantius Fortunatus. What is important here, however, is the way Bernard quickly linked this sentiment of individual friendship with the unity of the friends in Christ and in the brotherhood of the Cistercian Order:

> In all matters I am joined to you by the kind reception of our sons and brothers, who lately have gone to those parts, and whom you cherish, love and help in an efficacious manner. Although they did not come from our own house especially ⟨Clairvaux⟩, still they are not the less loved for being from one of our daughter houses, for we all, both near and far, are one in Christ, both these and those who come from our side to you, and specially commend them your fatherhood, asking that, what you have well begun, you will complete even better in the Lord.[13]

[12] Ep 545; SBOp 8:512–13 (my translation). For Bernard and Malachy, see chapter 3 below.
[13] Ibid.

The letter ends with an assurance to Malachy that he would be able to share in whatever good was done in the Cistercian Order. Bernard managed in the course of fewer than twenty lines to go from expressing his special friendship for Malachy, to a statement of the unity Malachy now enjoyed with the entire Cistercian Order. The link between individual friendship and monastic confraternity could emerge from Malachy's efforts towards assuring the presence of the Cistercians in Ireland. For Bernard friendship and cistercian foundations were intimately linked. Whether in Denmark or Ireland, he was willing to express his friendship for those who helped him in this process.

It might seem appropriate to end here, in acknowledging Bernard's capacity for friendship and in seeing this talent as coordinated with his more important goal of spreading the Cistercians. But Bernard is not as simple as that. His need for friendship was so great that he seems to have sought out and maintained individual friendships for their own sake. Thus, in Bernard's scheme individual friendships were both possible and desirable. The strongest defence of such bonds can be found in Bernard's lament on the death of his brother Gerard, where he described what a faithful support Gerard had been for him at Clairvaux and how difficult it was for him to accept the fact of Gerard's death.[14]

Another instance of a particularized friendship in Bernard's life is his relationship with Nicholas of Montiéramey. This bond has been looked upon carefully, but mainly in terms of Nicholas's great betrayal of his master and Bernard's virulent reaction. Recent writers tend to see Bernard as exaggerating the bounds of reasonable behaviour in accusing Nicholas of being a thief, and it is still not clear to what extent Nicholas had, in fact, acted in good faith.[15] But the

[14] SC 26:3–14. See the chapter "Monks and Tears . . .", later in this volume.
[15] A good background article on Nicholas is John Benton's entry on him in *Dictionnaire de Spiritualité* 11 (Beauchesne: Paris 1981) col 255–59. See also my treatment in *Friendship and Community*, pp 279–91, and, for the debate

finale of Bernard's and Nicholas's relationship should not distract us from the keen devotion Bernard showed him for several years. In Bernard's letters Nicholas can be seen as a bond and go-between for Bernard and Peter the Venerable. Bernard wrote to Peter how he on receiving a letter from Peter would shut himself up alone with Nicholas, 'of whom you are so fond. There I refreshed myself again and again with the charm that emanated from your letter'.[16]

For Bernard there was no doubt that a letter from a friend was to have first priority over the daily obligations he had as abbot and ecclesiastical personage. Bernard wanted, moreover, to share the contents of the letter primarily with the friend whom he already shared with Peter, the Nicholas who had originally come from Peter and who could be allowed to add his own sentence to Bernard's letter to express his own individual affection for the abbot of Cluny: 'And I Nicholas add my undying affection for you and for all your household'.[17]

The work of Jean Leclercq has shown how much care Bernard put into his letters in order to make them products of literary art.[18] One could even go further and say that the sensuality that some men invest in food, sex, or the pursuit of wealth Bernard placed in the pursuit of literary perfection. In allowing Nicholas to share in the process of writing a letter, and even to add his own explicit contribution to it, Bernard was showing confidence in a freindship. We tend to remember only that he was betrayed, or thought he was betrayed, but the letters we have make it clear that Bernard and Peter both loved Nicholas dearly and wanted to be with him. Once again, Bernard could not be without his

on Nicholas, n 147 (pp 482–3).

[16] Ep 389; SBOp 8:356–7 (trans. James, 379).

[17] Ibid., trans. James p 380: Ego Nicolaus vester saluto vos in aeternum, et ultra, et domesticam illam familiam, quae lateri et spiritui vestro adhaeret.

[18] See, for example, his 'Lettres de S Bernard: histoire ou littérature?', Studi medievali 12 (1971) 1–74.

friends when he was doing what he loved to do: entering the monastic life, reading a friend's letter aloud, or responding to it. He needed the acknowledgement, awareness and even physical presence of his friends.

Turning to Bernard's relationship with Peter the Venerable, it is once again the controversial part of a relationship, in this case Bernard's attack on Cluny, that is best known, while later letters of friendship get little attention. The first of these are cautious and full of expressions of humility.[19] They date from 1138, the time when Bernard was returning to France after dealing with the schism of antipope Anacletus. In the next years there were various disagreements with Cluny, such as that over the election of the bishop of Langres.[20]   But in 1143 Bernard wrote to Peter a letter which signalled that he wanted the two of them to share friendship. We do not have the letter of Peter to which Bernard responded, but from what Bernard wrote, it seems that Peter had been poking fun at him. As Bernard wrote, 'So you are pleased to jest? Courteously and kindly I would admit, if I could be sure you were not ridiculing me'.[21]

This time Bernard spoke directly to Peter and dropped the apparatus of humility. He chided him for not writing for a long time. Now that a letter finally had come from Peter, he hardly knew how to take it. Peter had shown an 'unexpected esteem' (*inopinata dignatio*) for Bernard, and now Bernard wanted to know what his exact meaning was in playing with language:

> I have only said this so as to be quite open with you and not to keep anything back from you, for this true friendship demands. Because charity believes all things, I have put away all my misgivings, and am glad that you have warmed to the memory of an old friendship, and

[19] Epp 147, 148, 149; SBOp 8:350–53.
[20] See for example Ep 166, SBOp 8:377, p 253 in James.
[21] Ep 228; SBOp 8:98–100 (trans. James, 375)

recalled a wounded friend. Being recalled, I am happy to return, happy to be recalled.[22]

There had been some kind of misunderstanding between Bernard and Peter, between Cîteaux and Cluny, but Bernard was not addressing it as an official matter between the two Orders. It was a matter of friendship.

Bernard had felt offended by Peter's standoffishness, and now he did not know what to make of Peter's indication of affection. But he had decided to take it in the best possible sense. True friendship requires faith in the good intentions of the friend and complete openness with him. These enabled Bernard to forgive and forget whatever had passed between them, and to return to his friend. The language here indicates that in 1143 Bernard considered his friendship with Peter to be one of longstanding. Did it go back to the time when Bernard and Peter had resolved their differences in the 1120s? We do not know, for the collection of letters only allows us to focus on the relationship of the two men at selected moments. In 1143, at least, Bernard could again embrace the bond and characterize it in terms of true friendship. He implies, however, that there had been some trouble that now was over:

> Here I am, now as ever, your devoted servant, and full of gratitude for being once more your intimate friend, as you were kind enough to write. If I had perhaps grown cold towards you, as you reproach me for having done, there is no doubt that cherished by your love I shall soon grow warm again.[23]

Bernard's references to Peter's letter allow us to reconstruct part of it: Peter had indicated, perhaps with gentle humour,

[22] Ibid, pp 98–99, James p 375.
[23] Ibid., p 99. The Latin is masterful and richly deserves quotation:
En ego, qui fueram vestrae profecto sanctitatis servus, et nunc, et ante. Gratias ago, optime locatus sum, intimus vobis denuo factus, sicut dignamini scribere. Si forte intepueram, ut arguitis, haud dubium quin velociter recalescam, fotus vestrae caritatis visceribus.

that Bernard had stopped caring for him but that he, Peter, considered Bernard to be his friend: *intimus vobis.*

If Bernard had been following the rules of letterwriting, the *ars dictaminis*, this section would have included a statement of good will: the *captatio benevolentiae.*[24] In general, Bernard showed his good will towards Peter here. But he did much more. He cut through the polite superficiality of rhetorical good manners and described to Peter something of what he had to experience, first because of the long silence, and then because of Peter's remarkable letter. Only once he had reestablished his own relationship with Peter could he accept the humour in a positive way:

> I must say I enjoy your fun. It is both pleasantly gay and seriously grave. I do not know how it is you are able to be gay and grave, so that your fun has nothing about it of frivolity, and your dignity loses nothing by your gaiety.[25]

Every word is balanced carefully and contrasted with its opposite: *iucunditate gratus, et serius gravitate.* Bernard as artist of the well-turned phrase is at work. This is his way of expressing his decision not to be insulted by Peter's fun and games but instead to join in them as an indication of friendship. He then sets about describing his situation at Clairvaux and says he would not be leaving it again, except for the General Chapter. Bernard was not well, but he was still able to join in on Peter's joking tone and to anticipate a possible humorous reply from Peter: 'I suppose you will not now dare to reproach me with my silence and, in the way you have, to call it sloth'. Bernard could not resist the temptation to give Peter something of what he had received from him. Instead of being sour and displeased with Peter's disturbing mixture of silence and jokes, Bernard decided to return both in kind!

---

[24] For a translation of the treatise, *Rationes dictandi*, 'The Principles of Letter-Writing', see *Three Medieval Rhetorical Arts*, ed. James J. Murphy (University of California. Berkeley 1971) 1–25.

[25] Ep 228, SBOp 8:99. James p 375.

Such passages are to my mind the mark of real friendship and much more than a literary pose. The friend adapts and plays with the tone of the letter he has received and shows that he has understood and can respond to the nuances of affection others might ignore or misunderstand. Just beneath the surface there is evidence of trouble and disagreement. Instead of suppressing this element, Bernard admitted that it had been there but indicated his desire to renew an old and important friendship.

If we were to study all the letters between Peter and Bernard, it would be possible to trace their friendship into the early 1150s and to conclude that Peter was almost always the diplomat, while Bernard usually seemed to convey what was on his mind in a much more direct way.[26] The two knew how far they could go with each other and respected boundaries. The result is one of the few friendships in the twelfth century that can be illuminated from both sides. No matter how much we try to explain away this friendship in terms of the advantage of maintaining good relations between Clairvaux and Cluny, the language of Bernard is too personal to dismiss it as pure verbiage of high literary quality. The only conclusion possible is that aside from all practical considerations, Bernard wanted and needed Peter's friendship. 'True friendships do not grow old; otherwise they were not true', he insisted elsewhere, echoing Cicero and Jerome.[27]

In the same letter, addressed to a 'W' who might be William of Saint Thierry, Bernard borrowed from the language of the Song of Songs in order to express what he felt for a true friend: 'I shall hold him and not let him go, until I shall bring him into the house of my mother and into the chamber of her who conceived me' (Sg 3:4). Bernard was determined to hold onto the friend, come what may: '. . . since you still turn to me, I am yours and will be as long as I live'.[28] In parting,

---

[26] For a more detailed study of their relationship, see my *Friendship and Community*, pp 255–58.

[27] Ep 506, SBOp 8:464 (my translation).

[28] *Ibid.*. My translation.

he told this unknown friend that the sermons for which he had asked would soon be ready and would be sent off. The correspondent was thus interested in Bernard's literary and theological inspiration, but Bernard expressed the bond in terms of friendship. The ecstatic language of the Song of Songs is appropriate here. This allegory of love could be applied to one friend's need for another: 'I draw tight in my arms one who is joined to me in the marrow of his being, and there is no one who can snatch him from my grasp'.[29]

This last statement can be seen not just as an indication of the strength in Bernard's bonds with his friends. It also points to his determination to be the one to decide which of his human relationships were true friendships and how to go about cultivating these bonds. To put matters bluntly, Bernard had to be in charge of his friendships. He preferred to take the initiative in beginning a friendship or breaking it off, as we can see from a striking letter to a man who had promised to come to Clairvaux but had not kept his word. Bernard indicated that he cared for his correspondent, and that the latter had failed not only Bernard but also himself:

> Although you care not for yourself, I still do not cease to care for you since I am fond of you and grieve over you. Because I am fond of you, I grieve over you; because I grieve over you, I think of you.[30]

Bernard linked the continuation of his personal relationship to the man with his decision to enter Clairvaux and become part of its fellowship. In rejecting Clairvaux, the correspondent cut himself off from Bernard:

> If there lives in you the faintest spark of your old love for me; if you have any hope at all of eventually escaping from your wretched captivity; if you do not wish that confidence in the prayers and friendship of this community, which I am told you have even while living as

---

[29] Ibid.. Cf. Deut 32:39.
[30] Ep 415, SBOp 8:398–99, trans. James p 511.

you are, to be utterly empty and false, come at once to Clairvaux.

Here *amicitia* is placed together with prayer in the context of the entire community of Clairvaux, not just the friendship of Bernard alone. But for him the two could hardly be separated. If the man refused to come to Clairvaux, then he cut himself off from the 'friendship of good men, because by refusing to take their advice, you will prove yourself unworthy of their fellowship'.[31] No compromise was possible for Bernard: the promise once given had to be kept. On its fulfillment depended the continuation and renewal of his 'old love' and the friendship of the entire community.

Once again we see that Bernard's individual friendships were intimately linked to his goal of seeing that as many good men as possible entered Clairvaux and spread the Cistercian Order. He acted here as a man without compromise. Maintaining a friendship with Bernard was no easy matter. This is the impression left by Peter the Venerable's long, careful letters to Bernard. He explained every phrase, every step he took, for Peter realized that Bernard would decide whether his intentions and actions were acceptable. If we return to the case of Hugh of Vitry, where Bernard was cross at first because he could not control Hugh's tears but was happy later because he had managed to make him shed the right kind of tears, this scene of tension and tenderness summarizes the way Bernard set the tone. If Hugh was going to continue being his friend, then he had to become a monk. Bernard did not care that Hugh had initially been disappointed in his own decision to choose the monastic way of life and abandon the secular clergy.

Bernard would not take no for an answer. We can see this in his letter to Aelred of Rievaulx ordering him to write a work on charity. Aelred had apparently objected that he was not fit for such speculative work, for his life experience had been

[31] *Ibid.*, p 399.

more with practical matters. Bernard took Aelred's arguments
and made them his own:

> I most gratefully accepted your excuses, they served
> rather to inflame than extinguish the spark of my de-
> sire, because knowledge that comes from the school of
> the Holy Spirit rather than the schools of rhetoric will
> savour all the sweeter to me.... [32]

There is no explicit declaration of friendship in this letter.
Aelred is treated as the pupil who has to follow the Rule of
Saint Benedict and learn humility and obedience. In humility
he was to accept that he was capable of doing what Bernard
asked. In obedience he was to follow the command of his
master.

Aelred must have met Bernard at Clairvaux in the spring
of 1142. It was probably then that Bernard had conceived the
task for Aelred. Once he did so, no compromise was possible.
Outwardly everything conformed to the standard benedictine
pattern of adherence to the Rule, but when one turns to the
product of Bernard's conversations with Aelred, the result is
a highly untraditional work of monastic theology, one that
combines Aelred's personal experience with his interpretation of divine creation and love.[33]

Bernard must have recognized in Aelred a man who would
be able to combine his own self-awareness with an understanding of the function of love in a christian context. The
strength of Bernard's will in manipulating and making people conform to his desires and goals can easily be seen as
a negative factor in his bonds with other men, but here in
the case of Aelred the opposite is apparent. Bernard saw in
Aelred a potential friend who could spread the doctrine of
charity in monastic life by showing how it worked. As a man
of will, Bernard could order Aelred to write a treatise on the
subject. Aelred could only obey. The result is one of the most

---

[32] Ep 523; SBOp 8:487 (trans. James, pp 246–47).
[33] The *Speculum caritatis*, trans. as *The Mirror of Charity*, CF 35 (1990).

intense formulations of the workings of love in human and especially monastic life we find in the twelfth century. Without the strength of Bernard's will, Aelred might never have articulated his ideas. Here friendship underlies the strict language of command and subordination, for Bernard needed Aelred to be his instrument in spreading the doctrine of love in the cistercian manner.

Bernard had to be in charge, but he was not a man who reduced friendship to sycophancy. He was willing to respond to friends who had unflattering things to say about him, and this trait provides the most convincing indication that Bernard could be a friend. He was open to criticism and able to answer it. His letters included many which reveal receptivity to criticism. Even if the letters to which he replied do not usually survive, Bernard's review of their contents and frequent citation of individual passages enables us to reconstruct charges against him and to see how Bernard dealt with them.

Peter the Venerable did the same, in even greater detail. He can be seen moving carefully through letters from Bernard and answering them point by point. Bernard was not as meticulous, but he could, for example, face the essence of complaints levelled against him when he replied to a charge by William of Saint Thierry that Bernard loved him less than William did Bernard:

'My affection for you is greater than yours is for me'. These are your very words, and I could wish they were not, for I do not know if they are true.[34]

Instead of dealing with this accusation by protesting the depth of his affection for William, Bernard pointed out that only God knows what happens in the heart of a man: 'You may be right. . .but I am certainly certain that you cannot be certain'. The word play on *certus* is intentional and makes the point well: certitude about human dispositions

[34] Ep 85; SBOp 7:221 (trans. James, p 125).

is reserved to God alone, and so Bernard could only be amazed at the confidence with which William put forth his observation.

If Bernard had stopped here, it would have looked as though he was trying to avoid answering the charge by bringing up a theological point, thus intellectualizing a matter of human emotion in order to avoid responding in kind (as men have done both before and since!). But Bernard was willing to assert his love for William. His problem was, he wrote, that he did not know whether he loved him sufficiently. He defined this love on the basis of the Gospels as willingness to lay down one's life for one's friends. So Bernard was faced by the dilemma that his love seemed wanting: 'Woe is me, if (as I greatly fear) I am either loved by this man more than I deserved or love him less than he deserves'.

The rules of letter writing and a zeal for edification did not allow Bernard to leave William with a sense of defeat. He ended the letter by reminding William that he, Bernard, loved him to the limit of his capacity, while he was sure that William could even increase his love for Bernard:

> . . . although you love more than I do, you do not love more than you are able. And I too, although I love you less than I should, yet I love you as much as I can according to the power that has been given me.

We might 'translate' Bernard's words into the language of our time thus: do not ask me to be what I am not. Try to find out who I am, so that you can love me as I am.

Was Bernard trying to keep William at a distance? Or was he telling a man for whom he cared deeply that William had been mistaken and should reconsider what it was that he sought in Bernard and to what extent Bernard could provide it? I cannot help thinking that Bernard was being as frank and open with William as he possibly could be, even belabouring his point to near-repetitiveness.

The last part of the letter provides one of the moments in the twelfth century when we are privileged to see one man trying to speak directly to another. Whatever the rhetorical and theological background of this letter, it is an appeal from Bernard to William not to expect too much of him, not to ask more than he can give, not to demand something he could not give at all. Bernard may have been indicating to William that he, as abbot of Clairvaux, could not take on the needs and cares of William in more than a secondary manner. William's own account of his stay with Bernard at Clairvaux when the two were ill shows how the occasional tension between them and a contest of wills could only be resolved when Bernard got his way and forced William to do as he wished (VP I.59–60 = PL 185:259).

Bernard nevertheless gave William enough of himself so that they could remain friends, despite the fact that William defied Bernard by leaving his abbacy in order to become a cistercian monk. Bernard and William were competitors in friendship and in theological knowledge, but within this tension Bernard was willing to explain himself, to reveal his own sources of motivation to his friend and to share some of his inner life with someone for whom he cared. In this letter to William we see how friendship was so important for Bernard that he did his best to explain himself and to try to get the friend to understand why he acted as he did.

A completely fair characterization of Bernard's friendships would require as careful a review of his relationships with other men as Jean Leclercq provided of his dealings with women. But since men were closer and more central to Bernard, while women remained at a distance, such a study would turn into a new biography of Bernard. Forthcoming work from Adriaan Bredero, Michael Casey and Christopher Holdsworth will certainly shed new light on the question of Bernard's friendships, but for the moment I would conclude that Bernard was a friend at least in his dealings with those who enhanced the monastic life at Clairvaux or the Cistercian Order as a whole. With such men, as Peter the Venerable, William of Saint Thierry, Eskil of Lund, and Malachy of Armagh, Bernard could be warm, open, responsive. While writing to them in careful literary formulae, Bernard could still manage to convey a unity of emotion and thought in the bond of love which in his own time inspired strong loyalties from those to whom he addressed himself.

I cannot help comparing Bernard's declarations of friendship with those Anselm wrote when he was still abbot at Bec and sent to former monks who had moved with Lanfranc to Canterbury.[35] Anselm was able to concentrate more exclusively than Bernard on the vocabulary of love and friendship. His letters are less often burdened by matters of business and the troubles of the world. But when Anselm spoke of his devotion to his friends, he referred to an objective state of being having little or nothing to do with any particular feeling on his own part. Anselm's friendships were part of a divine hierarchy of loves in the fullest platonic sense. Here friends were subsumed into Anselm's yearning for divine love. Anselm at times expected the same progression from human to divine in his friends and could be surprised and irritated by their demands for renewed attention and more letters.

Anselm believed in and wrote about friendship, but it was Bernard who was a friend. Anselm had to hold back, to reduce the requirements of friendship because of monastic obedience and humility, while Bernard invested his passions and loyalties in friendships, which he believed conformed to monastic requirements. This is not to contend that Anselm was a passionless human being in comparison to Bernard. Anselm's dealings with human beings were only shadows of his yearning for God, while Bernard in reaching out for other men on the way to God could not help getting involved with them. He had to explain himself because he wanted and needed to be understood and loved by his friends. Anselm sought love through understanding, while Bernard aimed at understanding through love.

[35] As analysed in my 'Love, friendship and sex in the eleventh century: The experience of Anselm', Studia Theologica 28 (Oslo: 1974) 111–52.

Postscript: Stephen Harding and Bernard's Model for Friendship

Almost all the friends mentioned in the preceding pages lived outside of Clairvaux. No matter how well we can describe Bernard's bonds with celebrated churchmen like Peter the Venerable, we are at a loss when we come to the practice of friendship at Clairvaux itself. Only Nicholas was a friend at Clairvaux, and with his special literary interests and cluniac connections, he remained outside the context of monastic community. Should one then conclude that we cannot say anything specific about friendship in Bernard's time at Clairvaux? The problem deserves further investigation, but for the moment it is possible to touch on one aspect of this problem: was the Bernard who entered Cîteaux in 1113 fully formed in terms of his views and practice of friendship? Should we consider him to have been only peripherally influenced by the existing bonds of the monks to each other? Is Bernard the originator of the cistercian ideal and practice of friendship, and should this be seen as a turning aside from a more ascetic ideal and way of life in the earliest Cîteaux, where there was no room for the cultivation of individual friendships?

Such a view might seem to gain support from the text of the earliest draft of the *Carta Caritatis*, where there is nothing about friendship.[36] The bond of charity implied by the document is a legal one, ensuring that the new group of monasteries maintains mutual love not for the purpose of friendship but to increase monastic discipline. There is much here, as Chrysogonus Waddell has pointed out,[37] that hearkens back to Cassian's *Conference* on friendship, but it is a non-particularized friendship of monastic harmony other than any

[36] Jean de la Croix Bouton and Jean Baptiste Van Damme, *Les plus anciens textes de Cîteaux* (Achel, 1974), parts of which are translated by Bede K. Lackner pp 443–66 in Louis Lekai, *The Cistercians: Ideals and Reality* (Kent State University Press, Ohio. 1977).

[37] 'Notes towards the Exegesis of a Letter by Saint Stephen Harding', E. Rozanne Elder, ed., *Noble Piety and Reformed Monasticism*, CS 65 (1981) 10–39.

special bonds among individual monks that are echoed in Cîteaux's texts.

As so often in dealing with early Cîteaux, we are hindered by a lack of contemporary documents and especially by a paucity of narratives. Father Chrysogonus provides help here in his article through an analysis of a letter from Stephen Harding to his former benedictine community at Sherborne. Dated to 1131, the letter can be seen as an assurance to an established english community that it had nothing to fear from the coming of the Cistercians to England (PL 185:1259).

In the first sentence of the letter, Stephen Harding provided a *captatio benevolentiae* which provides a classical-sounding definition of the purpose of letter writing in terms of maintaining love among those separated from each other: 'The function of a letter is to address the absent as though they were present, and to bring together through their fellowship of charity those still kept apart by long distances'. A careful search through earlier letter collections might reveal an exact source for this statement. For the moment, however, it is enough to characterize this as a statement of friendship and love from one community of monks to another, but especially from Stephen Harding himself to the monks of Sherborne. Some of them, he hoped, would remember him as 'their' monk.

By expressing himself in this manner, Stephen must have sought to disarm the hostility of Sherborne by appealing to a commonly accepted conception of monastic life as a *contubernium caritatis*. But is it possible to get even closer to the historical Stephen Harding and to see if he was as dedicated to the practice of friendship as Bernard was? There seems to be no contemporary or near-contemporary material, but in the *Life of Saint Peter of Juilly*, also an Englishman, we are told that he and Stephen were close friends in their youths and that they pursued studies in France before they became monks:

Peter became aware of his way of life and approved of it, so he joined ⟨Stephen⟩ to himself as a friend and companion ⟨familiarem et socium⟩. Thus both of them remained joined by the bond of holy companionship ⟨sanctae societatis⟩. . . . (PL 185:1259)

Since this biography was written sometime after 1160 and perhaps as late as 1185,[38] its value as historical evidence is limited. It refers to events that took place in the 1070s and so would have had to draw on a very long tradition. One cannot ignore the author's interest in making a link to Stephen, the renowned abbot of Cîteaux, in order to establish the holiness of his own Peter. But if we assume that there is some truth in this assertion of a strong friendship in Stephen's life as a cleric before he joined the reformed monastery of Molesme, then the pattern of his personal and religious development parallels that of Bernard: first there was the world of schools, friends, and competition for excellence in learning. Only then did the youth turn to the monastic life. If Stephen and Bernard had such similar backgrounds, rooted in the flowering of learning and the expression of friendship in clerical circles at the end of the eleventh century, then Stephen would immediately have been able to recognize in the young Bernard at the gates of Cîteaux the type of learned and enthusiastic young man he himself had been more than thirty years earlier at Molesme.

Because of Stephen Harding's own background in classical learning and clerical friendships, he could sympathize with the Bernard who brought his family and friends with him into his new life. Without the assent and encouragement of Stephen Harding, Bernard might never have been able to develop his practice and expression of friendship in the monastic life. Bernard might have done what he wanted in any case, but the presence of Stephen Harding still seems to have been essential for the new cistercian mode of friendship.

[38] See Lexikon für Theologie und Kirche 8:165.

The transformation from desert asceticism to a greater appreciation of the worth of human bonds in the process of monastic salvation will perhaps always remain an obscure process at early Cîteaux, but once Bernard becomes visible to us, the development is clear. He was a difficult and demanding friend, but one who could not imagine life without friends and friendship. He built on the tradition of Cicero as applied to monastic life by John Cassian but made the ethic and practice of friendship more personal and individual, a rightful aspect of monastic society's conversion of the world into God's image in man.

Bibliographical Note

For Bernard the saint I am deeply indebted to the work of Jean Leclercq, especially to the volumes indicated in the bibliographical note for the first chapter. The remark about hating or loving Bernard I have from my former student, Lars Grunnet, in a conversation with Dom Leclercq during a conference at the Medieval Centre in Copenhagen in September 1983. I am grateful to Lars Grunnet for many good talks on Bernard as a man, monk and politician. Also I owe a debt of thanks to the students who attended a class on Bernard at the Medieval Centre in Copenhagen in the autumn of 1990.

For clerical expressions of friendship, see especially *The Letters and Poems of Fulbert of Chartres*, ed. Frederick Behrends (Oxford 1976) and *Briefsammlungen der Zeit Heinrichs IV*, Monumenta Germaniae Historica: *Die Briefe der deutschen Kaiserzeit* 5, edd. Carl Erdmann and Norbert Fickermann. Böhlaus: Weimar, 1950.

A pioneering study of the difference between early cistercian ideals and those of the eastern desert in Late Antiquity is Benedicta Ward, 'The Desert Myth', in *One Yet Two*, ed. Basil Pennington, CS 29, 1976, 183–99.

Adriaan Bredero's interpretation of Bernard in terms of his zeal for spreading the Cistercian Order is found in his 'Saint

Bernard and the Historians', *Saint Bernard of Clairvaux*, CS 28, 1977, 27–62, especially the last pages.

Nicholas of Montiéramey or of Clairvaux is treated at length in Giles Constable, *The Letters of Peter the Venerable* 2, Cambridge, Massachusetts, 1967, 316–30. For the dispute between Bernard and Cluny, see Jean Leclercq's introduction to the *Apologia* to Abbot William, *Bernard of Clairvaux: Treatises* 1, CF 1, 1970. Also Adriaan Bredero, 'The Controversy between Peter the Venerable and Saint Bernard of Clairvaux', *Petrus Venerabilis*, edd. Giles Constable and James Kritzeck, Rome, 1956, 53–71.

Jerome's adage on true friendship appears frequently in medieval contexts: *amicitia, quae desinere potest, vera numquam fuit* (Ep 3.6, p 18 in I. Hilbert, Corpus Scriptorum Ecclesiasticorum Latinorum 54. Vienna, 1910.

On Aelred and Bernard, see Aelred Squire, *Aelred of Rievaulx: A Study*, CS 50, 1981, esp ch. 2, 'A Way of Life'.

For my remarks on Stephen Harding and Bernard, I would be able to say little at all without the published and unpublished work of Chrysogonus Waddell, as well as his letters to me. He is in the process of reevaluating the sources for the early history of Cîteaux, and his studies give them new life and meaning.

3. Bernard and Malachy Reconsidered

Intimacy or Confraternity?

In looking at the biographical materials for Bernard of Clairvaux, even the casual reader will notice that hagiography triumphs over biography. Except in a few passages in William of Saint Thierry's first book of the *Vita Prima*, Bernard is viewed from a distance as a saint-already-made, and so it is practically impossible to gain any intimate knowledge of him.[1] He is seen as a man of power and miracles, a new Martin of Tours who transformed the church around him, but he is hardly ever perceived from the inside.

A common explanation for this distance to Bernard the person lies in the fact that the *Vita Prima*'s later books were composed with a view to canonizing Bernard.[2] In the second

[1] The first book of the *Vita Prima* is usually dated to soon after 1145. The second book, by the benedictine abbot Ernald of Bonneval, was begun right after Bernard's death in 1153 and deals almost exclusively with Bernard's political career. The third, fourth and fifth books were composed after 1153 by Bernard's secretary, Geoffrey of Auxerre. See Adriaan H. Bredero, 'Saint Bernard and the Historians', *Saint Bernard of Clairvaux. Studies Commemorating the Eighth Centenary of his Canonization*, ed. M. Basil Pennington, CS 28 (1977).

[2] The pioneering work on the connection between the *Vita Prima* and

75

half of the twelfth century, sainthood was no longer an automatic process of acclamation. In order to obtain papal approval, Bernard had to be shown to be a saint in the mould of the miraclemaker or thaumaturge. To penetrate his interior life was of secondary interest, except when it mirrored the decisiveness of his actions.

The Vita Prima's reticence about the inner person may also be due to a second consideration. The abbot of Clairvaux had himself provided a model for hagiography in his Life of Malachy, the archbishop of Armagh in Ireland who had died at Clairvaux on 2 November 1148.[3] In describing Malachy's career, Bernard kept close to traditional models for hagiography. He emphasized power and miracles. In only a few instances did he break out of the mould to reveal intimate details about Malachy. In this one venture into hagiography, Bernard set a pattern that would confine his own biographer, Geoffrey of Auxerre.

Bernard's traditional approach may explain why it is so difficult for us today to gain a sense of the exact relationship between Bernard and Malachy. It is common to find mention of their 'friendship', even 'intimate friendship' in modern treatments of Bernard.[4] Yet when we look into the Life of Malachy, there is only limited information about their relationship. One Cistercian once confided to me that as far

---

Bernard's canonization is that of Adriaan Bredero, Études sur la Vita prima de saint Bernard (Rome, 1960). Bredero's conclusions are summarized in his 'The Canonization of Bernard of Clairvaux', CS 28 (note 1 above) 27–62, esp. 31–34.

[3] V Mal is to be founded in SBOp 3:307–78. I use the english translation by Robert T. Meyer, The Life and Death of Saint Malachy the Irishman (CF 10, 1978).

[4] Louis Lekai, The Cistercians: Ideals and Reality (Kent State University Press, Ohio, 1977) p 271, wrote of 'the intimate friendship between Saint Bernard and Saint Malachy'. Anselme Dimier, 'Mourir à Clairvaux', Collectanea Ordinis Cisterciensis Reformatorum 17 (1955) 272–85, mentioned (p 279) the first visit of Malachy to Bernard in 1139 as forming a 'friendship which would last until death'. David Hugh Farmer's entry on Malachy in The Oxford Dictionary of Saints (Clarendon Press, 1978) 258–59, interestingly did not use the term friendship. Farmer considered the V Mal to be 'biased'.

as he could tell, there was no friendship at all. Malachy was cultivated as a matter of political convenience in Bernard's plan to spread the Cistercian Order into Ireland.

This sceptical view provides one extreme in understanding Bernard and Malachy, while the assertion of an intimate friendship between the two men gives another point of reference. I shall try in what follows to argue for a compromise solution. In reviewing carefully the text of Bernard's *Life of Malachy* and the models behind it, I find a close bond between the two men. But their relationship is not described in detail. Only in his account of Malachy's death at Clairvaux did Bernard provide some information about his own closeness to the irish churchman.

It may seem a waste of time to try at a distance of almost nine centuries to dig up evidence about something as subtle and fragile in human life as a friendship.[5] However ill-equipped we are to answer the question of friendship, the matter can intrigue anyone who takes the trouble to penetrate the difficult facade of Bernard's language. In dealing with hagiographical materials, Bernard gave his followers a model and kept cistercian biography clear of the intimate portraiture that appears, for example, in Eadmer of Canterbury's *Life of Saint Anselm*, a work that Bernard could have known.[6]

Despite his central position in cistercian life, Bernard did not succeed in imposing his type of hagiography on the order. Cistercian descriptions of saintly figures eventually did concern themselves with matters of interior life. The visionary dimension that underlies so much of Bernard's language in his other works, but was largely kept out of the *Life of Malachy*, managed to surface in later cistercian biographies.

[5] For a definition of friendship in its medieval and monastic context, see my *Friendship and Community* pp xiv-xvi.

[6] Several of the twelfth-century manuscripts of the *Vita Anselmi* are of french cistercian provenance. One of them, Troyes MS 6, comes from Clairvaux. See *The Life of Saint Anselm by Eadmer*, ed. R. W. Southern (Oxford Medieval Texts. Clarendon Press, 1972) p xviii.

This process of spiritual and literary osmosis is not easy to trace, but in taking the *Life of Malachy* as a point of departure, we will see how the genre of cistercian hagiography developed from the mid-twelfth to the mid-thirteenth century.

Recent Interpretations

After the publication of the *Life of Malachy* in the standard edition of Bernard's writings in 1963, useful studies have looked at the work in terms of its content and purpose. A canadian historian, J. S. Maddux, provided in 1976 one of the most thorough treatments, 'Saint Bernard as Hagiographer'.[7] Here he showed how Bernard used his description of Malachy in order to provide a model bishop for imitation by other churchmen. Just as in the *De consideratione*, also written during Bernard's last years, the abbot of Clairvaux told the pope how to behave, so too in the *Vita Malachiae* he provided a programme for episcopal reform.

Concentrating on models for episcopal life, Maddux pointed out that Bernard divided up his treatment of Malachy into alternating periods of outward involvement as a churchman and inward withdrawal into a monk-like discipline.[8] This rhythm of life is broken only in the last chapters, where Bernard described Malachy's final visit to Clairvaux and his death there. What Maddux calls the dynamic of ascent from one stage of episcopal activity to another is ended when Malachy came for good to Clairvaux, the claustral paradise

[7] *Cîteaux: Commentarii Cistercienses* 27 (1976) 85–108, esp. p 86. Another interesting analysis of the V Mal is that of Thomas J. Renna, 'Saint Bernard and Abelard as Hagiographers', *Cîteaux* 29 (1978) 41–59, but the article is open to the objection that Abelard's autobiography cannot fruitfully be placed in the genre of hagiography. Maddux provides a full bibliography in his notes for earlier work on the V Mal. I will not try to reproduce his references unless they have direct relevance to my own interpretations.

[8] Maddux, p 97: 'He takes over the principle of the saint's history as a continually greater manifestation of God's presence in him . . . and at the same time shapes the narrative into a cycle of alternating monastic and episcopal periods.'

which he entered as the first step on a new journey, this time as a citizen of heaven.

Maddux's rich interpretation of the *Life of Malachy* does not answer one vital question. Whom did Bernard intend as his audience? What group or groups in the church did Bernard want to influence through his writings? Maddux implies that Bernard was concerned with the episcopacy and anyone in a position of authority. But what about the monks of Clairvaux themselves? Did not Bernard see that in providing such a tale of adventure and ascent in the secular church, he might be distracting his monks from the content of their own lives?

We will have to look more closely at Bernard's hints about his audience, and we will also have to consider Bernard's information about Malachy's early life. As the australian historian Barry O'Dwyer has shown in a brief but penetrating article, the abbot of Clairvaux probably could not have known about Malachy's childhood from his irish monastic sources.[9] They could not have provided him with the details about Malachy's considerations in leaving the world that Bernard provided. Influenced by Jean Leclercq's willingness to provide psychological explanations in interpreting Bernard, O'Dwyer made the point that Bernard in writing about Malachy's family, education and deliberations on a way of life was actually reflecting on himself and his own choices in youth.[10]

With O'Dwyer's and Maddux's analyses, and as ever relying on the pioneering work of Jean Leclercq, we can turn to

[9] 'Saint Bernard as an Historian: The *Life of St Malachy of Armagh*', *Journal of Religious History* 10 (1978) 128–41, esp. pp 136–37. I am most grateful to Professor O'Dwyer for sending me this article. His further work on the *Life of Malachy* will be published in a forthcoming german language edition of the works of Saint Bernard.

[10] O'Dwyer, p 137. '. . . Bernard's reversion to the events and the meaning of his own life in recounting the events of Malachy's early years would suggest that he was unconsciously under the influence of the psychological theme of repetition.' O'Dwyer here refers to Jean Leclercq's article, 'Literature and Psychology in Bernard of Clairvaux', *The Downside Review* 93 (1975) 1–20.

the *Life of Malachy* itself. The purpose of what follows is not to challenge previous results but to consider the text and its contemporary context in order to look at the hagiography in what it reveals about Bernard. The *Life of Malachy* reflects Bernard's ongoing effort to interpret the world in terms of God's will. This he saw primarily within the monastery but also in a larger community of believers of which the monastery was only a part.

Bernard's Autobiography

Geoffrey of Auxerre, Bernard's secretary and biographer, long ago anticipated O'Dwyer's psychological interpretation of Bernard's link to Malachy in the hagiography: 'Our father commended his ways and in the blessed Malachy left his own image, though not on purpose.'[11]   This fascinating remark can provide a point of departure for understanding Bernard's work. He described himself in Malachy, for Malachy was everything Bernard wanted to be: a man of God who brought order and peace to his contemporaries in spreading the good news of the Gospel, reforming the church, while at the same time insisting on a monastic centre to his life.

Bernard took his point of departure in the cloister, while Malachy moved in and out of the cloister in his path through the irish church.[12]   In emphasizing Malachy's yearning for

[11] 'Suos vero sanctissimus Pater noster commendavit mores, in beato Malachia suam expressit imaginem non advertens', Leclercq, 'Etudes sur saint Bernard et le texte de ses écrits', *Analecta Sacri Ordinis Cisterciensis* 9 (1953) 164. The next sentence, as Leclercq admits, is none too clear: 'Nam ego fateor, dictante eo, in tabulis quae proferebat excipiens, sine dilatione notavi quod domi abiit ut disceret.' The statement shows that Bernard dictated the *Life of Malachy* to Geoffrey, as one would expect. Geoffrey may be pointing out that what Bernard learned from Malachy he could also have learned from himself. Thus Geoffrey saw Bernard at Clairvaux going out to meet Malachy and learn from him about a way of life that Bernard himself already led.

[12] Maddux, p 98: '. . . Bernard always takes care to present Malachy as the ideal monk each time the saint is about to accept a new office or undertake a new apostolic activity.'

quiet and for community, Bernard described his own vocation. In showing how the churchman could not avoid con-
frontation with powerful interests which had different uses
for the church, Bernard recalled the incidents of his own life
and his frequent absences from the monastery in order to
deal with ecclesiastical matters in themselves unconnected
with monastic life.

It was probably also Geoffrey of Auxerre who composed
the first proper office for Malachy at Clairvaux. This was
made, as has been shown, in the preparations for Malachy's
canonization.[13] The first efforts to make him officially a saint
were not successful. Malachy was not canonized until 1190.
When Bernard obtained sainthood in 1174, the Cistercians
took part of the office intended for Saint Malachy and applied
it to Saint Bernard. Thus what Bernard originally had written about Malachy was used in several instances to describe
Bernard himself. The passages, which Chrysogonus Waddell
has compiled, are brief formularies in the liturgical mould.
They do not provide any striking information about the personalities of Bernard or of Malachy. But the cistercian ease in
transferring malachian epithets from one liturgy to another
shows that Geoffrey's insight was not unique. In recycling
Bernard's words on Malachy into the liturgy for the feast of
Saint Bernard, the monks of Clairvaux saw that Bernard in
describing Malachy as a man of God, close to the monastic life and at the same time a church reformer, also had
described himself.

The early chapters of the *Life of Malachy*, in which Bernard
dealt with the saint's early life, contain many parallels to
Bernard's own experience.[14] Malachy was seen as very close

[13] Here as so often I am deeply indebted to Father Chrysogonus Waddell
for his published and unpublished work. His letters have been faithful
companions in guiding me onto the right track in this complex area of
cistercian liturgical history. See his 'The two Saint Malachy Offices from
Clairvaux', *Bernard of Clairvaux. Studies presented to Dom Jean Leclercq*, CS 23
(1973) 123–59, esp. 150–51.
[14] Compare V Mal I.l–III.6 (SBOp 3:309–15) with VP I.l–9 (PL 185:227–32).

to his mother, who encouraged him to cultivate learning. Like Bernard, Malachy was attracted to learning but at a crucial moment decided not to make a career of it. Malachy, like Bernard, had to deal with a sceptical, critical sister who did not understand or appreciate his vocation. Malachy, like Bernard, looked for a master who could teach him what he wanted to know about the religious life. In searching for a place apart from men, Malachy inevitably attracted men and created his own community, just as Bernard had done.[15]

In these chapters we recognize a pattern of separation from family and school familiar from William of Saint Thierry's portrait of Bernard, a pattern surely drawn from William's conversations with Bernard. At the same time Bernard may have used earlier hagiographical models in describing the young Malachy. One possible point of reference is Bernard's assertion that as a child Malachy did not like to play. In Bede's *Life of Cuthbert* the saint as a child is said to have enjoyed play but was told that this activity was not appropriate for his future life as bishop.[16] In some instances Bernard had to depend on information that was specific to Malachy, as in a story that the youth had been repelled by his teacher when he found him playing with a shoemaker's awl.[17] Bernard seems to have arranged his material to make Malachy's experience conform to his own. He may not have known that

[15] Compare V Mal II.5 (SBOp 3:314): 'Ita qui primo solitarius sedit et unicus patris sui, fit iam unus ex multis, fit ex unigenito primogenitus in multis fratribus' with VP I.10 (PL 185:232): '. . . sic ignis quem miserat Dominus in cor servi sui volens ut arderet, primo fratres ejus aggreditur, solo minimo ad conversionem adhuc minus habili, seniori patri ad solatium derelicto, deinde cognatos, et socios, et amicos. . . . '

[16] See Bertram Colgrave, ed., *Two Lives of Saint Cuthbert* (Cambridge 1940), Bede ch. 1.

[17] V Mal I.2 (SBOp 3:311), CF 10, p 17, a very striking anecdote: 'Intrans vero domum, vidit virum ludentem subula crebrisque fulcantem tractibus, nescio quo notabili modo, parietem. Et solo visu offensus puer serius, quod levitatem redoleret, resilivit ab eo. . . . ' Notice that even here, however, Bernard admitted he did not have all the details: *nescio quo notabili modo.*

Malachy's first school teacher was his own father,[18] but his
failure to mention this fact may as well be due to a desire
to emphasize the mother's role in the boy Malachy's life.

At one point Bernard provided an inner monologue for
Malachy, revealing his thoughts about breaking away from
the life of secular schools in order to lead another kind of
life.[19] Malachy is described as considering the gifts God had
given him, and wondering if he would be able to make secure
what he had received. He decided that for a time he would
lose his life so that he did not lose it forever. He would hand
himself completely over to the Lord, who would repay him
with interest:

> What I am and what I have, where would they both
> be safe if not in the hands of the Author? Who is so
> solicitous for their preservation, so powerful to keep
> them and so faithful in restoring them? He will preserve
> them in safety and bring them back in his own good
> time. Without restraint I give myself over to serve him
> by his own gifts.[20]

Even if Malachy at some point later in life actually told his
companions or Saint Bernard himself about similar deliberations, the abbot of Clairvaux would not have known their
content in such detail. If we look closely at the language, with
its collage of biblical references and reminiscences, there is
no doubt Bernard provided here a classic description of arguments for conversion to monastic life and at the same time
gave his audience his own reasons for his choice. In his view,
our lives are fragile and can easily be crushed. In a moment
everything can be lost. The young man in search of meaning,
purpose and permanence asks:

> Shall I lose in a moment all the blessings of goodness
> which have anticipated me from the beginning? Much

[18] V Mal I.l (SBOp 3:310—See the note for lines 1–3). CF 10:129, n.7.
[19] V Mal I.3 (SBOp 3:312), CF 10:18–19.
[20] Ibid. = CF 10:19.

rather do I resign myself and them to him who is their source, for I also belong to him.[21]

As a necessary conclusion, Malachy is shown as going to a holy man in Armagh, Imar, who lived next to the church and provided Malachy with what he needed, a pattern of life (*formam vitae*). The rest of the biography is basically concerned with the pattern that Malachy followed, not in becoming a monk, but in combining monastic solitude with ecclesiastical commitment, just as Bernard did.

Bernard's audience, to which we later will return, would have been familiar with such deliberations. The augustinian strand of self-examination was stronger than ever in twelfth-century clerical and monastic circles. As hagiographer, Bernard could draw on this tradition by making a mosaic of appropriate biblical passages emphasizing the brevity of life and our total dependence on God's goodness. The conclusion, *conversio*, was foregone, but the decision and its circumstances were worth dwelling on as a decisive moment in human life and the history of salvation. Bernard knew it all from his own experience. In describing Malachy, he generalized from his own conversion.

A second area where Bernard tread on familiar ground is revealed in his description of Malachy's conflicts with secular or ecclesiastical authorities who did not share his programme of reform.[22] In such confrontations Malachy and Bernard were on the same side, favouring an episcopal church in which secular power could have only a limited influence. Here Bernard did not make it clear to his audience that the irish church had for centuries functioned in a different way from the roman one.[23] Insular bishops had lived in monasteries and had provided the sacraments

---

[21] Ibid.= CF 10:18.

[22] See, for example V Mal XI.22; CF 10:40–41 (the defeat of Malachy's enemy Nigel) or XIII.28; CF 10:45 (Machprulin, who slandered Malachy, was punished).

[23] V Mal X.19 (SBOp 3:329; CF 10:37–8), the note for line 8: 'S. Bernardus hic confundit abbates et episcopos monasticos . . . . '

without having territorial dioceses. They were usually subject to abbots whose election could often reflect secular rather than ecclesiastical concerns. Bernard was not interested in how different the irish church had been. His concern was to show how Malachy enhanced the episcopal position and brought the irish church into line with Rome. Like Bernard, Malachy had to go to Italy to see the pope and to iron out vexed questions of discipline and authority.

Here we find an emphasis on the *vita apostolica* that was an important concern in twelfth-century life and finally led in the next century to the foundation of the mendicant orders: 'The apostolic way of life which was all the more wondrous in Malachy as it was rare in others'.[24] Like the biographer of Saint Martin, Sulpicius Severus, Bernard used his saint to lash out against the bishops of his own day. He contrasted the activities of his holy bishop with those of average bishops in his own time.[25]

Heroic Biography

To mention Sulpicius Severus is to bring to mind how traditional Bernard was in his description of Malachy. Especially in the earlier chapters of the *Life of Malachy*, Bernard preferred familiar images of battle and war to describe Malachy's efforts. When his sister died, his prayers for her are described as weapons breaking down the gates of heaven.[26] The offering of mass for her is seen as a powerful weapon against

---

[24] V Mal XIX.44 (SBOp 3:349; CF 10:58): 'Forma apostolica haec, et inde magis mira in Malachia, quo rara nimis in aliis'. For an insightful presentation of such thought and language in the period, see M.D. Chenu, 'Monks, Canons and Laymen in Search of the Apostolic Life', *Nature, Man and Society in the Twelfth Century*, trans. Lester K. Little and Jerome Taylor (University of Chicago Press, 1968) 202–38.

[25] See the comparisons made in V Mal XIX.44 (SBOp 3:349; CF 10:58) in which Bernard started with the behaviour of the bishops (*illi*) and then pointed out Malachy's contrasting actions: 'Illi dominantur in clero; iste, dum esset liber ex omnibus, omnium se servum fecit.'

[26] V Mal V.ll (SBOp 3:320; CF 10:28): '. . . quando peccatrix mulier fraternis obtinuit armis, quos suis meritis negabatur.'

the devil, a conception of the sacrifice of the mass far from thirteenth-century hagiographical literature, where the offering of mass opened up visions of heaven.

Time and again Malachy had to fight the devil. When a sick monk tried to kill him, his response is described in terms of fighting. His prayers were the arms with which he put the devil to flight.[27] Malachy was Christ's warrior (*bellator tuus*) who suffered greatly for him.[28] This new recruit of Christ recalls the language of Saint Paul and repeats an image to readers of early medieval hagiography.[29] Malachy in his confrontations with the devil can be seen as a new Martin of Tours. He is a saint in the mould of the first medieval centuries, when powerful men and women seemed necessary in order to cleanse society of devils able to roam about at will and ravage human lives. We are a long way from the tenderness and intimacy that the cistercian spirit is supposed to have brought into its surroundings. Here we reach the fringes of a Europe where reason and order were absent.

Malachy's main weapon in conquering the devil was the miracle. The account of his miracles makes up more than half the hagiography. Because of the predominance of miracles, Bernard could link Malachy's prowess to the patterns evident in earlier times. He could compare Malachy with such Old Testament prophets as Elisha and Elijah. When a woman tried to interrupt Malachy's sermon, he said nothing, but some force oppressed and almost suffocated her. 'Thus the miserable wretch taking up against Malachy the reproach that was made to Elisha found out that he was indeed a second Elisha.'[30] Those who challenged Malachy found to their

[27] V Mal VI.14 (SBOp 3:324; CF 10:28).
[28] V Mal VIII.17 (SBOp 3:326; CF 10:34): 'Quanta passus est pro nomine tuo bellator tuus a filiis sceleratis!'
[29] V Mal XIV.32 (SBOp 3:339; CF 10:48): 'Et ecce rursus accingitur, quasi novus Christi tiro, ad spirituale certamen.' Cf. Eph 6:10–11. See the *Vita S. Martini* 4.3, where Martin addressed the emperor with his defiant words, 'hactenus...militavi tibi; patere ut nunc militem Deo.' *Sulpice Sévère. Vie de Saint Martin*, ed. Jacques Fontaine. Sources chrétiennes (Paris, 1967) I:260.
[30] V Mal XXIII.52 (SBOp 3:337), CF 10:46. Cf 2 Kgs 2:24.

dismay that he was under God's special protection. Just as the prophets of old, he brought news of God's dispensation and conveyed divine wrath to those who refused to believe. In some cases Malachy is seen as being even more effective than his Old Testament models. When a woman was dying, he came and stopped her flow of blood. This action is compared with that of Elisha, who had sent a boy servant unable to provide the help needed.[31] Bernard was keenly aware of the biblical text and development of story. In his narrative he presented every detail to make the parallel more complete and striking for his audience.

In a highly dramatic parallel to the Old Testament, Malachy caused a storm that wreaked havoc and death only on his enemies: 'This brings me to the deed of Saint Elijah, bringing clouds and rain from the ends of the earth, now calling over the blasphemers fire from heaven.'[32] Bernard saw Elijah and Elisha as much more than lonely saintly figures. They were politically concerned, willing to challenge the secular authorities of their time. Their involvement reflected that of both Bernard and Malachy.

In summing up the different miracles of Malachy, Bernard pointed out that the types corresponded to those found in the Bible and in previous lives of the saints:

> For in what type of ancient miracles did Malachy not excel? If we pay earnest heed to those few which I mentioned above, he did not lack prophecy or revelation or revenge upon the ungodly, or the grace of healing, or changing of mind and even raising of the dead.[33]

Bernard was guided by the miracles of Christ, as in the many healings of sick and lame people.[34] At the same time he may have had in mind some of the saints described by

---

[31] V Mal XXIII.52 (SBOp 3:356; CF 10:66): '. . . alterum se exhibens puerum Elisaei, nisi quod huius efficacio opera fuit.' Cf. 2 Kgs 4:29.

[32] V Mal XI.23 (SBOp 3:333; CF 10:41).

[33] V Mal XXIX.66 (SBOp 3:370), CF 10:84.

[34] As V Mal XXVII.40–41 (SBOp 3:345–47; CF 10:54).

Gregory the Great in the 590s in the first book of his *Dialogues*.[35] These italian abbots and bishops were renowned not for what they said but for what they did in transforming a countryside plagued by barbarians (the Lombards) into one where orthodox Christians could live in peace and worship God without harassment. Although Bernard does not refer directly to Gregory in the *Life of Malachy*, his hagiography shows the same interest in presenting God's power as working through the holy and virtuous man who safeguarded the church and defeated God's enemies. In this crude world of good and evil, there is little room for doubt about right and wrong. Moral subtleties are absent. The naked power of God is transmitted through heroes fighting for him.

Bernard's primary hagiographical model for a bishop-monk was Sulpicius Severus's *Life of Saint Martin of Tours*.[36] Jean Leclercq has shown how for centuries saints' lives based on Martin had emphasized miracles, while Bernard in his sermon on Martin also made use of Sulpicius's hagiographical emphasis on poverty.[37] But in the *Life of Malachy*, Bernard was more traditional. Certainly Malachy, by his lack of interest in acquisitions and his criticism of materialistic bishops, provided references to Martin's poverty. But the theme of poverty is almost drowned in miracle stories.

Like his model Martin, Malachy is first of all a thaumaturge. His *virtus* consists primarily in being a lightning rod for God's power. At one point Bernard does insist that a change in someone's attitude is a greater event than any

[35] For the latin text, Umberto Moricca, *Gregorii Magni Dialogi* (Rome, 1924), translated by Odo John Zimmerman, *Saint Gregory the Great. Dialogues*, The Fathers of the Church 39 (New York, 1959). In the responses of Gregory's deacon, Peter, who, as at the end of ch. 3 (p 15 in the trans.) could remark, 'I see how unfounded my previous impression was that Italy had no wonder-workers.'

[36] As above, note 29. Trans. in F.H. Hoare, *The Western Fathers* (London: Sheed and Ward, 1954, 1980).

[37] 'S. Martin dans l'hagiographie monastique du moyen age', *Saint Martin et son temps*, Studia Anselmiana 46 (Rome, 1961) 175–87, esp. 186–87.

external miracle.[38] This emphasis points to new directions in hagiography, but here it is only a hint, not a major shift in the direction of the narrative.

Bernard was acutely self-aware when he wrote. He told his audience that he deliberately omitted a description of Malachy the inner man.[39] This little-noticed declaration comes in the text just after a more celebrated passage in which Bernard claimed Malachy was his own greatest miracle.[40] This assertion so pleased Geoffrey of Auxerre that he copied it when he wrote about Bernard.[41] Just when it would be appropriate to pass from the saint's acts to his inner life, Bernard gives us a description of Malachy in terms of the way he appeared to his contemporaries. Literary devices take over in providing apt juxtapositions: *per omnia serius, sed non austerus. Remissus interdum, dissolutus numquam.*[42] However pleasing to the ear Bernard's latin phrases might be, they do not provide any new revelations about Malachy. Bernard did not want to penetrate beneath the surface of Malachy's life. He revealed little of Malachy's speech, nor did he provide many personal or memorable anecdotes reflecting Malachy's inner life.

This view of Bernard's presentation of Malachy is not intended as a criticism of the writer for failing to be more 'modern' in his approach to biography. Bernard was faithful to traditional models and can hardly be taken to task for sticking to what would have been familiar to his audience. But Bernard did not have to be so cautious. There were other possible models, like the *Vitae Patrum*, the Lives of the Desert

[38] V Mal XXV.54 (SBOp 3:358; CF 10:68–69): '. . . ego istud superiori suscitatae miraculo mortuae censeo praeferendum, quod exterior quidem ibi, hic vero interior revixerit homo.'

[39] V Mal XIX.43 (SBOp 3:348; CF 10:57): 'Ut enim taceam interiorem hominem eius. . . . '

[40] Ibid.: 'Et meo quidem iudicio primum et maximum miraculum, quod dedit, ipse erat.'

[41] VP IV.1 = PL 185:303: '. . . sicut Malachiam sanctum idem ipse commendat, primum maximumque miraculum quod exhibuit, ipse fuit.'

[42] V Mal XIX.43 (SBOp 3:348; CF 10:57).

Fathers, with their brilliant dialogue. However much he had been a man of action, Malachy could also have been remembered for what he had said to his disciples during their trials and tribulations. But the sayings neither of Malachy's teachers nor of Malachy himself are recorded. This may have been because Bernard did not know Malachy very well. It is possible, of course, that Malachy was not one for memorable sayings and Bernard deliberately glossed over his silence. But Bernard's main reason for keeping a distance may well lie in a desire to heroize the saint, to place him in well-known categories and to show his attitudes through striking actions rather than any significant words.

In a few of the miracle stories, Bernard did provide a dialogue that makes the situation come alive and renders it into more than a repetition of a biblical story. This is the case, for example, when Malachy's plans for a church built in stone were challenged. Malachy assured his opponent that his work would be finished, but his enemy would not live to see it. Even here, however, the dialogue, instead of making Malachy more an individual, emphasizes his traditional background. He is like the Old Testament prophet predicting doom for those who had no faith in the rightness of his vision.[43]

Bernard the Traditionalist

The language and style of Bernard of Clairvaux, as well as the impact of the Cistercians on twelfth-century society, are so striking that it is easy to forget that Bernard and his monks considered themselves traditionalists. They thought of themselves as reasserting values and ways of life that had been lost.[44] In writing the *Life of Malachy* Bernard had no desire

[43] V Mal XXVIII.62 (SBOp 3:366; CF 10:78): 'Tu vero, quia non vis, non videbis; et quod non vis, morieris: attendito tibi, ne in peccato tuo moriaris.'

[44] As we see in the text of the *Exordium Parvum* (to which Bernard would have contributed), which describes the reasons why the first monks left Molesme: 'Nam viri isti apud Molismum positi, saepius inter se Dei gratia aspirati, de transgressione regulae beati Benedicti patris monacho-

to provide a new pattern for the bishop-monk who reformed the church and restored its liberty. He wanted to assert the values that he found already established in the lives of such bishops as Augustine, Martin of Tours, and Gregory the Great. Bernard was appalled that before Malachy irish Christianity had long existed without the administrative forms that he took for granted as necessary for the spread of the Gospel:

> For a thing unheard of from the very beginning of Christianity occurred: bishops were changed without order or reason and they were multiplied at the whim of the metropolitan.... [45]

For Bernard, Malachy brought order and reason (*ordo et ratio*) back into the life of the irish church, and so Bernard deliberately used these same words in describing the death and burial of Malachy: *cuncta geruntur ex ordine, cuncta ex ratione procedunt.*[46]

The reason and order that Malachy actually brought to Ireland were quite different in their hierarchical forms from anything that had earlier existed. But Bernard had no great interest in the past as it really had been. His job was not that of the fact-oriented historian but of the tradition-bound reformer. Bernard could not accept that in Ireland bishops could be multiplied in number, live in monasteries without territorial dioceses, and be subject to semi-secular abbots. Once Malachy had asserted himself, everything was changed.

---

rum loquebantur, conquerebantur, contristabantur, videntes se ceterosque monachos hanc regulam sollempni professione servaturos promisisse, eamque minime custodisse, et ob hoc perjurii crimen scienter incurrisse, et propter hoc apostolicae sedis legati auctoritate uti praelibavimus, ad hanc solitudinem convolaverunt, ut professionem suam observantia sanctae regulae adimplerent.... ' Text in Jean de la Croix Bouton and Jean Baptiste Van Damme, *Les plus anciens textes de Cîteaux*, Cîteaux. Commentarii Cistercienses. Studia et Documenta 2 (Achel, 1974).

[45] V Mal X.19 (SBOp 3:330), CF 10:38: 'Nam quod inauditum est ab ipso christianitatis initio, sine ordine, sine ratione mutabantur et multiplicabantur episcopi pro libitu metropolitani.'

[46] V Mal XXXI.74 (SBOp 3:378; CF 10:92).

To Bernard's mind, Malachy created an order that was eternal and necessary.

Bernard's attention to tradition helps explain why he was not so eager to plunge the depths of Malachy's mind. In casting about for models, Bernard found in Malachy the bishop, church reformer, and advocate of cistercian monasticism whom he needed. What mattered to Bernard was not so much what Malachy thought and felt but what he actually did to carry out his policies. Only at the end of Malachy's life, in his last few days at Clairvaux, could Bernard concern himself with Malachy as a man of flesh and blood. This rapprochement took place on the threshold of Malachy's transformation into a saint.

It is important to realize that until Malachy's last stay at Clairvaux, Bernard never really had a chance to get to know him well. In all, Malachy visited Clairvaux three times. The first two visits, which probably took place in 1139 on the way to and from Italy, could each not have lasted more than a few days. Bernard's own description of his meeting with Malachy is sketchy and provides no memorable anecdotes.[47] The main result of the first visit is said to have been Malachy's request to the pope that he be allowed to become a monk of Clairvaux. According to Bernard, Malachy was deeply moved by the sight of the brothers of Clairvaux. They in turn were 'not in a small way edified by his presence and speech.'[48] We are not told, however, what the monks and Malachy actually said to each other. Bernard's only indication that a close bond was formed between himself and Malachy is contained in the phrase *intimis visceribus colligens*, indicating that he was taken into Malachy's intimacy.[49]

[47] V Mal XVI.37 (SBOp 3:343; CF 10:51–52).
[48] Ibid.: '. . . visis fratribus, compunctus est, et illi non mediocriter aedificati in praesentia et sermone eius.'
[49] Ibid. Robert T. Meyer in his helpful notes to the translation points out (CF 10:139, n. 113) that this phrase may be connected to 'Hebrew symbolism' which 'made the bowels the seat of the affections.'

When Malachy returned to Clairvaux, the main order of business was to establish that some of his companions would remain there in preparation for being sent back to Ireland as cistercian monks. Malachy's own words are quoted, to the effect that the monks will be a seed in whom the irish people will be blessed. These people had from ancient times heard the word monk but had never seen any.[50] This idea of a barbarian people that had not seen monks was repeated fifty years later in the *Exordium Magnum Cisterciense* in describing the swedish people.[51] Once again Bernard provided a language that would be recycled in later cistercian literature.

The description of Malachy's return visit to Clairvaux is especially noteworthy because Bernard allowed himself the freedom of departing from his narrative and describing how the men left at Clairvaux eventually did return to Ireland and establish a monastery. These included Christian, the first abbot of Mellifont, founded north of Dublin in 1142. Malachy's visit to Clairvaux is thus interpreted mainly as a point of departure for a new cistercian foundation. Clairvaux is seen as a powerhouse, a centre of learning for men to be trained in the monastic life so that they could later spread it in Ireland. By the time Bernard wrote the *Life of Malachy* in 1149, he could boast that the new house had already founded five daughters: 'and so, the seed having been multiplied, the number of monks grows daily, according to the desire and prophecy (*vaticinium*) of Malachy.'[52] This is the only time in the narrative that the word *vaticinium* is used. Malachy is remembered

---

[50] V Mal XVI.39 (SBOp 3:345; CF 10:53): 'illae gentes, quae a diebus antiquis monachi quidem nomen audierunt, monachum non viderunt.'

[51] EM IV.28, p 260: '. . . qui monachi quidem nomen audierant, sed monachum antea non viderant.'

[52] V Mal XVI.39 (SBOp 3:345; CF 10:53): '. . . augescit in dies numerus monachorum, iuxta desiderium et vaticinium Malachiae.' For the spread of cistercian monasticism in Ireland, see Geraldine Carville, 'The Cistercian Settlement of Ireland (1142–1541)', *Studia Monastica* 15 (1973) 23–37, and Roger Stalley, *The Cistercian Monasteries of Ireland* (London and New Haven: Yale University Press, 1987) 7–16. It is notable that Stalley in describing the bond between Bernard and Malachy does not use the term 'friendship' but instead writes of their 'profound respect and admiration for each other.'

as a prophet for furthering the spread of cistercian monasticism in Ireland.

Two visits, each of three or four days, do not in themselves 'disqualify' Malachy and Bernard from forming a friendship. Anyone who ever has had the privilege to come as a guest and participate even for a few days in the life of a flourishing monastic community knows that friendships quickly arise in such a context. But what was important for Bernard to describe here was not the formation of an intimate bond between himself and Malachy. His purpose was to show that Malachy, in coming to Clairvaux, entered into its fellowship or confraternity and made himself instrumental in the spread of the Cistercians to a new part of the world. Malachy's role was that of God's instrument in the growth of the Cistercian Order. Through his visit and its practical results he became forever joined to Clairvaux.

Only in the description of Malachy's third and final visit to Clairvaux did Bernard sketch the outline of a personal friendship. Bernard started by using the ecstatic language of the Psalms about the day which the Lord has made as full of joy.[53] He described, however rhetorically, his own response to Malachy's arrival: 'How quickly and leaping I, though weak and shaking, came to him. How happily I rushed into his embrace.' Bernard here used the type of language concerning the meeting of friends that he included in some of his letters of friendship, as in writing to Peter the Venerable, abbot of Cluny.[54] Introducing the language of the Song of Songs, Bernard hinted that he had spent time alone with Malachy.[55]

[53] V Mal XXXI.70 (SBOp 3:374; CF 10:88): 'Quam iucundus ad eius introitum dies festus illuxit nobis.' Cf. Ps 117:24: 'Haec est dies quam fecit Dominus; exsultemus et laetemur in ea.'

[54] See, for example, Bernard's description of how he felt at receiving a letter from Peter the Venerable: Ep 389; SBOp 8:356–57.

[55] V Mal XXXI.70 (SBOp 3:374; CF 10:88): 'Quam alacri vultu et animo, mi Pater, introduxi te in domum matris meae et in cubiculum genitricis meae!' Cf. Song 3:4.

Once again, however, we are not allowed to hear Malachy's voice or to get an idea of the content of his conversation. Bernard merely insisted on the joy of an occasion when the brothers could be together in unity with their guest (Ps 132:1). Already here Malachy is being converted into a saint whose physical presence in life was less important than what remained with the brothers after his death: 'Then we heard his wisdom, we held his presence and we still hold it' (*tenuimus praesentiam eius et tenemus*).[56]

The four or five days of Malachy's spiritual feast with the brethren of Clairvaux quickly passed and gave way to two weeks of illness (18 October- 1 November 1148). Here Bernard let go his restraint and turned to a cistercian language of tenderness. This type of personal warmth we know from elsewhere in his writings, especially from some of his letters and the Sermons on the Song of Songs.[57] But until now this tone had been almost conspicuously absent in the *Life of Malachy*. Bernard described the scene of Malachy's illness in some detail. The brethren busied themselves, trying to get Malachy to take medicine or to eat. At last we have Malachy's own words, as he protested that it was *sine causa*, to no purpose, to take medicine, but he would do whatever the brethren ordered 'because of love'.[58]

Here are the detail and sense of an individual human presence that the literary genre of heroic biography rarely provides. Bernard had broken through his own self-imposed habits and now gave a slow, loving description of the friend's last days. There are no more miracles, except for a single brief incident after Malachy's death. Instead we read his last words, looking forward to the end, promising the brothers that they in death would not be parted: 'Take care of me. I

---

[56] V Mal XXXI.70 (SBOp 3:374), CF 10:88.

[57] I think especially, of course, of Bernard's lamentation on the death of his brother Gerard. See Chapter 5 below, 'Monks and Tears'.

[58] V Mal XXXI.70 (SBOp 3:375; CF 10:88): '. . . caritate vestri facio quidquid iniungitis.'

shall do my best not to forget you'.[59]   Malachy's last words
are a prayer for the community of Clairvaux and for all who
had served him faithfully.

Hagiography normally devotes great attention to the
saint's death scene, so there is nothing surprising in Bernard's care here. What is new is that Bernard based his
description on his own observation and allowed himself to
describe in detail what he saw. Now in Malachy's last days,
when there were world and time enough, Bernard could allow
himself to turn to Malachy the friend. When it was almost
too late, the bond could find expression.

Friendship with Sanctity

The Malachy who came to Clairvaux and died there did
indeed become Bernard's friend, but the *Life of Malachy* does
not give us a detailed description of intimate friendship. The
relationship that was established took as its point of departure the sharing of a monastic way of life. Because of
Malachy Clairvaux could be a centre from which Ireland was
to be settled with monks. The work that Malachy had begun
in reforming the church and especially monastic life would
be continued by the monks of Clairvaux.

For centuries Ireland had been the home of the saints.
Now Clairvaux would be. Bernard wanted Malachy's body as
a relic, a depository of grace and miracles and a reminder
of Clairvaux's position. I think Bernard's desire was genuine
and had nothing cynical or calculating about it. Bernard saw
people as potential allies or enemies in his desire to reform the church and spread monasticism.[60]   In Malachy he
saw a reflection of himself and his own programme, and he
was delighted, even overjoyed, that Malachy concentrated his
piety and activities so much on Clairvaux. Malachy's death at
Clairvaux may have been a lucky accident for Bernard, but it

[59] V Mal XXXI.73 (SBOp 3:377; CF 10:91): 'Habete . . . curam mei; ego
vestri, si licuerit, non obliviscar.'
[60] As Adriaan Bredero has pointed out, 'Saint Bernard and the Historians' pp 57–58.

ensured that Clairvaux became in its own time what Ireland previously had been, the burial place of God's champions and heroes.

For Bernard the death of Malachy and his burial at Clairvaux signalled a *translatio sanctitatis* from Ireland to his monastery. The old repository of sanctity had transferred itself to a new home. Clairvaux could respect the importance that Armagh as archiepiscopal seat had as the burial place of Saint Patrick. Bernard described how many bodies of saints slept in the monastery of Bangor. Malachy's purpose had been to replant the 'paradise' that once had been there.[61] But the monastic reform could only be done through Clairvaux, and so it was natural that all the cistercian houses founded in Ireland in Malachy's lifetime and afterwards were from the Clairvaux filiation.[62]

Some years ago the outstanding cistercian scholar, Anselme Dimier, wrote a seminal article, 'Mourir à Clairvaux'. In it he went through all the available evidence, source by source,[63] and concluded that Clairvaux became in Bernard's lifetime and especially after his death a magnet that attracted monks, bishops and other churchmen to come there to die. Dimier was correct in pointing to a wealth of literature on this point, but he might have added that dying at Clairvaux was in itself not the goal. Most important for the monks and churchmen who came to Clairvaux was the hope of being buried there. Malachy was probably the first outsider to receive this privilege. His place of burial is noted in the clarevallian literature, as the *Chronicon Clarevallense* from the early thirteenth century.[64] Bernard himself, in ending

---

[61] V Mal VI.13 (SBOp 3:322;CF 10:31): 'Malachias, velut quemdam replantaturus paradisum, amplexus est, et quia multa corpora dormirent ibi.'

[62] See the studies cited in n. 52 above.

[63] See note 4 above.

[64] The burial place of Malachy next to Bernard is noted in connection with the burial of Henry of Marcy, abbot of Clairvaux and then cardinal, 'behind the altar, between Saint Malachy and Saint Bernard.' (*Chronicon Clarevallense*, PL 185:1252).

the *Life*, spoke of Malachy's body as 'a treasure which is buried with us.' The monks would keep charge of it until the last day last day.[65]

For Bernard, the spread of the Order and burial at Clairvaux were signs of divine blessing. Because Malachy achieved both, he could be counted as one of Bernard's friends. Malachy shared not in a type of personal bond which we associate with friendship but in a confraternal bond of great intensity. With this interpretation of their relationship, we can turn to Bernard's preface to the *Life*, where he described his 'sleeping friend' in language taken from the Song of Songs as the voice of the turtle dove. Bernard pointed out here that Malachy considered him to be among his 'special friends', second to none. When he lay dying, Malachy gave Bernard his blessing.[66]

Bernard wanted his audience to be clear from the start about the link between himself and Malachy. 'He blessed me and I possess the blessing in inheritance', he asserted. The inheritance was not an individual one. It was linked to the whole community of Clairvaux. Only in this community context can we understand Bernard's appreciation of Malachy. The saints of Ireland were being joined by the saints of Clairvaux.

Lessons for a Clairvaux Audience

Bernard's *Life of Malachy* provided encouragement to the monks of Clarivaux to celebrate a distinguished guest who had come to stay with them and helped transform their monastery. If we concentrate on the spiritual significance of Malachy's life, instead of on his political role, we find

[65] V Mal XXXI.75 (SBOp 3:378; CF 10:93): '. . .tuus thesaurus, qui reconditur penes nos.'

[66] V Mal Praefatio (SBOp 3:309; CF 10:13): '. . . me inter speciales amicos Sanctus ille habebat, et eo loci, ut nulli in hac parte gloriae secundum fuisse me credam . . . . At ille, cum iam membra alia movere non posset, fortis ad dandam benedictionem, elevatis sanctis manibus super captum meum, benedixit mihi.'

several potential lessons for Bernard's monks. Malachy's conversion showed that young men entering monastic life were to expect hardship. They should consider it normal that in coming from privileged backgrounds they would have had a hard time making their choice. Like Malachy they would have to deal with difficult family members. Even after the choice was made and the world left behind, monks could not consider their battle over. At times they would have to go out into the world on difficult journeys. Some of them would have to venture forth to make new communities. Like Malachy they would want to end their lives at Clairvaux. There could be no guarantee for them, but some of them would be able to return, as he did, to be buried together with the other saints.[67]

The cistercian parallel is evident in the description of the irish brethren's displeasure with Malachy's long absences from them. Like Bernard, Malachy often had to leave his community. In the *Life of Malachy* Bernard described the understandable resentment of the Irish.[68] He added stories about travels and even a touching anecdote about a supposedly inferior nag offered to Malachy which turned out to be an excellent mount.[69] Similar tales about cistercian travels contained in the *Exordium Magnum* continue this genre and reflect the movement of cistercian life in founding new houses far from Clairvaux and in returning regularly to the General Chapter.[70] Even in describing Malachy's problems with building a stone church and local resistance to the project, Bernard may have been thinking about discussions at

[67] See for example, the story in EM IV.28, pp 259–60, of Gerard, monk of Clairvaux, whom Bernard sent to Sweden but promised would die at Clairvaux.

[68] V Mal XV.33 (SBOp 3:340; CF 10:49).

[69] V Mal XV.36 (SBOp 3:342; CF 10:51).

[70] See, for example, the moving story of a lay brother who managed to herd buffalo from Italy across the Alps on the way back from a trip (EM IV.34, p. 270). See also my 'Oral Sources in Caesarius of Heisterbach's *Dialogus Miraculorum*', *Analecta Cisterciensia* 36 (1980) 223–30.

Clairvaux concerning the transfer of the monastery to larger sites and the building of a new church.[71]

For Bernard the cistercian ideal was made manifest in Malachy's commitment to monastic life. He is seen several times as a part of a monastic community, where he would humble and obscure himself among the brethren:

> At places where he was pleased to make a stopover, he adapted himself to the customs and observances of the place, content with the common way of life and table. There was nothing in his food or in his apparel by which Malachy could be distinguished from the other brothers.[72]

The Malachy whom Bernard in the preface called 'my friend' (*amicus meus*) became by the end of the narrative 'our friend' (*amicus noster*).[73] The 'our' is undoubtedly the community of Clairvaux, if not the larger Cistercian Order. Especially in describing the scene of Malachy's death, Bernard spoke directly to his fellow Clarevallians, 'Brothers, let us not leave in death him whom we have followed in life.'[74] Bernard made sure in his language that the Cistercians who read the story of Malachy would realize that he was speaking to them directly. Thus in describing how Malachy left the cistercian house of Soulseat in Scotland on his way to Clairvaux, he spoke of the monks here as his 'sons, our brothers, the convent of monks and abbot.'[75] This formulation is not a tautology. Malachy's last foundation was made up of his sons, who thereby became *brothers* of Bernard's monks at Clairvaux. It is for them, as well as the irish brothers, that Bernard wrote.

[71] V Mal XXVIII.61 (SBOp 3:365; CF 10:77–8). Cf. VP II.28–31, PL 185:283–85.

[72] V Mal XIX.43 (SBOp 3:349; CF 10:58).

[73] V Mal XXXI.75 (SBOp 3:378; CF 10:92): 'Malachias amicus noster dormit.... '

[74] V Mal XXXI.72 (SBOp 3:376; CF 10:90): 'Fratres, non relinquamus in morte quem in vita prosecuti sumus.'

[75] V Mal XXX.68 (SBO 3:373; CF 10:87): 'Et relicto illic de filiis suis, fratribus nostris, monachorum conventu et abbate.... '

The *Life of Malachy* was not exclusively attuned to the Clair-
vaux community. Malachy in Bernard's eyes was an international figure who as a saint belonged to the entire church.
But in his work for the spread of the Cistercian Order in
Ireland and especially in his death and burial at Clairvaux,
Malachy became a very special friend to Clairvaux. Bernard
did not mention two anecdotes that his own hagiographer,
Geoffrey of Auxerre, has provided for us. At Malachy's death,
according to Geoffrey, Bernard exchanged clothes with him.
He took Malachy's tunic and kept it for himself as a remembrance of his friend, while he buried Malachy in his
own clothes.[76] At the mass in his memory Bernard deliberately read the text for a saint-confessor as if to announce to
his contemporaries that in his eyes, Malachy was already a
saint.[77]

Bernard may have omitted such stories because he wanted
to avoid concentrating too much on his personal bond with
Malachy and instead was concerned with putting Malachy
into the context of the Clairvaux community. Intimacy was to
be subordinated to confraternity. Malachy belonged to everyone at Clairvaux, just as he belonged to the irish cistercian
brethren to whom the *Life* was addressed. In death as in life
he gave help and guidance to the monastic communities of
which he had made himself a part. The welcome guest had
become the eternal guide: *quem habuimus hospitem, habeamus
ducem.*[78]

---

[76] VP V.23, PL 185:364–65: 'Ipsius enim tunicam, in qua sanctus ille
feliciter obdormierat, ad missarum sibi servaverat celebrationem, et morit-
urus in ea sese jusserat sepeliri, sicut et sanctum illum in sua sepelierat
veste.'

[77] VP IV.21, PL 185:333: '. . . formam mutavit orationis, et collectam in-
tulit, quae ad sanctorum pontificum celebritates, non ad commendationes
defunctorum pertinet. . . . '

[78] V Mal XXXI.75 (SBOp 3:378; CF 10:93). There are several mentions of
Malachy in the EM. As Chrysogonus Waddell has pointed out in a letter
to me, Malachy always appears here in the company of Bernard, as his
associate, in protecting the monks of Clairvaux. He is once called Bernard's
collateralis, which one is tempted to translated in a positive if demeaning
manner as 'sidekick'. See EM VI,4, p. 352: '. . . specialis patroni et tutoris

The same Malachy portrayed in the *Life* can be glimpsed in Bernard's letters to him. Bernard subordinated declarations of love and support to the subject of monastic expansion. Bernard in one letter counselled patience in Ireland until his monks were sufficiently prepared to go there.[79] In another, he emphasized how the monks who had been sent provided a bond between him and Malachy.[80]

Impact on Cistercian Hagiography

When Geoffrey of Auxerre sat down to complete the *Life* of Bernard, he was influenced by Bernard's own *Life of Malachy*. Besides realizing that Bernard had written indirectly of himself in describing Malachy, Geoffrey also felt literarily beholden to Bernard's portrait of a saint. Thus it was natural for him to follow Bernard in considering a saint's greatest miracle of all to be his way of life. Bernard provided in Malachy a pattern hard to avoid: many miracles, few sayings, a concentration on external matters for the saint and the communities to which he was linked. Geoffrey once provided a glimpse of Bernard's delight at returning to his monastery and regaining a sense of reality from talking about spiritual matters to his monks, something he had missed on the outside.[81] How one would like to know the contents of such conversations! But Geoffrey does not lift the veil. It is only with some of the stories collected in the 1160s and later and not included in the *Vita Prima* that Bernard's ways

---

eiusdem loci, sancti scilicet Bernardi nec non et insignis collateralis ipsius beati Malachiae.'

[79] Ep 341, SBOp 8:282–3, trans. in Bruno Scott James, *The Letters of Saint Bernard of Clairvaux* (London, 1953) 452–53.

[80] Ep 357, SBO 8:301, James pp 454–55.

[81] VP III.22, PL 185:316: 'Denique, sicut nobis saepius fatebatur, inter summos quosque honores et favores populorum, vel sublimium personarum, alterum sibi mutuatus hominem videbatur, seque potius reputabat absentem, velut quoddam somnium suspicatus. Ubi vero simpliciores ei fratres, ut assolet, fiducialius loquerentur, et amica semper liceret humilitate frui, ibi se invenisse gaudebat, et in propriam rediisse personam.'

as abbot to his monks at Clairvaux are described in greater detail.[82]

Geoffrey maintained this conservatism in following Bernard's hagiographical method later in life when he wrote the *Life* of another cistercian saint, Peter of Tarentaise.[83] Here we are told little about Peter as abbot and a great deal about him as archbishop. The imprint of the *Life of Malachy* remains. Miracles vastly outnumber incidents from daily life. Generalizations about edifying habits leave scant room for bits of conversation or memorable sayings that could characterize the man.

This initial pattern of cistercian biography did not persist. Bernard and his followers had released too much energy and had themselves so much valued individual human spiritual experience that cistercian lives could not be kept in a literary straitjacket. Walter Daniel's *Life of Aelred of Rievaulx*, composed soon after Aelred's death in 1167, is a harbinger of a new, sweeter style with personal anecdotes.[84] Outside Clairvaux's immediate sphere of influence we can detect a new direction, a concentration on intimate detail. The spirit of 'simplicity and ordinariness', pointed out by Chrysogonus Waddell in cistercian hagiography, eventually triumphed even at Clairvaux in the *Life* of abbot Peter Monoculus.[85] In the thirteenth century at Villers in Brabant, this interest in inner life was combined with a new insistence on revealing the contents of visions and other spiritual experiences.[86] Cistercian

---

[82] See Chapter 6 below, 'The First Cistercian Renewal'.

[83] His *Vita* is in the *Acta Sanctorum Maii* 2:317–45.

[84] Trans F. M. Powicke in Nelson Medieval Texts (Edinburgh, 1950) and reissued in Oxford Medieval Texts, 1978.

[85] 'Simplicity and Ordinariness: The Climate of Early Cistercian Hagiography', *Simplicity and Ordinariness*, ed. John R. Sommerfeldt, Studies in Medieval Cistercian History 4, CS 61 (1980) 1–47, which concentrates on the *Lives* of Amadeus Senior, monk of Bonnevaux, who died around 1150, and of Peter, abbot of Clairvaux, who died in 1186, but whose *Life* was not written until after 1200.

[86] See the translations of the *Lives* probably composed by Goswin, chanter of Villers, by Father Martinus Cawley of Our Lady of Guadalupe Monastery, Oregon, forthcoming in Cistercian Publications.

hagiography became linked to visionary literature, a far cry from the traditional miracles and dramatic external events described in the *Life of Malachy*. A new more tender spiritual-ity emerged, concentrating on Jesus as a person, the suffering human being with whom we share our fate.

Friendship After All?

Bernard and Malachy spent no more than a few weeks of their busy lives together. Bernard never visited Ireland. He deliberately left out Celtic place names, which confused him as much as they do us.[87] He probably had little first-hand knowledge of Malachy's background, and so attached to his friend a story of youth and conversion close to his own. Only in experiencing the last days of Malachy did Bernard have an opportunity to approach the human being behind his ideal of the new monk-bishop securing the church's freedom from secular authorities and spread reformed monasticism.

Were they friends in the end, in any sense we could rec-ognize? Bernard in his preface to the *Life of Malachy* claimed they were. Malachy's own response is visible only through Bernard's interpretation. His sense of purpose and mission, what we might call Bernard's Clairvaux centralism, makes the bond seem rather one-sided. But his attractiveness is at-tested not only by Malachy. Other powerful churchmen from the fringes of Latin Europe, like Archbishop Eskil of Lund, also came to Clairvaux to see him and called on Clairvaux to send monks to their provinces.[88] In Eskil's Denmark we see the story of Malachy's Ireland repeated with minor variations.

The problem with friendships between figures like Bernard and Malachy is that the protagonists reveal themselves to us as men of power rather than as figures of tenderness. The intimacy that Bernard could share with some of his monks is paralleled with Malachy only during the irish archbishop's

---

[87] V Mal XX.45 (SBO 3:351): '. . . cuius nomen tacemus, quod nimis barbarum sonet, sicut et alia multa.'
[88] See my *The Cistercians in Denmark*, CS 35 (1982) 51–53.

final days at Clairvaux. Until that point there was a clear programme of getting the Cistercians to Ireland, and Malachy was seen only as an instrument, not as a person of flesh and blood.

Geoffrey of Auxerre provided the story that Bernard did not offer about how the abbot, on Malachy's death, wore his tunic when he celebrated mass, and asked to be buried in it.[89] It became a relic of Malachy's holiness but also a token of Bernard's bond with his friend. In this story, so conspicuously absent from Bernard's own narrative about Malachy's death, we have a vital piece of evidence that Bernard wanted personal closeness with Malachy and genuinely missed him after his death. In writing the *Life of Malachy*, Bernard expressed this bond in the context of the monastic community. He presented his friendship mainly in terms of the confraternity of Clairvaux. In this context Bernard's attachments became a part of his way of life as an abbot who drew monk-bishops to himself and created their legend.

An historian cannot read hearts and minds. But we can see something of Bernard in the loyalties he engendered in his monks and in the churchmen who came to Clairvaux. Malachy's desire to die at Clairvaux is known to us only through Bernard, but the fact remains that Malachy more than once routed himself through Clairvaux so that he could see Bernard. Malachy left some of his best men with Bernard to be trained in cistercian life. A political-institutional bond probably gained strength in mutual recognition of a deep concern about the content of christian life for monks and for laity.

At their final reunion, Bernard may well have hurried out to meet Malachy, as he claimed, in spite of his bodily aches and pains. The arrival of a friend from such a distance, long anticipated, would have created great excitement. When Malachy became ill, his condition caused the entire community concern. He had become one of their greatest champions, and

[89] See note 76 above.

so Bernard did not have to distinguish between his feelings for Malachy as a person and his devotion to him as an ally and instrument for the spread of cistercian houses.

Malachy in death was for Bernard as well as for his community a beautiful sight: 'That liveliness of countenance, that peacefulness such as is apparent in a sleeper.'[90] Bernard described death as a realization of the full potentiality of the human being. Malachy's death created a sense of peace, order, and victory for the forces of good.[91] The friend could rest forever at Clairvaux, sharing in the benefits of the monks' prayers and providing spiritual strength to the monastery. What more could Bernard ask for from a friend who had already spread his monks to Ireland? In this friendship of confraternity, with undertones of intimacy, Bernard expressed a traditional approach to hagiography and wrote of his own search for God.

---

[90] V Mal XXXI.74 (SBOp 3:377), CF 10:91: 'Eadem vivacitas vultus, serenitas eadem, qualis apparere solet in dormiente.'

[91] Ibid. (SBOp 3:378): 'Vicit fides, triumphatur affectus, res in suum devenit statum.' The translation (CF 10:92), 'things fall back into routine', does not, I think, grasp Bernard's meaning. His biographer wanted to indicate that in the death of Malachy, as the triumph of his life, there was achieved a state of affairs appropriate for the life of a cistercian house. It was not routine which was reestablished; rather Malachy's death reestablished the monastery's intimate participation in the divine order. A possible translation might be: 'the divine order is reasserted'.

4. Bernard and Eskil

Friendship and Confraternity[1]

The last years of Bernard's life reveal to us a relationship with another prelate whom we can consider to be a second Malachy: a churchman in charge of an area on the outskirts of Europe who had discovered Bernard of Clairvaux and did his utmost to bring Cistercians to his ecclesiastical territory. This is Eskil, archbishop of Lund from 1137–77, one of the most controversial figures in danish medieval history. Traditionally Eskil has been seen as an exponent of the Gregorian Reform in the North, and he has been praised as a figure who brought the scandinavian church closer to european developments.[2]

---

[1] This chapter is a complete revision of my article, 'Why Scandinavia? Bernard, Eskil and Cistercian Expansion in the North 1140–80', *Goad and Nail. Studies in Medieval Cistercian History* 10, ed. E. Rozanne Elder, CS 84 (1985) 251–82. There I concentrated on the scandinavian scene, while here I am more concerned with Eskil, Bernard, and the milieu of Clairvaux.

[2] See, for example, Hal Koch, *Danmarks Historie* 3. *Kongemagt og Kirke* 1060–1241 (Copenhagen. Politikens Forlag, 1963) 180–85, as p 181: 'One can hardly name other ⟨figures⟩ from the danish medieval period of corresponding international format and importance' (my translation). Hal Koch, an important teacher and politician in Denmark under the german occupation and in the years afterwards, intended to write a biography of Eskil

In recent years, however, an 'Eskil noir' has become visible, a man of narrow family interests and an arrogant aristocrat whose main fear in life was of being relegated to the status of servitude.[3] It is not my purpose in what follows to resolve this perennial debate in danish history, for it goes back to the great historian Saxo. In his *Gesta Danorum* from the late twelfth century, he revealed a personal distaste for Eskil, while he was devoted to Eskil's successor as archbishop of Lund, Absalon (1177–1201).[4] Instead of an historiographical approach, I will try to describe what we know and what we can assume about the links between Eskil and Bernard. This attention will provide a further dimension in understanding Bernard as a friend of important ecclesiastical figures. This involvement we will see in terms of the bond of confraternity his monastery of Clairvaux could offer such a friend.[5] Once again we will consider the question of a friendship and its content, but my main concern will be to show how the personal relationship that Bernard in life forged with Eskil managed to continue after Bernard's death and gave Eskil a bond with the Clairvaux Cistercians.

Bernard did not write a biography of Eskil, as he did of Malachy, and so we have to reconstruct the content of their

---

but had to give up because, he claimed, the materials were too scarce. See his *Danmarks Kirke i den Begyndende Højmiddelalder* (Copenhagen: Universitetsforlaget, 1972) p 7: 'The point of departure for this work was the desire to write a life of Eskil, the most important person in the danish medieval church, towards whom the judgment of history has been only partly just.'(my translation).

[3] Niels Skyum-Nielsen, *Kvinde og Slave* (Copenhagen. Munksgaard, 1971) p 166.

[4] *Saxonis Gesta Danorum*, ed. J. Olrik and H. Ræder (Copenhagen, 1936) pp 436–37. See my remarks in *The Cistercians in Denmark* p 68.

[5] I use the term 'confraternity' here in the broadest possible sense of a bond of community with spiritual benefits, extended to lay people and churchmen who were close to the Cistercians in the twelfth century. Thus Bernard extended letters 'of confraternity' both to Malachy and to a king of Ireland. SBOp 8:512–13, epp 545–546, as p 513 to Malachy, '. . . participem vos facimus omnium bonorum quae fiunt et fient in ordine nostro usque in sempiternum'.

relationship from the few contemporary sources available. First, however, it might be in order for a non-scandinavian readership to review what we know about Eskil's life.[6] He was born in the early years of the twelfth century, into a rich landowning family, the Thrugots, in the danish province of Scania, which since the seventeenth century has been a part of Sweden. The most distinguished member of this family was Eskil's uncle Asser, who from 1103 to 1137 was the first archbishop of Lund.[7] Eskil was destined from an early age for an ecclesiastical career and was sent to some of the best cathedral schools in Germany, including the one at Hildesheim. After he returned home, probably in the late 1120s or early 1130s, he became provost of the cathedral of Lund, and here he probably assisted Asser in the fight against the danish king Niels in securing the independence of the danish church from the primacy of the archbishopric of Hamburg-Bremen. In 1134, after a number of bishops had been killed at a terrible battle near Fodevig in Scania, Eskil became bishop of Roskilde and made a name for himself as a defender of ecclesiastical freedom.

On the death of Asser in 1137, Eskil was elected to the archbishopric of Lund. In August 1139, he held a synod for the entire church of the North in order to mark his independence of the Hamburg church. But his main problem lay at home, not abroad, for Denmark in the 1140s was scarred by dynastic conflicts. At one point in the early 1140s a claimant to the throne invaded Scania and imprisoned Eskil, but the middle years of the decade brought a modicum of peace before civil war broke out in 1146 and continued until 1157, when King Valdemar I assumed power over all of Denmark. A sign of the mid-decade pause was Eskil's consecration

[6] Unless other sources are given, I am dependent for my sketch on the excellent portrait by Aksel E. Christensen in *Dansk Biografisk Leksikon* 4:256–9 (Copenhagen; Gyldendal, 1980).

[7] Asser's central importance in the nordic church is described masterfully in Aksel E. Christensen, 'Archbishop Asser, the Emperor and the Pope', *Scandinavian Journal of History* 1 (1976) 25–42.

of the only partly completed new cathedral at Lund on 1 September 1145.

In 1143, at the request of the swedish king and queen, Eskil cooperated with the foundation of the first cistercian houses in Scandinavia, Alvastra and Nydala.[8] Both of them were daughters of Clairvaux. In 1144, Cîteaux became mother house to the first danish cistercian monastery, Herrisvad in the diocese of Lund, not far from the archepiscopal seat.[9] Here Eskil's involvement must have been significant, even though the loss of the early sources for the monastery means that it is impossible to say whether he contributed any lands to the new foundation.

In the early 1150s, in the midst of the danish dynastic struggle, Eskil turned to Bernard of Clairvaux in order to get help in his own conflict with the archbishop of Hamburg for primacy in the North.[10] In late 1152 or early 1153 Eskil was in Clairvaux and met Bernard, who sent him back to Denmark with a group of monks who founded the cistercian house at Esrum north of Copenhagen.[11] In 1156, on the way home from another trip to Clairvaux and Rome, Eskil was taken prisoner by an ally of Frederick Barbarossa, an event that became an international incident in the dispute between papacy and empire. Once back in Denmark, Eskil cooperated with the new danish monarch Valdemar I, known as 'The Great', but he also spent many years abroad, partly because of his disagreements with the king in the papal schism of the

[8] See James France's *The Cistercians in Scandinavia*, forthcoming from Cistercian Publications.

[9] For the beginnings of Herrisvad, my *Cistercians in Denmark*, pp 40–41, and my article 'Herrevad' forthcoming in *Dictionnaire d'Histoire et de Géographie Ecclésiastiques* (Louvain).

[10] Stella Maria Szacherska, 'The political role of the Danish monasteries in Pomerania 1171–1223', *Mediaeval Scandinavia* 10 (1976) 122–55, esp. 134–6.

[11] In most contemporary annals, 1153 is given as the date when the Cistercians arrived at Esrum (*Conventus venit in Esrom*). In my article in *Goad and Nail*, pp 269–71, I have given my reasons for seeing 1153 as the actual foundation date of Esrum, even though there is a papal privilege for the monastery from 29 December 1151.

1160s. In the years 1161–67, Eskil was abroad in Jerusalem, Paris, Rheims, and probably also Clairvaux. In 1174 he was again in Paris, and finally in 1177 he gave up his archbishopric, consented to Absalon as his successor, and withdrew to Clairvaux, where he apparently became a monk and died in 1181, to be buried close to his friend Bernard, just as Bernard had been laid to rest close to Malachy.[12]

This crowded and complex career brought a scion of a rich and violent danish magnate family into the orbit of the Cistercians. As with Malachy, Bernard seemed to exercise a special fascination on a churchman who wanted to participate in the european reform movement and could turn to the abbot of Clairvaux not only for monks but also for a personal and political bond. This link brought the churchman to Clairvaux, to meet Bernard and finally to become a member of his community. The confraternity of Malachy with Clairvaux in Bernard's lifetime is paralleled by the confraternity of Eskil with Clairvaux, finally leading in the late 1170s to Eskil's reception into the monastic community itself as a monk.[13] In the two prelates we can sense something of the way Bernard's personality and attractiveness could make him and his monks irresistible.

[12] *Monumenta Claraevallensis Abbatiae*, PL 185:1555: 'Item ibidem in arcu ad sinistram ipsius altaris jacent: primo in prima parte ipsius sepulturae requiescit vir magnificus et insignis ac de stirpe regia oriundus, felicis recordationis Dominus Eskilus, quondam Lundensis Archiepiscopus et totius Daciae ac Sueciae Primas, qui tempore B. Bernardi veniens Claramvallem, et Monachus factus ibidem summae humilitatis et totius honestatis ac religionis se speculum exhibuit, et monachalis perfectionis exemplar suis posteris dereliquit. Obiit autem anno incarnationis Dominicae MCLXXXI.' Eskil was thus buried to the left of the altar of Our Saviour, next to Garnier, ninth abbot of Clairvaux and afterwards bishop of Langres.

[13] We can be confident that Eskil, in spite of age, did become a monk and not just an old age pensioner at Clairvaux, for the near-contemporary *Chronicon Claraevallense*, whose reliability is solid, says that Eskil 'took on the habit of the order': 'Anno Domini 1181, apud Claramvallem mortuus est venerabilis Eskilus Danorum archiepiscopus, sumpto habitu ordinis: qui diu manserat in Claravalle, et sibi substituerat archiepiscopum in Dacia, Absalonem nomine' (PL 185:1249–50).

Bernard's Letter to Eskil

The most important indication of Bernard's relationship to Eskil is a letter, dated to early summer 1152, but possibly already from the autumn of 1151, from Bernard to Eskil.[14] It used to be thought that Bernard here alluded to Eskil's desire to come to Clairvaux.[15] Recent work has established that the letter concerns Eskil's fear of Hamburg's hegemony over Lund.[16] A new inspection of the language of the letter, however, has led me to conclude that Eskil had two quite different matters on his mind when he sent an envoy, the monk William, to Bernard. First, Eskil had a business matter, *negotium*, which needed to be forwarded to the pope, Eugenius III; secondly, Eskil harboured a *secretum*, for which he needed Bernard's very special assistance. The 'business matter' involved the foundation of a cistercian house on land where Eskil apparently a decade earlier already had established a monastery.[17] The envoy William continued from Clairvaux to Italy and the pope, where he on 29 December 1151 obtained a papal authorization for the foundation of the new house, with William himself as its first abbot.[18] The 'secret' was not Eskil's desire to retire to Clairvaux or even to visit the monastery: it was his perennial problem with the archbishop of Hamburg-Bremen and the need to clarify Lund's independence of any german ecclesiastical authority.[19]

[14] SBOp 8:358–9, ep 390.

[15] See Niels Skyum-Nielsen's conclusion in *Diplomatarium Danicum* 1,2, edd. Lauritz Weibull and Niels Skyum-Nielsen (Copenhagen, 1963) p 203.

[16] Note 10 above.

[17] This was Esrum, which was first a benedictine house, as I tried to prove in *Goad and Nail*, pp 266–68.

[18] *Codex Esromensis. Esrom Klosters Brevbog*, ed. O. Nielsen, Selskabet for Udgivelse af Kilder til Dansk Historie (Copenhagen, 1880–81, 1973), pp 3–4.

[19] It is clear from the Latin that Bernard here was dealing with two separate matters: '. . . et negocium tuum quantumcunque potuimus munivimus ad dominum papam. De secreto autem verbo illo quod tam ardenter ascendit in cor tuum. Respondebit tibi ex parte nostra Guillelmus tuus.' (SBOp 8:359, ep 390) The use of *autem* provides a transition between the two concerns.

Such is the official content of the letter. At last, after so much uncertainty, we can be fairly sure about what it was Bernard was doing for Eskil.[20] At the same time, however, it is important to look at the 'filling' in the letter, in which Bernard characterized his bond with Eskil. He started by stating his love for Eskil in no uncertain terms: 'Your letter and greetings, or rather the expressions of affection coming from your heart, I received from you all the more happily as I specially love you and am loved by you.'[21] Bernard could say similar things to a friend such as Peter the Venerable, but this is not the type of greeting he gave to just anyone.[22] From the very first a tone of intimacy is set.

Indicating his participation in Eskil's difficulties, Bernard thereby made them into his own. Here Bernard used his most articulate prose, building up phrases whose words rhyme and accentuate the mood of distress and concern he wanted to create:

'Tangit et angit cor meum quidquid tuum exasperat, et quidquid illud sit quod te persequitur, non solum te persequitur, sed me tecum.' (Whatever frustrates you also touches and wrenches my heart, and whatever it be that persecutes you, it not only concerns you, but me with you.)[23]

---

[20] Evidence of Bernard's activity for Eskil is a passage in a letter of his to Eugenius III, dated to 1152, where he pointed out that the archbishop of Lund's problem no longer existed (SBOp 8:194, ep 280).

[21] SBOp 8:358, ep 390. This is my own translation. Bruno Scott James simplifies the complex language of this letter and does not allow the linguistic nuances that Bernard here created.

[22] As ep 387, SBOp 8:355, to Peter: 'Utinam sicut praesentem epistolam, ita vobis mentem meam mittere possem! Sine dubio tunc clarissime legeretis quid in corde meo de amore vestro digitus Dei scripserit, quid meis impresserit medullis.' In writing to the visionary Hildegard of Bingen, in contrast, Bernard concentrates on her achievements and his admiration for her but by no means indicates love or affection for her (SBOp 8:323, ep 366).

[23] SBOp 8:358, ep 390 (my translation).

Instead of limiting himself to sympathy, Bernard explained this bond with Eskil in terms of friendship. This is a reciprocal relationship in which the two friends have to be aware of each other's needs: 'For whatever affection and love absent friends can hand over to each other, I think I owe you and I am owed by you.'[24] Bernard made a number of word contrasts that seem to be there for their rhetorical effect (*audax sum, non mendax*) but he seemed to be making a solid point, that because he and Eskil are friends, they owe a debt to each other and have to take each other into consideration. As far as Bernard was concerned, Eskil had made the initial contribution. Now Bernard asked how he could repay Eskil.[25]

For us who put Bernard at the centre of twelfth-century church life, this may seem like purely rhetorical humility. But if we think in terms of Eskil's position as the archbishop of an important see and Bernard's as abbot of Clairvaux, then Bernard represented official reality correctly. It was a gift for him to be sought out by such a man. The only reciprocity he could provide was through the Lord, 'And if I cannot redeem ⟨you⟩, then my redeemer is not dead, for the Lord will redeem ⟨you⟩ for me (Ps 137:8)'.[26] Because of Jesus, Eskil could embrace Bernard with such devotion, and so Bernard in turn could rejoice 'in the privilege of the love' that Eskil had bestowed upon him through 'our brother, your son' William. The messenger thus became an envoy not just of business but of the love and friendship that existed between Bernard and Eskil: 'I am refreshed through your envoy, refreshed through your letters, refreshed through all who can come from you to us or through us'.[27]

---

[24] Ibid.

[25] Ibid.: 'Quando tantam tantillus, et a tanto, gratiam sperare auderem'. Bernard here alluded both to Eskil's high position in the church and to his generosity. He may be well indicating his gratitude for Eskil's cooperation in the bringing of Cistercians to Scandinavia, a dimension in this letter not previously noticed.

[26] Ibid.: 'Et si ego retribuere non potero, non est mortuus retributor meus, quia Dominus retribuet pro me'.

[27] Ibid., p 359: 'Refectus sum per nuntium tuum, refectus sum per

These remarks, which make up more than half the letter, are not only a very astute *captatio benevolentiae*. They are a theological expression of the bond that Bernard envisioned between himself and Eskil. This union could flourish because of their mutual love in Jesus and because of the presence of a dependable go-between, William, who belonged to Bernard as monk and Eskil as envoy: *fratrem nostrum filium tuum Guillelmum*.

Bernard added here a commonplace about desiring to see the friend in person rather than through letters:

> Would that I had the power from on high to say all this to you and not write it, so that I might open my heart to you by word of mouth rather than by the written word. Certainly the living word is more welcome than the written word, and the tongue more eloquent than the pen; for the eyes of the speaker lend credence to his words, and the expression of the face conveys affection better than the pen. But being absent from you, this is beyond my power and so I must satisfy myself with the second best alternative of a letter.[28]

Such statements are common in Bernard, and they may indicate the influence of his secretary Nicholas of Montièramey.[29] One can wonder why Bernard dawdled at such a moment before going onto the essential message of the letter about matters of business and secrets. But again one thinks of Bernard's letters to Peter the Venerable, which also carried important business, but where Bernard, also in harmony with his secretary Nicholas, gave himself time to indicate the

litteras tuas, refectus sum per omnes qui a te usque ad nos, vel per nos, evadere possunt.'

[28] SBOp 8:359, ep 390. I have used the translation in James, pp 493–4.

[29] See Jean Leclercq, *Recueil d'Etudes sur Saint Bernard et ses écrits* 1 (Rome, 1962) p 16: 'Nicolas, en particulier, a mêlé ses propres productions à celles de Bernard. . . . ' In my *Friendship and Community*, pp 484–85, note 168, I have pointed out the many phrases in this letter that point to the style of Nicholas.

tensions and excitement of a living friendship.[30] Even if the desire to see the absent friend were a cliché in Bernard, it may well have been sincerely meant.

As if to underline the reality of the bond, Bernard ended the letter by apologizing for not writing more and stated that Eskil as friend had a *ius amicitiae* over him. In this relationship brother William was the bond in Christ: *tuus, et specialiter tuus in visceribus Iesu Christi* (Phil 1:8). Once again the duality of friendship is strengthened through the presence of a third person, William, who became Eskil's stand-in for Bernard and in turn could be sent back to Eskil as Bernard's stand-in. The letter is packed with subtleties of language that are not even approached in James's translation, but the main point is that the triangle of Eskil-William-Bernard reciprocal friendship is made possible by their union in Christ.[31]

Bernard's final assurance of the right of friendship seems to indicate his desire to make absolutely clear to Eskil that the archbishop could count on him, as he would on the archbishop: 'He is always with you, who has his own right, and he will be with you as long as he lives, so that you can cultivate his friendship with every right.'[32] Friends can count on each other, for they can expect something of each other by right. This seems to be the sense of Bernard's simple yet infinitely complex statement dealing both with personal bonds and theological union.

A Possible Point of Departure for Friendship

It has usually been assumed that Bernard and Eskil first

[30] As SBOp 8:356–7, ep 289, where Nicholas was clearly present, for he affixed his 'signature', as it were.

[31] The possible presence of Nicholas in this bond would provide yet another dimension and would have made possible a relationship also between William and Nicholas, yet another reason for dating the letter to late 1151 and not to 1152, when Nicholas fell into disgrace.

[32] SBOp 8:359, ep 390: 'Ille semper tecum est, qui sui iuris est, et tecum erit quamdiu fuerit, omni mihi amicitiae iure colende, pie ac reverendissime Pater.' The Latin is so compact that it is almost impossible to do justice to it in translation.

met each other sometime after this letter was written, in late 1152 or 1153, during the last year of Bernard's life.[33]

Bernard's secretary Geoffrey of Auxerre must have been present at some of the encounters between archbishop and abbot, and it was to Eskil he turned when Bernard died on 20 August 1153:

> The fear we feared has come to us, and it has happened which alone or most greatly we were dreading. I know, I know it has already come to your eyes, now it comes to your heart, and that sword has run through your soul.[34]

The language tries to approximate Bernard's compact intensity but falls far short and verges on the sentimental, except with the fine sentence, reminiscent of the Song of Songs: 'Indeed Bernard your friend sleeps; but he does not wholly sleep; for his heart keeps watch. It keeps watch' (Song 5:2).[35]

It is no surprise that Geoffrey could not live up to the linguistic mastery of Bernard, but it is significant that he chose Eskil as the recipient of his notification to the world outside the monastery that his abbot was dead. For Geoffrey there was no doubt: Bernard was his friend. There is no hedging here: the classical word *amicus* is employed instead of any vaguer term. Eskil's closeness to Bernard is something that Geoffrey takes as a basic point of departure for his entire letter.

And what about Eskil? We know nothing of his immediate reaction to the death of Bernard. Assumedly he had brought monks back with him from Clairvaux in the early months

---

[33] Niels Skyum-Nielsen, *Kvinde og Slave* p 141.

[34] *Diplomatarium Danicum* I,2, nr 114, p 206: 'Timor quem timebamus evenit nobis; et accidit quod vel solum vel maxime verebamur. Scio scio iam pervenit ad aures vestras. iam pervenit ad cor. et vestram ipsius animam gladius iste pertransiit. . . . '

[35] Ibid.: 'Siquidem Bernardus amicus vester dormit; sed non totus dormit; vigilat vigilat cor illius.' Geoffrey here borrowed from Bernard's description of Malachy's death (SBOp 3:378): 'Malachias amicus noster dormit. . . . '

of 1153.[36] He was himself caught up in surviving the last
years of civil war that brought him to leave Denmark again
in 1156. But his devotion to the Cistercians is clear in the
way he in 1157, when Valdemar was victorious, encouraged
the king to take over a group of monks from Clairvaux and
find them a home in Denmark after they had been thrown
out of Sweden.[37] The foundation of Vitskøl on the Limfjord
in 1157 is usually seen as Valdemar's victory declaration, but
it also points to Eskil's continuing loyalty to the Cistercian
Order.

There is no doubt that for the rest of his life, Eskil maintained his bond with Clairvaux Cistercians and supported the
Order in Denmark, as can be seen in his statement of Esrum
abbey's privileges from 1158.[38] But what about Eskil's bond
with Bernard? Did personal loyalty have anything to do with
his continuing involvement with the Cistercian Order? We
have some indication of Eskil's debt to Bernard in a letter he
wrote from german captivity in 1157 to the danish church to
describe his situation. If we recall the language of Bernard,
based on Ps 137:8 *Dominus retribuet pro me*, we find Eskil echoing a similar theme:

> I indeed have already been redeemed by the blood of
> Christ, and I do not need to be redeemed again . . . His
> blood is my redemption. His blood is my price. It is
> unworthy that I be given a price, for the price of re-
> demption is without price.[39]

[36] As he claimed in his 1158 privilege to Esrum abbey, *Diplomatarium Danicum* I,2, nr 126: '. . . ac ne Cisterciensis ordinis fratres nobis deessent. ad
beatissimum Clarevallensis cenobii patrem dominum Bernardum quamvis
multo labore et sumptu pervenimus . . . nobiscum in terram nostram ad-
duximus.'
[37] See *Scriptores Historiae Danicae Minores* II, p 140, a thirteenth-century
narrative on the foundation of Vitskøl: 'Archiepiscopus autem Eschillus,
abbatem Henricum intelligens literatum et honestum virum esse, sicut
syncerissime omnes religiosos honorans, summo studio eum Waldemaro
regi commendabat, monens ac consulens, ut in abbatia, quam se rex fun-
daturum esse promiserat, talem virum abbatem constitueret.'
[38] Note 36 above.
[39] *Dip. Dan.* I,2, nr 119, p 224: 'Ego etenim, semel Christi sanguine

This passage has recently been interpreted as an arrogant magnate's refusal to be ransomed like a slave.[40]   But if we take Eskil's statement in the context of Bernard's earlier letter to Eskil, we can see how the prelate had learned from the abbot. For Bernard, only Christ can repay our debts. Through him, all debts are cancelled out and human and divine love made possible.[41]   Eskil says the same thing in his letter. His vocabulary is different, but his meaning similar. Christ's blood has paid for us, once and for all. No human being can purchase or redeem any other. Consequently Eskil could assert his own interior freedom and the freedom of his church from german aggression.

A debate on the workings of the redemption characterized the period from 1050 to 1150. Was it a question of the manifestation of God's love for us, as Abelard would have had it, or was it essential to show exactly what the God-man paid in terms of satisfaction, as Anselm wrote in his *Cur Deus Homo*?[42] This debate took on a significance that involved the very definition of humanity in relationship to God. For Eskil, being a human being and a christian meant being bought back by Christ from the captivity of the devil. If any person tried to take him into captivity again, he was the instrument of the devil, and Eskil could assert to the whole world his freedom. He had learned well from Bernard that Christ is our *retributor* or redeemer. He is the one who has paid back whatever was owed.

---

redemptus, iterum non requiro redimi . . . . Sanguis eius redempcio mea. Sanguis eius precium meum. Indignum est ut sub precio redigar, cuius precium sine precio est.'

[40] Niels Skyum-Nielsen, *Kvinde og Slave*, p 166: ' . . . the rich man's fear of being bought free, which would make him into a pseudo-slave'.

[41] For Bernard on the Redemption, *Tractatus contra quaedam capitula errorum Abaelardi*, PL 182:1053–72, which is the same as his letter 190, to Pope Innocent, SBOp 8:17–40, esp. p 38: 'Magnum profecto et valde necessarium humilitatis, magnum et omni acceptione dignum caritatis exemplum; sed non habent fundamentum, ac proinde nec statu, si desit redemptio.'

[42] See R. W. Southern, *Saint Anselm and his Biographer* (Cambridge 1966, now under revision) esp pp 95–7.

I have devoted so much space to three letters—Bernard to Eskil in late 1151 or early 1152, Geoffrey of Auxerre to Eskil in 1153, and Eskil to the danish church and people in 1157—because they provide our central sources for the relationship of Bernard and Eskil. I cannot draw many conclusions from this material, but I think its hints at intimacy between the two point to the possibility of their already having known each other before their meeting at Clairvaux in 1152/53. I cannot prove this thesis, but the more I have studied Bernard's letter to Eskil, the more I have become convinced that he was writing to someone whom he already knew.

If we compare this letter with others from Bernard to people he had never seen but to whom he felt a bond, we find that in the latter case, he often would specifically indicate that he never had met them.[43] Another indication that Eskil may have been at Clairvaux as early as 1143/44 and have met Bernard can be found in the letters of the distinguished benedictine abbot and letterwriter Peter of Celle, who in one letter stated that he had known Eskil since his youth (*ab adolescentia*).[44] Since Peter was born in 1115, and youth hardly could go beyond the age of 30 in the medieval view, this would have meant that the two got acquainted before about 1145. Eskil in his youth already had been south, at least to Germany. I see no reason why he could not have journeyed to Rheims in the 1140s, visited Peter, and then gone on to Cîteaux and perhaps Clairvaux in 1143 in connection with

[43] As to David king of the Scots, SBOp 8:478, ep 519: 'Iamdudum amplector te, rex illustrissime, ac desidero faciem tuam videre praeclara nominis opinione provocatus.' Also to William the Englishman, who later became a monk of Clairvaux, SBOp 7:259: 'Etsi facie ignotus nobis, etsi corpore remotus a nobis, amicus tamen es, et amicitia notum iam nobis, et praesentem te facit.' We notice that Bernard to Eskil did not use any such formula of physical ignorance yet friendship.

[44] *Dip. Dan.* I,3 nr 73, dated to 1177–80: Peter, as abbot of Saint Rémi at Rheims wrote to Eskil at Clairvaux of the friendship they had. 'Iam illum convenio oculum, qui de vobis amicabiliter sollicitus. Lustrat vias nostras et studia ab adolescentia'.

the negotiations to send the first cistercian communities to Sweden and Denmark.

If we trace Eskil's own involvements at the time, there is nothing that would have hindered him from making such a trip. Similarly with Bernard, we know that he was at Clairvaux much of the time during these years, before he started in 1145 a series of journeys that would bring him into Southern France and Germany.[45] After the involvements of the 1130s in the papal schism and a three year stay in Italy, the 1140s brought Bernard back to Clairvaux for some years. He even wrote to Peter the Venerable that he hoped his ailments would make it possible for him to stay home for good.[46] This was not possible, but in the first half of the 1140s Bernard's main concern was more regional than international: disputes between Count Thibaut of Champagne and King Louis VII.[47] Louis in fact invaded Champagne, and Bernard became closely involved, but the unsettled domestic situation did not prevent Clairvaux from sending out new daughter houses.

By the early 1140s Bernard had a european reputation based on the success of his order and his efforts to maintain the independence of the church from secular interference. Eskil, from 1137 archbishop of Lund and eager to guarantee his independence from Hamburg, could already then have turned to Bernard as an ally. What we find in Bernard's letter to Eskil from the early 1150s would have been an expression of continuing support from an already established friend. Thus the contact between Bernard and Eskil does not have to have existed through the medium of the Cistercians in Sweden and Denmark. The two could have met face to face in 1143 or

---

[45] Watkin Williams, *Saint Bernard of Clairvaux* (Westminster, Maryland, 1952) p 356.

[46] SBOp 8:99, ep 228: 'Fractus sum viribus, et legitimam habeo excusationem, ut iam non possim discurrere ut solebam.'

[47] Williams (note 45 above) pp 207–16.

1144 and have realized that they could make use of each other and trust each other.[48]

All this is hypothesis, for there is no decisive proof. Yet it is worth considering the possibility that Bernard and Eskil did meet in the early 1140s. Bernard's devotion to Eskil, the loyalty of Geoffrey to Eskil, and the debt of Eskil to Bernard's thinking on the redemption of humankind all point to a relationship that had had time to mature. An earlier dating for their first meeting is not necessary to explain the fact of their friendship at the end of Bernard's life, but it would place the first cistercian foundations in Scandinavia in a clearer context, the fruit of a bond that was personal as well as political.

Confraternity at Clairvaux 1156–1181

When Eskil in 1153 visited Clairvaux, he told Geoffrey of Auxerre how expensive it had been for him to get there.[49]

[48] A tantalizing indication of Eskil's direct role in bringing the first monks from Cîteaux to Herrisvad in 1144 is provided by the Øm Abbey Chronicle: 'Ipse ⟨Eskillus⟩ *eduxit* duos conventus, unum de Cistercio, alterum de Claravalle, et fundavit duo monasteria, Herivadum in Scania et Esrom in Selandia, de quibus plura examina monachorum diffusa sunt per Daciam.' (*Scriptores Minores* II, p 169) Since we can assume that Eskil physically led monks from Clairvaux to Esrum in 1153, the use of the verb *educere* for his actions in both new foundations would point to his also having been south to bring the monks from Cîteaux to Herrisvad. This is a late source, 1207, but it may base itself on a solid tradition among the Cistercians in Denmark.

One source that apparently indicates Eskil's first journey to Clairvaux as being in 1152/53 is Geoffrey of Auxerre's reference in the *Vita Prima* to how Eskil was not content to see Bernard in his sons and so himself went to Clairvaux to meet him (VP IV.25, PL 185:335). This passage is usually seen as referring to Eskil's preparations for the founding of Esrum. But the subjunctive tense in the passage can be read as an indication that Eskil had the desire to found cistercian houses, and so as a consequence went to Bernard before any cistercian houses at all were founded in Scandinavia: 'Patrem sanctum unico venerabatur affectu, unica devotione colebat. Nec contentus est in filiis eum videre, cum novum coenobium exstruxisset, et impetrasset ab eo desideratum sacrae congregationis examen.'

Geoffrey, writing in 1155/56 may have conflated a trip by Eskil to Clairvaux in the 1140s with his later trip in 1152/53.

[49] VP 4:25, PL 185:355: 'Nam de expensis dicere non est magnum,

Eskil impressed both Geoffrey of Auxerre and later Herbert of Clairvaux with stories of his previous life and what he risked in choosing the Cistercians. Eskil's material contribution to the Cistercians in Denmark has been a matter of controversy,[50] but one of the explanations for his limited involvement in the danish houses after the 1150s may well have been the fact that he spent most of his time away from Denmark. His heart was at Clairvaux, not at Esrum, and it is in Champagne, not Northern Zealand, that one must look for Eskil's commitment to the Cistercians. He was back at Clairvaux in 1156, as Geoffrey of Auxerre witnessed in speaking of a miracle that Bernard had performed for Eskil.[51] In Denmark for the foundation of Vitskøl in 1157, Eskil could enjoy a few years of relative peace under the new king Valdemar and may have cooperated in the foundation of a cistercian house at Sorø in 1161.[52] This, however, was almost completely the work of the Skjalm family, led by bishop Absalon of Roskilde. Soon afterwards Eskil was out of the country, away to his longest period abroad, lasting until 1167, a result of the papal schism. Thus when the magnate Buris Henriksen in 1163 founded Tvis cistercian house in Western Jutland, Eskil was absent. It is only in 1170 that we again find him in Denmark, at the new benedictine church at Ringsted, where he cooperated in accepting Valdemar's father Canute Lavard as a saint and crowned Valdemar's son Canute VI.[53]

---

quamvis eumdem audierimus protestantem, quod expenderit in itinere ipso argenti marcas amplius quam sexcentas.'

[50] See Svend-Erik Green-Pedersen, 'De danske cistercienserklostres grundlœggelse og den politiske magtkamp i det 12. aarhundrede', *Middelalder, metode og medier: Festskrift til Niels Skyum Nielsen* (Copenhagen 1981) 41–65 and the riposte by James France, 'Saint Bernard, Archbishop Eskil and the Danish Cistercians', *Cîteaux* 39 (1988) 232–47.

[51] PL 185:335, speaking of the three years that had gone by since Bernard had blessed bread and given it to Eskil. Now the archbishop, back at Clairvaux, could witness that the bread was still fresh.

[52] *The Cistercians in Denmark*, p 64.

[53] Hal Koch, *Kongemagt og Kirke*, pp 285–6.

For Eskil it may have been much more enjoyable (and much less traumatic) to have been able, a few years later in 1174, to celebrate the canonization of his friend Bernard. At this time Eskil again went abroad. We find him at Paris retrieving some of the money back that he had deposited at the monastery of Saint Victor. Assumedly he also visited Clairvaux. By now he was probably making his preparations for his final entrance to Clairvaux.[54]

These decades of Eskil's life show the continuing importance of his bond with Bernard. The archbishop could find no better exit from his troubled life than to become a member of the Clairvaux community. Here he had eager listeners to his stories of his early life and schooling, to gruesome descriptions of what happened to schismatics and adulterers in Denmark, and to a narration of his uncles' pilgrimage to Jerusalem at the beginning of the century.[55] Many of these stories were so violent that they were excluded from the great chronicle of cistercian stories, the Exordium Magnum Cisterciense, but others, such as the pilgrimage narrative, were included even though they had no connection with monastic history.[56] Conrad of Eberbach took his predecessor Herbert of Clairvaux's narrative and justified his inclusion by adding that just as Eskil's uncles were pilgrims to Jerusalem, so too Eskil became a pilgrim to Clairvaux.

Clairvaux normally was not interested in pilgrims, as we can see from another Exordium Magnum story telling how the monastery put a stop to pilgrimages to the tomb of Bernard.[57] But Eskil was always welcome: the monks were willing to bring him into the confraternity of the monastery and in the end let him become a monk. His bond with Bernard provided a living witness to Bernard several decades

---

[54] Hal Koch, p 307.

[55] Lauritz Weibull, 'En samtida berättelse från Clairvaux om ärkebiskop Eskil av Lund', Scandia 4 (1931) 270–90.

[56] EM III:28, pp 214–7: 'De felici consummatione duorum peregrinorum sepulcri domini, avunculorum domni Eskili archiepiscopi'.

[57] EM II.20, pp 116–7.

after the saint's death. Eskil must have enjoyed this status, but he had not forgotten his home and family. At one point he told the brothers in chapter about a vision he had of one of his brothers by blood, who appeared to him only with head, neck, and the tops of his shoulders visible.[58] Eskil was convinced from the man's sad look and silence that he was appealing for prayers. After a violent life, he was in pain and needed monastic assistance. The biological family exerted a continuing pull on Eskil in the midst of his spiritual family, to whom he felt free to go for help.

Eskil's last years at Clairvaux and his burial there underline the strength and continuity of his bond with Bernard from the 1140s onwards. Eskil could assure the monks that Bernard remained powerful after his death, as a story he told them in the mid 1150s indicates. A relative of his, known as Niels Grevsun or Count Niels, had entered a cistercian house, probably Esrum.[59] There he became a good brother and died faithful to the community. This made the devil very angry, for he had long considered Niels as one of his own. In vengeance he invaded another brother and created what appears to us like an epileptic fit. The symptoms are described in detail, as well as the remedy: the application of 'the sacred relics which had been brought there the same year by the archbishop himself, the hair and beard, as well as a tooth of our blessed father Bernard.'[60]

When these were applied to the man's chest, the demon began to cry out in german: 'Take it away, take it away, remove Bernard. . . . Alas, how heavy you have become, Bernard, how weighty, how unbearable you are for me'.[61] This use of

---

[58] Weibull (note 55 above), p 283: 'Veruntamen ex eodem mortuo non poterat aliquid agnoscere nisi tantum caput et collum ac summitatem scapularum. Reliqua namque pars corporis tota ardere videbatur, et nichil ex eo penitus apparebat, nisi tantummodo flamma que totum occupabat.'

[59] PL 185:335–37 (VP 4:26–7).

[60] Ibid.: '. . . de capillis et barba, et dentem unum beati patris nostri Bernardi afferri monet, et ejus pectori superponi.'

[61] Ibid.: 'Tollite, tollite, amovete Bernardum . . . Heu, quam ponderosus factus es, Bernarde! quam gravis, quam intolerabilis factus es mihi!'

Bernard's relics a short time after his death is paralleled by a similar incident from a spanish house, Moreruela.[62] For cistercian houses on the fringes of Europe, Bernard's relics were a powerful remedy against the attacks of the devil.

In such stories we can see how Bernard lived on through his physical remains and continued to exercise power over everyday life in cistercian monasteries. At Clairvaux Eskil could be as close as possible to the body of Bernard himself. He could commemorate the friendship of Bernard and Malachy and think of his own parallel friendship with Bernard. When Conrad began putting his materials together for the *Exordium Magnum*, this parallel was not lost on him, and he recorded that both archbishops had been friends and allies of Bernard. Malachy is mentioned eight times in Conrad's great work, Eskil four. Both figures were seen as being important in Bernard's life.

Two Twelfth-Century Ecclesiastical Types

Eskil has been called the first European from the North.[63] He found the meaning of his life in a european monastic movement which he brought to Denmark and in the end joined. The bond between Eskil and Bernard has long been celebrated in danish history writing, and yet at the same time there has been an ambivalence towards Eskil and his commitment. What surprises me is the fact that Eskil managed to become Bernard's ally and friend. The two men came from vastly different backgrounds and reflect two different types of Christianity.

Eskil revealed much about himself when he spoke to Herbert at Clairvaux in the late 1170s. He talked about the

[62] I am grateful to Andrea Liebers, Seminar für Lateinische Philologie des Mittelalters und der Neuzeit der Universität Heidelberg, for sending me the text of MS Salem IX 31 from the early thirteenth century, which contains ff 104v–106v the story of a novice's visions at Moreruela, dated to 1184, in which Saint Bernard and his relics play a special part.

[63] Weibull (note 55 above) p 270: 'Man skulle kunna kalla Eskil den förste europeen på nordisk mark.'

terrible nightmare he had had at school in Hildesheim when he was a teenager.[64] He had been about to burn up in a hell-like room but was ushered into the presence of an angry woman, Mary. Eskil the youth tried to bribe her with money, but Mary refused it. She insisted he promise he would found monasteries for her. The dream is accounted as the origin of Eskil's desire to found monastic houses, but it reveals at the same time a view of Mary in marked contrast with that which emerges in cistercian writings of the twelfth century. Her demands and harshness reflect an older form of Christianity, bargaining the purchase of paradise and asking for direct compensation from human beings for their offences. This view can lead to the consequence that the individual human being has little hope of salvation.[65] Eskil's ransom in his childhood dream is a far cry from the ransom he could announce to the world that Christ already had paid for him. His dream revealed a world that was narrow and constricted, with cold cash payments and the bribing of high officials.

Bernard's world was vastly different, for here no metaphysical payment could ever be made that was worth anything, except the one that Christ made for all of us. The human being had to flee to him, to the mystery of the Incarnation and the child Jesus which Bernard as a child saw in his first recorded vision.[66] The gentleness Bernard envisioned here was a long way from the violence that characterizes Eskil's stories to Herbert. The archbishop seems almost to have enjoyed telling about the terrible end of adulterers and schismatics, how they would be found hung by a demon or dead in bed.[67]

[64] Weibull (note 55 above) pp 276–9. The narrative was included in the EM III.27, pp 210–13.

[65] This perception is what Southern described as the epic view of life in his brilliant final chapter to *The Making of the Middle Ages*, 'From Epic to Romance'.

[66] VP I.4; PL 185:229.

[67] Weibull (note 55 above), pp 280–82.

Eskil lived in a tough, unforgiving world. He had relatives who meant well as christians but who respected naked force more than anything else. The devil's savage attack on a monk of Esrum in revenge for his loss of a soul he had considered his own may well symbolize the problems of a cistercian monastery in defending its position in a hostile society.

Eskil's relatives had to fight for what they thought were their rights, while Bernard's relatives relatively quickly found the peace and tranquility of the monastery. Eskil could not feel safe and secure in his life until he withdrew as an old man to Clairvaux, while Bernard as a youth actively chose the monastery and then used his position there to settle the feudal disputes of his time. Bernard, in his withdrawal, could influence outside events, while Eskil, in his involvement, often became the victim of events and had to leave his country for shorter or longer periods.

Bernard's self-chosen exile in the monastery thus contrasts with Eskil's many involuntary exiles. Bernard's abandonment of power gave him immense influence, while Eskil had to fight for himself, his relatives and his church. In Eskil's combativeness we find the aggressivity of his class, ready to conquer the Baltic by the end of the twelfth century once its own inner disputes had been resolved. In the fighting of the middle years of the twelfth century Bernard in France-Champagne could be an arbitrator, while Eskil in Denmark was a participant and often a victim.

These two aristocrats, burgundian Bernard and scanian Eskil, grew up with vastly different mentalities but came to have a high regard for each other. Eskil's stories to Herbert in the 1170s indicate that he never quite gave up the pessimistic view of power with which he grew up. One even detects a streak of sado-masochism of the kind that would have been common in a member of the aristocracy whose position prevented him from using force but who could rejoice in what looked like God's punishment of evil men.[68] But Bernard did make a profound difference in Eskil's life, for he brought to him the realization that salvation comes through total surrender to a Christ whose blood offering replaces all the offerings that any magnate could make to bribe the powers of the world. Eskil perhaps never became a full member of this new gentler world, but Bernard's presence in his life gave him an alternative to total immersion in a young, macho society thirsty for power and prestige.

Friendship at Clairvaux as Seen In Retrospect

Eskil's childhood fear of hell and damnation turned into an adult confidence in the power of Christ's redemption. At Clairvaux he could recall his origins and at the same time share in the community of friendship that the Cistercians had made. The scenes of Eskil's life at Clairvaux can perhaps tell us something not only of his situation there but also of the atmosphere at the monastery in the decades after Bernard's death. It was during this period that Clairvaux monks, such as John, prior in the 1170s, could make a collection of stories about Bernard that presented him in a more intimate manner than Geoffrey of Auxerre allowed himself in the *Vita Prima*.[69] We catch a glimpse of Eskil's bond with Prior John in a scene included in the *Exordium Magnum*. Eskil and Alan, former bishop of Auxerre, visited Prior John when he lay dying (1179).[70] The two bishops insisted that John get out of his usual monastic garb, made of coarse material, and put on

---

[68] There is perhaps a parallel between Eskil's glee at the death of schismatics and Guibert of Nogent's descriptions of the terrible end in store for those who caused civil disorder. See John Benton, *Self and Society in Medieval France: The Memoirs of Abbot Guibert of Nogent* (University of Toronto Press, 1985).

[69] See my 'A Lost Clairvaux Exemplum Found: The *Liber visionum et miraculorum* compiled under Prior John of Clairvaux (1171–79)', AC 39 (1983) 27–62.

[70] EM 4.27, pp 257–8.

something more comfortable. But John refused. He wanted to die as humbly as he had lived.

John, who had collected stories about Bernard's humility and devotion to his monks, here is remembered for the same type of virtue. In the cistercian literature of the last decades of the twelfth century we find a frequent assertion that the ideals which Bernard brought to the order were being continued, at least at Clairvaux.[71] Whether or not this is completely true, we can look upon Eskil as feeling attracted to Clairvaux in the 1160s and 1170s because he felt it was indeed carrying on the heritage of his friend Bernard. At the same time the monks of Clairvaux may have turned to Eskil because he had been a friend of Bernard who represented a venerable tradition. Eskil could tell edifying and entertaining stories about themselves and the world from which the Cistercians were never very far.

When Eskil saw his dead relative in his oratory at Clairvaux, he felt a need to tell all the monks about his vision. He wanted to share his experience with them. He trusted that they would understand his concern for the dead man and that they would join with him in prayer for the man's soul.[72] By the same token he could have been certain that the monks would take care of him at his death and bury him close to his beloved Bernard. This natural confidence reveals the existence of friendship in the context of a monastic community: sharing stories, asking for prayers, trusting that one will be taken care of, in life as in death. A sceptical observer might add that the Cistercians could also make good use of such stories in their propaganda describing the attractiveness of

[71] As in the words of Conrad himself on the basis of his stay at Clairvaux in the 1180s and 1190s: 'Testis enim nobis est Dominus, quia, cum in Claravalle disciplinis claustralibus et sacri ordinis observantiis subditi essemus, tantum ibi religionis et gravitatis tantumque puritatis et honestatis vidimus. . .' (EM 6.10, p 367).

[72] Weibull (note 55 above), p 283: '. . . etiam postera die veniens in capitulum monachorum multa missarum et oracionum impendia pro eodem mortuo impetravit.'

their order. This is true, but it is only part of a larger cistercian sense of being the centre of a monastic experiment that
was renewing the church.

If there is one word that characterizes this reciprocity of
bonds at Clairvaux as we see it through the Eskil sources, it
is generosity. Eskil could sense the hospitality of the monks
in taking him in and looking after his physical and spiritual
needs. The monks in turn could be grateful for the generosity
of the former archbishop. His material generosity seems to
have been of little concern to them when compared with the
wealth of his presence, his stories, his link with the past.
While Malachy was a brief acquaintance for the monks of
Clairvaux and was memorialized because of Bernard, Eskil
formed a long and lasting friendship with them.

Even deeper than this sense of reciprocal generosity lies
the conviction that the Cistercians take care of their own.
Monks have been doing this since the earliest days of monasticism, imitating the practice of the first christians in community at Jerusalem. But now the monks could see their care
in terms of a great international network of contacts that included a powerful prelate who eventually joined them for
good. Clairvaux's relative openness to Eskil, its ability to ab-
sorb him into its daily life, and its willingness to link his life
to its own sense of history point back to Bernard's own time
and his attitudes. For all that we do not know about bonds of
friendships among individual monks in Clairvaux at the time
of Bernard, we can assume from the bond between a monk
like Herbert and Eskil that the brethren of Clairvaux were eager and willing to speak to each other about their inner lives,
their dreams and visions, and thus to share themselves with
each other.

This dimension of cistercian spirituality needs more attention, however difficult it is to study. The link between Bernard
and Eskil or Eskil and Herbert made it easier and more natural for monks to cultivate friendships with each other. In
a monastery where common concern had high priority, it
was legitimate for members to get to know each other as

they were, not only in terms of their present lives, but also in terms of past experiences. Bernard often in his Sermons drew on personal experience, and we can assume that he encouraged the brethren to do the same in talking about conversion to the monastic life, temptations and trials, and the desire for heaven.

I do not want to suggest that the Cistercians had an easy time of it in seeking out and finding each other in everyday life. But their success in attracting difficult and complex people like Eskil shows how Bernard had been able to make the Order into a european rather than a provincial movement. Bernard was no easy person himself, yet in the emotional and spiritual ferment his person and writings created, the most talented men of the twelfth century found a centre of spiritual meaning and activity. Rough-hewn Eskil found his match in the classic form of Bernard's life. The person of Bernard and the institution of the Cistercians provided friendship and confraternity for a son of the North, the first danish european.

5. Monks and Tears

A Twelfth-Century Change[1]

Tears are as much a part of the history of our culture as are universities and economic systems. It is, in fact, impossible to deal with life in the Middle Ages without taking tears into account. Decades ago, the great dutch historian Johan Huizinga pointed to the facility of emotional expression in the later Middle Ages. He proved his point by quoting from what he considered to be a flood of tears in literary sources.[2] Even if we reject some of these accounts of secular weeping as textual embroidery, monastic life has a long and venerable

[1] This chapter is based on a paper originally read at the conference 'The Mind of the Middle Ages', sponsored by the Medieval Centre, Copenhagen University, in September 1983. I would like especially to thank Sir Richard Southern for a number of invaluable conversations in Oxford in the summer of 1983 on this and related subjects.
[2] *The Waning of the Middle Ages* (Harmondsworth 1965, first published in English in 1924) p 13: 'All this general facility of emotions, of tears and spiritual upheavals, must be borne in mind in order to conceive fully how violent and high-strung was life at that period.'
For a totally different approach to the phenomenon of tears, in terms of the mechanics of rhetoric, see Peter von Moos, *Consolatio. Studien zur mittelalterlichen Trostliteratur*, Münstersche Mittelalter Schriften 3 (Munich: Wilhelm Fink Verlag, 1971).

tradition of tears.[3] To dismiss monastic tears as literary embellishment would be to deny one of the most important sides of monasticism in the West from the Rule of Saint Benedict onwards: its ability to combine individual human emotions with collective religious practices.

I first met monastic tears in an historical context when I read the cistercian Caesarius of Heisterbach. His *Dialogue on Miracles* (written 1219–23) has an account of a monk of Villers in Brabant who wanted to obtain the grace of tears (*gratia lacrimarum*).[4] His abbot allowed the monk to go to a holy woman in a nearby town. The passage has been noticed because it contains one of the earliest appearances of the word *begginae* for the religious women living in informal communities in the Low Countries.[5] But the story is equally interesting because it shows that at the beginning of the thirteenth century it was possible for a monk to step outside the normal bounds of monastic life in order to gain the grace of tears.[6]

Tears for what? Caesarius's account makes clear that the monk wanted to be able to shed tears of regret for sin. The holy woman in his story rightly pointed out that to be a monk meant to be able to weep for one's sins: 'Are you not a monk?' she asked. 'Someone who does not weep for his sins is not a monk'.[7] Even if the main cause of tears is one's

[3] For the eastern development, see Irénée Hausherr, *Penthos: The Doctrine of Compunction in the Christian East*, CS 53 (1982).

[4] DM II.20, ed. J. Strange (Cologne 1851 and reprinted Ridgewood, New Jersey, 1966). The monk who tells the story is named Walter. By the time Caesarius wrote his account, Walter had become abbot at the great cistercian house of Villers.

[5] As in Ernest W. McDonnell, *The Beguines and Beghards in Medieval Culture* (New York: Octagon Books 1969) p 438.

[6] For the bonds between men and women that could arise out of such contacts, see my 'The Cistercians and the Transformation of Monastic Friendships', AC 57 (1981) 1–63.

[7] DM II.20: '. . . rogavi eam, ut oraret pro me. Quae cum diceret: Quid vultis ut orem pro vobis? Respondi: ut possim deflere peccata mea. Et illa: Numquid non estis monachus? Qui peccata sua non potest deflere, monachus non est.'

own sins, tears in general were welcome in cistercian life. In our time, when tears often dry up completely on the death of loved ones, but flow freely at the prompting of the 'tear-jerker' film, we may well have something to learn from the experience of monks.

I have no doubt that medieval monks did weep, not only for their sins but also for their loved ones. I look upon the shedding of tears as part of a christian monastic ideology of self-expression, which I shall define in the course of this chapter. Monastic tears are not necessarily an hysterical reaction to a life bereft of some sensual experiences. The tears of monastic Villers in 1200 are not in the same category as those of freudian Vienna in 1900.

Tears and compunction, the pricking of conscience in regret for sin, are almost interchangeable through much of monastic experience.[8] Many of the eastern fathers saw weeping as a necessary sign of contrition. One of the desert fathers, Barsanuphios, had to warn that the link is not reciprocal: 'It is not compunction that comes through tears, but tears through compunction.'[9] Tears in themselves are not a sign of closeness to God. They can be shed for the wrong reasons, as out of sentimentality. As the novice in one of Aelred of Rievaulx's dialogues conceded, he had an easier time weeping over arthurian legends than over his own sins.[10]

In the Latin Systematic Collection of the Sayings of the Desert Fathers, an entire section is reserved for compunction, and here again an outer manifestation of sorrow for sins is the flow of tears.[11] John Cassian, as in so much else, brought the eastern tradition of tears with him to Marseille and thus to the West in the early fifth century. He warned against

---

[8] The best general guide to this subject is the article 'Larmes' by Pierre Aduès in *Dictionnaire de Spiritualité* 9 (Paris, 1976) col. 290–303.

[9] *Barsanuphe et Jean de Gaza. Correspondance* (Solesmes 1972) nr 285, p 220.

[10] *Speculum Caritatis* II.17,51. CC CM 1 (Turnholt 1971) p 90.

[11] PL 73:860–64, 'De Vitis Patrum Liber V: Verba Seniorum, Libellus 3, De Compunctione'.

forcing tears to come, but in general he accepted them as evidence of compunction.[12] Here as elsewhere, Benedict of Nursia drew on Cassian. His Rule makes it clear several times that the monk is to pray with tears, as in ch 49 where 'prayer with tears' is mentioned as part of the monk's lifelong Lenten observance. Benedict did not use the term 'tears of compunction', but the context indicates that monks are to show open contrition for their past sins. Summing up this development is Gregory the Great, the writer who introduced the phrase Caesarius later used, the grace of tears.[13] One weeps first because of the remembrance of sin, he pointed out, and later because of a desire for heaven. Gregory thereby made tears more than a sign of compunction. They could also manifest a yearning for better things to come.

Gregory's two-fold definition of tears remained standard until the twelfth century in monastic circles. Tears indicated the distancing of self from a sinful past and the anticipation of a glorious future. They had nothing to do with regret for human loss at the death of a friend or a family member. This is by no means to claim that monks on such occasions refrained from crying. But such tears were thought to be sensual and indicative of too close bonds to the world. Augustine in his *Confessions* admitted his tears, but in his letters of guidance on the monastic life he had room only for tears of compunction. Ambrose of Milan, however, accepted the place of tears in writing about the death of his brother. His lament is both eloquent and dignified.[14] But Ambrose

---

[12] 'Larmes', col. 295: 'A partir au moins de Jean Cassien larmes et componction sont intimement associées. Ce sont souvent des mots interchangeables, une espèce de tautologie, *compunctio lacrimarum.*'

[13] *Dialogi* III.34; PL 77:300: 'Principaliter vero compunctionis genera duo sunt, quia Deum sitiens anima prius timore compungitur, post amore. Prius enim sese in lacrymis afficis, quia dum malorum suorum recolit, pro his perpeti aeterna supplicia pertimescit . . . . Quae suspirans a patre terram irriguam petit, quia a creatore nostro cum magno gemitu quaerenda est lacrymarum gratia.' Trans. Odo John Zimmerman, *Saint Gregory the Great. Dialogues,* The Fathers of the Church 39 (New York 1959) 173–74.

[14] *De excessu fratris sui Satyri,* PL 16:1345–1414, trans. as 'On His Brother

was not a monk. For a long time his sentiment failed to find a place in the monastic tradition.

The monastic refusal to allow a place for tears in connection with the death of friends is summarized in the mid-twelfth-century *Consolatio de morte amici*, written in the 1140s by the Benedictine, Lawrence of Durham.[15] In this carefully-wrought and highly literary composition, Lawrence tried to prove that tears for a dead friend are both irrational and unnecessary. Borrowing from both Boethius and Ambrose, Lawrence constructed a dialogue between himself and Reason. He starts out as a monk who refused to abandon the desolation he felt on the death of his beloved friend: it is I who am being rational in weeping, he insists at first, and you, reason, who are being irrational in trying to convince me not to do so.[16] But Reason naturally wins. In strict argumentation reminiscent of the logic of Saint Anselm, the likelihood of the friend's joy in heaven becomes the major consideration. Lawrence's own sorrow is turned to happiness for his friend. Now he could be secure in the knowledge that his friend was saved, something he could never count on while his friend was alive. An augustinian awareness of the fragility of all human life and its relationships provides encouragement that helps eliminate the tears of sorrow.

In Lawrence of Durham tears are neither disregarded nor condemned. They are, however, abolished through the processes of reasoning. Gregory the Great might hardly have recognized such erudite reasoning and high-flown literary style, but he is the point of departure for Lawrence's insistence that monks cry for their sins and not for the loss of each other when hope of heaven lies before them.

Satyrus', John J. Sullivan and Martin R. P. McGuire, *Funeral Orations by Saint Gregory Nazianzen and Saint Ambrose*, The Fathers of the Church 22 (Washington, D.C., Catholic University of America Press, 1968).

[15] Ed. Udo Kindermann (Inaugural Dissertation: Erlangen 1969).

[16] Ibid., pp 143–44: 'Quodsi omisso tantotamque multiplici bono me sine causa lugere credis, constat te potius quam meum luctum a ratione peregrinari.'

Monastic tears of compunction and sorrow at human loss have little to do with each other in the Early Middle Ages, but in a new era of sentiment after about 1050, we find in many monastic writers an opening towards tears within the context of human attachments. One of the first writers to indicate this new attitude is John of Fécamp in Normandy (d. 1078). Just as he developed a way of prayers that is more personal than standard carolingian formulae, John accepted expressions of emotion in moments of sorrow.[17]

John legitimized tears by recalling situations in which Christ wept: at the tomb of Lazarus, and at the sight of Jerusalem.[18] He recalled the words of the Sermon on the Mount, 'Blessed are they who mourn, for they will be comforted.' But if we read on in his central passage on tears, it soon becomes apparent that John of Fécamp was asking God for the grace of tears in order to repent for his sins. In saying, 'Come tears, I ask, in the name of my Lord Jesus Christ, come', he seeks tears of regret for what he himself had done, and not tears of love for dead friends. Despite his new sweet style of prayer, John is solidly anchored in the monastic tradition of compunction going back to the egyptian desert.

If we turn to John of Fécamp's close neighbour and near contemporary, Anselm of Bec (d. 1109), we begin to find evidence of tears not only of compunction but also of human compassion. Anselm's prayers and meditations as well as his early letters contain floods of tears. Caution is necessary, however, for Anselm is a master of language. Just as his expressions of devotion to friends can be meant in a collective rather than a personal sense,[19] so too his declarations of tears are often meant more to symbolize his yearning

[17] Benedicta Ward, *The Prayers and Meditations of Saint Anselm* (Harmondsworth 1973) 47–50, an excellent introduction to the development of medieval prayer.

[18] Jean Leclercq and Jean-Paul Bonnes, *Un maître de la vie spirituelle au onzième siècle* (Paris: Vrin, 1946). See the 'Confessio theologica' pp 151–52.

[19] As pointed out so well by R. W. Southern, *Saint Anselm and his Biographer* (Cambridge, 1966) 72–76.

for salvation for himself or his friends rather than a need for their individual presence.[20] Only at the death of his young charge Osbern do we find Anselm weeping, and here his biographer Eadmer allowed only a momentary glimpse of his master's state of mind.[21] Tears are almost interchangeable with prayers for the dead friend, but they are not allowed to take a prominent place in Eadmer's account. With Anselm and John of Fécamp we get just a hint of what is to come in the tears of compassion that allow expression of emotion in monastic life. The incorrigible reformer Peter Damian (1007–72) reminds us, however, how conservative the monastic tradition remained in this area. Peter's ideal was the life of the hermit. In writing on how the grace of tears is to be acquired, he emphasized the need for isolation and withdrawal from other men in order to gain the tears that come from compunction.[22] Damian's monastic heroes were hermits who found a place apart, not monks in a community of friendship.

Into the early twelfth century I find no monastic representative for tears on the loss of a friend. Good tears are invariably those of compunction. It comes almost as a shock to read in one of the sermons of Saint Bernard of Clairvaux on the Epiphany that there is another type of tears which 'greatly exceeds' these. Bernard wrote that these have 'the taste of wine'. They are tears 'of brotherly compassion going forth with the fervour of charity'. They even produce 'a certain sober drunkenness' (*sobria quadam ebrietate*).[23] Apparently on

---

[20] See my 'Love, Friendship and Sex in the Eleventh Century: The Experience of Anselm', *Studia Theologica* 28 (Oslo, 1974) 111–152.

[21] *The Life of Saint Anselm by Eadmer* ch 10, Oxford Medieval Texts, ed. R. W. Southern (1972) p 18: '. . . Anselm withdrew to a more private part of the church where he might more freely pour out prayers for him ⟨Osbern⟩. While he wept, his body was worn down with the great sorrow of his heart. . . . '

[22] *De institutis ordinis eremitarum*, ch. 26, PL 145:358: 'Quomodo lacrymarum gratia possit acquiri'.

[23] In *Epiphania Sermo* 3.8, SBOp 4:30: 'Nec parum distat inter has lacrimas devotionis at aetatis utique iam virilis, atque eas quas primaeva aetas inter infantiae vagitus emisit, lacrimas utique paenitentiae et confusionis. Verumtamen longe amplius utrisque praecellunt aliae quaedam lacrimae,

his own initiative, Bernard added a new category of tears to Gregory's standard tears of compunction and of heavenly desire. He did not deny the importance of tears of repentance for sin. Elsewhere he preached, 'If you do not weep, you will not fully feel the wounds of the soul and the lesion of the conscience'.[24] But there is something better and fuller in the monastic life.

If we return to the Sermon on the Epiphany and look at the whole passage, we find Bernard presenting three types of tears: those of devotion, those of penance, and those of brotherly compassion. The first corresponds to Gregory's tears of desire for heaven, the second to the Desert Fathers' tears of compunction, while the third, so far as I can tell, makes up a new category in monastic spiritual writings. Bernard was an artist in dividing concepts into discrete categories, and at times it can be difficult to accept the worth of his three- and four-fold distinctions.[25] In this case, however, Bernard is not just being conceptually innovative. He is dealing with the content of monastic experience and is legitimizing tears shed because of the suffering or death of friends and other loved ones.

Despite the critical apparatus of the Leclercq-Rochais edition of Bernard's works, I find little help there in placing this sermon chronologically. But one event in Bernard's life might help explain his acceptance of the tears of brotherly compassion. In 1137, Bernard was at Viterbo with his brother and fellow monk, Gerard.[26] When he became ill, Bernard prayed that his brother be spared at least until they returned to

---

quibus et infunditur sapor vini. Illas enim lacrimas vere in vinum mutari dixerim, quae fraternae compassionis affectu in fervore prodeunt caritatis, pro qua, etiam ad horam, tui ipsius immemor esse sobria quadam ebrietate videris.'

[24] *In Quadragesima Sermo* 2.4; SBOp 4:362, 'Si non plangis, plane non sentis animae vulnera, conscientiae laesionem.'

[25] Especially in his *Sententiae* (SBOp 6/2).

[26] *Sermones super Cantica* 26.14; SBOp 1: 180–81. For the date, see Watkin Williams, *Saint Bernard of Clairvaux* (Westminster, Maryland: Newman Press, 1953) 148–49.

Clairvaux, so that Gerard could die among his friends. Gerard did improve, but a year later he died at Clairvaux. Bernard himself tells us that during the final illness and the funeral of his brother, he did not weep at all.[27] He performed all his necessary duties as abbot of the monastery. Only when it was all over did he allow the pain to rise up in him.

Bernard chose the occasion of a sermon on the Song of Songs to describe the outbreak of this emotion. I do not think it likely that Bernard actually burst out in the midst of his sermon in an abrupt way, as suggested by the written text of the twenty-sixth sermon, but this is possible.[28] Whatever the exact situation, Bernard used a literary vehicle to describe his own state of mind. Part of this description of Bernard's sorrow on the death of his brother was later included in the *Exordium Magnum Cisterciense*, but the compilator telescoped the passage and left out some of the strongest and most passionate parts.[29] Bernard composed a long, heartfelt lament, a tribute to his brother, but also a description of his own state of mind and reflections on the loss he had suffered.

The most important aspect of Bernard's statement lies for us in his defence of his right to weep. He realized that some monks might disapprove of his self-indulgence, but he insisted that he had a right to admit openly the loss of the friend, brother and helper he had suffered in Gerard's death. Let the tears come forth, he insisted: the time for holding them back was over:

> Flow on, flow on, my tears, so long on the point of brimming over; flow on, for he who dammed up your exit is here no longer. Let the floodgates of my wretched

[27] SC 26.3; SBOp 1:171: 'Denique plorantibus aliis, ego, ut advertere potuistis, siccis oculis secutus sum invisum funus, siccis oculis steti ad tumulum quousque cuncta peracta sunt exsequiarum solemnia.'

[28] See Jean Leclercq's introduction to *The Works of Bernard of Clairvaux* 3: *On the Song of Songs* 2, CF 7 (1976), 'Were the Sermons on the Song of Songs Delivered in Chapter?'

[29] EM III.1, pp 149–51. The EM excerpt starts with section 4 from Bernard's lament and so leaves out his abrupt opening and description of his immediate reaction to the death of Gerard.

head be opened, let my tears gush forth like fountains, that they may perchance wash away the stains of those sins that drew God's anger upon me. When the Lord shall have been appeased in my regard, then perhaps I shall find the grace of consolation, but without ceasing to mourn: for those who mourn shall be comforted.[30]

Bernard indicates in his description of his actions that so long as he performed his official function as abbot, he had to maintain the dignity of his office. But now he must be allowed to be a man again, a man with weaknesses and failings, one born of Adam, who had a right to need other men:

I have made public the depth of my affliction, I make no attempt to deny it. Will you say then that this is carnal? That it is human, yes, since I am a man. If this does not satisfy you then I am carnal. Yes I am carnal, sold under sin, destined to die, subject to penalties and sufferings. I am certainly not insensible to pain; to think that I shall die, that those who are mine will die, fills me with dread. And Gerard was mine, so utterly mine. Was he not mine who was a brother to me by blood, a son by religious profession, a father by his solicitude, my comrade on the spiritual highway, my bosom friend in love? And it is he who has gone from me. I feel it, the wound is deep.[31]

---

[30] SC 26.8; SBOp 1:176, trans. Kilian Walsh (CF 7:67): 'Exite, exite lacrimae iampridem exire cupientes; exite, quia is, qui vobis meatum obstruxerat, commeavit. Aperiantur cataractae miseri capitis, et erumpant fontes aquarum, si forte sufficiant sordes diluere culparum, quibus iram merui. Cum consolatus fuerit super me Dominus, tunc fortassis et ego merear consolari, si tamen non pepercero a maerore: nam qui lugent, ipsi consolabuntur.'
[31] SC 26.9, SBOp 1:177; CF 7:69: 'Affectum confessus sum, et non negavi. Carnalem quia dixerit? Ego humanum non nego, sicut nec me hominem. Si ne hoc sufficit, nec carnalem negaverim. Nam et ego carnalis sum, venumdatus sub peccato, addictus morti, poenis et aerumnis obnoxius. Non sum, fateor, insensibilis ad poenas: mortem horreo meam et meorum. Meus Girardus erat, meus plane. An non meus, qui frater sanguine fuit, professione filius, sollicitudine pater, consors spiritu, intimus affectu? Is recessit a me: sentio, laesus sum, et graviter.'

Here, as in so much else, Bernard is full of surprises. Certainly Bernard could be a powerbroker and a polemicist, but he also lets us see him as a man in contact with his own emotions, able to mould his inner life into a christian form without denying his natural impulses.

Bernard distinguished between his own loss and Gerard's gain. Gerard is in heaven, and there is no reason to feel sorry for him in his passing. But Bernard still had a right to dwell on his own loss. At times it might appear as if Bernard's main reason for regret was the absence of someone who had taken care of many practical affairs and thus had given Bernard time for his spiritual life.[32] But Bernard insisted that what he missed most of all was the companionship of a dear friend. This loss brings tears of compassion. As human beings, he insists, we have a need for each other's company. Just as much as we rejoice in each other's presence, so we feel sorrow at each other's absence, especially when this becomes a permanent separation:

> It is but human and necessary that we respond to our friends with feeling, that we be happy in their company, disappointed in their absence. Social intercourse, especially between friends, cannot be purposeless; the reluctance to part and the yearning for each other when separated, indicate how meaningful their mutual love must be when they are together.[33]

In Bernard the West learned the dignity and usefulness of tears of human loss. Bernard realized that sorrow must have a chance to get out of one's system. It cannot remain within

---

[32] SC 26.6; SBOp 1:173–74: 'Ad omne quod emerserit, respicio ad Gerardum, ut consueveram, et non est. Heu! tunc ingemisco miser, sicut homo sine adiutorio. Quem consulam in ambiguis? Cui in adversis fidam? Quis portabit onera? Quis pericula propulsabit?'

[33] SC 26.10; SBOp 1:178; CF 7:69: 'Humanum, inquam, et necesse affici erga caros, sive delectabiliter, cum praesto sunt, sive, cum absunt, moleste. Non erit otiosa socialis conversatio, praesertim inter amicos; et quid effecerit mutuus amor in sibi praesentibus, horror indicat separationis, et dolor de invicem in separatis.'

forever: human pain needs a means of expression. He chose a public moment in the life of his monastery to proclaim his own witness to faith in God and love for Gerard. Once tears were shed, homage paid to Gerard's memory, and degree of loss made evident, then Bernard could go on to the next sermon. But not as if there had been pause. He began the twenty-seventh sermon by reminding his listeners/readers why he had stopped in the middle of the preceding one.[34]

Whether or not all these words actually were spoken in the chapter house is not of great importance. What matters is Bernard's decision, in giving the sermons literary form, to include a lament for his brother. He may have been influenced by Ambrose's model. In any case a thoroughly human expression of sorrow was now merged into a monastic milieu. Faithful to the lesson of Christ at the tomb of Lazarus, Bernard set a precedent no later Cistercian could ignore. His witness to tears of compassion was not just tucked away in the corner of a minor sermon. It was placed prominently in his most celebrated literary and theological product, the *Sermons on the Song of Songs*. In Bernard spiritual and emotional life could become one in the monastic experience. Tears of human loss could become an expression of faith, hope, and love.

Bernard and Aelred

Aelred of Rievaulx met Bernard at Clairvaux a few years after the death of Gerard.[35] It is likely that his own lament for the death of his friend Simon was patterned on Bernard's.[36] Like Bernard Aelred broke off in the midst of an intellectual exposition in order to express personal distress on the death of a friend. Like Bernard, Aelred eventually returned to his

---

[34] SC 27.1; SBOp 1:181: 'Sed si nostras defleamus aerumnas, ne id quidem oportet nimis, ne non tam amasse illum, quam nostra quaesisse de illo commoda videamus.'

[35] F. M. Powicke, *The Life of Ailred of Rievaulx by Walter Daniel* (London: Thomas Nelson, 1950; reprinted in Oxford Medieval Texts 1978) lvi-lix.

[36] *Speculum Caritatis* I.99, CC CM 1:57.

subject, while at the same time acknowledging why he had gone astray. Also like Bernard, Aelred conceded the importance of tears and their rightful place in monastic life. The monk mourns for those who die and admits openly the loss he feels.

Both Aelred and Bernard were superb literary artists. They found nothing unacceptable in drawing on their own inner lives in order to express their ideas. But they could not have written about their losses without believing that their experiences could be used in the monastic programme of spiritual growth within community. Aelred's sense of loss and tears were meant to be shared with other monks.

Monastic tears do not correspond to Tennyson's 'Tears, idle tears; I know not what they mean'. Aelred and Bernard had no idle tears. They knew exactly what their tears meant: the expression of the pain they felt at the loss of friends who could only be returned to them when they themselves died. Both Aelred and Bernard wrote about a frustrated desire to have preceded the friend in death and revealed that they found it hard to remain behind. For both writers, there was no reason to resist the impulse to tears. Tears were to be encouraged, for they provided witnesses to love, care and need.

> Do not keep back these tears, for the sweet memory of you, my brother, brings them forth. Let this sight not be a burden for you, for it is not despair that causes it but affection. Do not choke these tears which religious feeling, not lack of faith, elicit.[37]

Aelred's meaning is easy to grasp. So long as tears are not a sign of despair, a loss of faith in Christ's promise of individual salvation, then we have a right to weep on the deaths of those whom we love. We cry not because they are in another

[37] *Spec car* I.99: 'Noli has lacrimas prohibere, quas dulcis memoria tui,mi carissime frater, educit. Non sit tibi onerosus hic gemitus, quem non excitat desperatio, sed affectus: nec cohibeas has lacrimas, quas pietas elicit, non fidei defectus.'

world, but because they no longer are with us in our world. Like Bernard, Aelred was aware that others might disagree with his tears and call them carnal. Even more defiantly than Bernard, Aelred rejected such critics.[38] The panegyric of his friend Simon became an exposition of Aelred's own psychic state. Aelred drew on the condition of his inner being to grow further in the love of the God who gave him Simon, and who also took him away. Bernard had to depart from the subject of his sermon in order to mention Gerard, but Aelred could add to his theoretical exposition on love by providing a concrete instance of love: his own for Simon and Simon's for him. As in so much else of cistercian life in the twelfth century, individual experience contributes to the collective articulation of monastic spirituality.

Tears after Bernard and Aelred

With Aelred and Bernard tears of compassion became part of monastic spirituality. This new expression was soon taken up by others. In a letter from the Paris master Stephen of Tournai, probably dating from the 1190s, to the prior at a monastery in Orléans, we find a division into tears of compunction and penance, those of compassion and mercy, and those of mutual joy and faith.[39] To the twofold distinction of Gregory the Great has been added the category of compassion. Stephen looked for authority in the three occasions on which Mary Magdalene was seen to have wept: for herself, for her brother, and for Christ. She wept for herself when she washed Christ's feet; for her brother, on the death of Lazarus; and finally for the Saviour when she saw the risen Christ.

[38] Spec car I.112; CC CM I:63: 'Sed forte iudicant nunc aliqui fortes lacrimas meas, nimis carnalem existimantes amorem meum. Interpretentur eas, ut volent; tu autem, Domine, vide eas, respice eas.'

[39] Ep 159; PL 211:448: '. . . primae lacrymae, frater, compunctionis et poenitentiae; secundae, compassionis et misericordiae; tertiae, congratulationis et fiduciae.'

Even if this explanation mixes up the biblical Marys, as medieval exegesis usually did,[40] the point is clear. Just as one should weep for one's sins, it is also good and right to weep for dead kin and friends. In Simon of Tournai the personal witness of Bernard and Aelred received a more systematic expression, even though Bernard already had anticipated Simon's threefold division.

Alongside the formalization of theology in the universities in the thirteenth century, tears continued to maintain some place, especially in the spiritual writings of the friars. The Dominican Thomas of Cantimpré, for example, told an apt story about tears of sorrow in his collection of anecdotes for sermons, *Bonum universale de apibus*.[41] It is based on is own family's experience. His mother had told Thomas how his grandmother had two sons, the first virtuous, the other wayward and prodigal. When the first-born son died, she was therefore desperately unhappy. But then the woman had a vision of youths walking along and seeming quite content. When she did not see her son among them, she began to weep. Finally she saw him coming far behind the others. 'Why, my son, are you alone and not with the others?' she asked. He replied that he had to carry with him the weight of all his mother's tears because they had been shed uselessly (*inaniter*). Instead she should offer her tears to God through the sacrifice of the mass and communion, as well as in offerings to the poor, and then he would be freed from the weight keeping him behind his companions.

In this simple tale the monastic theology of tears has been translated into the medium of lay life. Tears are appropriate and acceptable on the death of loved ones, but they are to be used as part of the efforts made to help the dead, and not in order to indulge in one's own loss. Bernard himself had warned against those who wept 'because of the misfortunes

[40] See *The Life of St. Mary Magdalene*, trans. David Mycoff (CS 108, 1989).
[41] II.53 (Douai, 1627) 500–01.

of the present life'.[42] Tears can be offered to God together
with other manifestations of devotion. They can help the
dead instead of adding to their burden.

We are a long way here from Bernard's elegant prose and
his exquisitely articulated emotions, but the underlying as-
sumption is the same. Tears of human loss have a place in
the spiritual life, so long as they are used rightly. Appropriately enough, Bernard was remembered in the exemplum
tradition for his tears, and also for the temptation to show
tears in public and gain admiration for his gift. In at least two
fourteenth-century collections he is said to have shed tears
of compunction in church and then to have been tempted
to let the brethren see him in such a state.[43] Bernard immediately and bitterly regretted this temptation, and an angel
came to comfort him. Bernard and tears had become associated with each other. This perhaps indicates a medieval
awareness that Bernard's sense of self could at times border
on pride.

The later Middle Ages are bathed in tears. Here one thinks
of Huizinga's account in his brilliant chapter 'The Violent
Tenor of Life'. Fourteenth and fifteenth century writers por-
tray tears in terms of violence. People fall into uncontrollable
fits of crying at the savageness of life and death. We would
find it difficult to relate such tears to any programme of spiritual growth. But there is no doubt that religious sentiment
in the period did encourage the shedding of tears. The great
art historian Emile Mâle has pointed out in a chapter on
'le pathétique' that in late medieval religious art, concentration on the sufferings of Christ and especially on Mary's

---

[42] SC 26.8; SBOp 1:176: '. . . vitae praesentis incommoda.'

[43] See J. A. Herbert, *Catalogue of Romances in the Department of Manuscripts
of the British Museum* (London, 1910) p 28: BL Additional 26770, f 76rb,
and BL Additional 27909 B, f 6r (Herbert p 466): 'Quadam die beatus
Bernardus solus in ecclesia habundanciam lacrimarum effudit et cogitavit
hec intra se: si scirent monachi mei tantas effudisse lacrimas multum
meam commendarent sanctitatem et postea penituit de tali cogitatione et
secum erubuit et valde confusus et desolatus et dixit ei angelus domini:
Noli desolari . . . . '

experience of them (as we see in the hymn *Stabat Mater*) encouraged the shedding of tears.[44] Here it is difficult to distinguish between sentiment and sentimentality. We are, however, in a different realm of human expression from that of twelfth-century cistercian monasticism, where tears had a place but were under strict literary and group control.

The cistercian tradition of tears seems to have remained faithful to twelfth-century conceptions, at least according to the surprising witness provided in a fourteenth-century manuscript from the augustinian house of Waldhausen in Austria.[45] This is an exemplum collection mainly made up of cistercian materials, but also containing some stories not found in the standard repertoire which had developed by that time. In one of these tales, a cistercian novice saw her *magistra* weeping before a statue of Christ and his mother. The Christ child acknowledged the nun's tears by drinking some of them, washing himself with some, and finally he bathed her face in the remaining tears.

The Virgin Mary then explained what had happened. The tears drunk by the Christ child are those that the nun offered in trying to know the divine will. The tears with which he bathed himself are those brought forth in compassion for others (*ex compassione proximorum*). The tears with which Jesus washed the woman are those she shed for her own conscience.[46] Here we meet again the three categories of tears described by Bernard: the last are those of compunction (even though the nun apparently had few sins of which to repent), while the others were tears of compassion for loved ones and of desire for heaven.

[44] *L'art religieux de la fin du Moyen-Age en France* (Paris, 1925) 86–107.
[45] British Library Additional MS 15833, ff 93v–94r; Herbert, p 581.
[46] Ibid., f 94r: 'Ego tibi exponam. lacrimas quas bibit filius meus, ipse sunt que pro cognoscenda divina voluntate funduntur. Lacrime vobis quibus lotus est filius meus ipse sunt que ex compassione proximorum funduntur. Lacrime vobis quibus ipsa lota est ipse sunt que pro consciencia propria mundana effunduntur et quia signo visibili pure consciencie esse. demonstrata est. gratias decetero age dono dei pro consolatione tam felici.'

Even here, in the literature of the exemplum genre and long after the spiritual flowering of the twelfth century, there is a clear method in what to us might at first have appeared to be the medieval madness of tears. Tears have a place in the religious life of the individual, but the story also makes clear that tears have a role in the life of the monastery as a whole. The nun's vision is seen by one of her most devoted novices. The girl's participation means that ultimately the rest of the house will come to share in the event. The nuns, as well as future readers of the story, are meant to perceive not just the miracle, but also divine acceptance of the efficacy of tears.

This late medieval story that emerged from an originally cistercian milieu could draw on the twelfth-century break-through that accepted the place and efficacy of shedding tears for loved ones. Bernard's sober drunkenness of tears could provide an alternative to hysterical bouts of weeping. Behind Bernard is the tradition of the desert that welcomes tears but sees them only as a byproduct of the spiritual life and does not associate them with human affection.

If we return here to the story in Caesarius about the grace of tears, we discover it reveals not only the importance of compunction in the monastic life but also an awareness that spiritual men need each other's help, as well as the help of spiritual women, in unblocking their inner lives. This means of expression can easily get out of control and does seem to have done so at times in late medieval religious life. But the very prominence of Bernard in spiritual texts of the period shows how his passionate sobriety could still appeal.[47]

What importance does all this weeping have for us to-day, when tears are manufactured by clever people to make money? In the first place, we can realize how different our

---

[47] See Giles Constable's two important articles, 'The Popularity of Twelfth-century Spiritual Writers in the Late Middle Ages', *Studies in Honor of Hans Baron* (Florence, 1971) 5–28, and 'Twelfth-century Spirituality and the Late Middle Ages', *Medieval and Renaissance Studies* 5 (1971) 27–60. I will return to these articles in my chapter 'Bernard and the embrace of Christ'.

culture would have been if there had been no intellectual acceptance of the importance of tears of compassion. Twelfth-century monks may have merely rediscovered the weeping Christ of the New Testament. But if they had not done so, such sorrow could have been looked upon as 'unmanly'. Christian spirituality would have developed in ways that had less room for the needs and pain of the individual person. A second point, closely associated, is that the acceptance of tears in the twelfth century strengthened concentration on the humanity of Christ. The moment at Lazarus's tomb became a central scene for an understanding of the link between individual emotion and fraternal love based on a human Christ. Thirdly the new place for tears made it possible for monastic life to concern itself with catharsis in human experience. Tears could have been limited to the cleansing brought about by penance for sins, but Bernard and his followers insisted that individual human loves should receive a prominent place in this process of self-renewal. Life might be a journey through a vale of tears, but on this journey were groups of people who cared for each other and who could admit that they missed each other when some completed their travels before others.

The Cistercians insisted on knowing themselves. For them self-knowledge also meant self-expression. Bernard and his friends were interested not in 'letting it all hang out', as recent cultural fads in the West have preached, but in acknowledging the bonds formed in human life and death. Partly thanks to the Cistercians, tears of compassion have meaning and context within communities based on love.

6. The First Cistercian Renewal and a Changing Image of Saint Bernard[1]

Most of us are attracted by the idea of human and corporative development. Implicitly or explicitly we think of organizations and institutions as bodies whose development resembles that of human beings: birth, growth, maturity and decline. Those of us who return time and again to the cistercian fount of knowledge and friendship at Kalamazoo probably each has his own explanation of how and when the Cistercian Order declined from its early prominence and vitality. When I received the catalogue of the 1988 congress, I was surprised to find I had been placed in a session entitled 'The Golden Age'. I myself do not think of the twelfth century in such terms, but I can imagine that for many scholars, the twelfth was the greatest of all cistercian centuries. The Order and its chroniclers have ever since been dwelling on the myths and ideals that arose during that period.

[1] This chapter is based on a paper given at the Cistercian Studies Conference in Kalamazoo, May 1988, and was first published in *Cistercian Studies* 24 (Gethsemani, Kentucky: 1989) 25–49 and is used with kind permission. I have made a few changes (See, for example, note 11).

The Cistercian Order in its first century can fascinate us because it advanced in both material and spiritual terms. The Cistercians produced an appropriate 'success story' in an age that saw great growth and even more optimism about the capacity of men (and women) to change themselves and their world. This success caused jealousies and rivalries, both inside and outside the Order, problems that only fully emerged into the light of day in the thirteenth century or even later. But it is already apparent from the events of the two decades between Bernard of Clairvaux's death in 1153 and his canonization in 1174 that individuals and groups in the church did not look uncritically at his work.[2] The phenomenal spread of the cistercian experiment, which was generally seen as Bernard's achievement, did not always inspire praise. In an age when growth in itself was not necessarily considered something good, churchmen asked why the Cistercians were taking their lands—and with them the sons of local nobles who otherwise would have become secular clerics or joined the Benedictines. The courtier and cleric Walter Map summed up in a diatribe the elegant and poisonous talk of a generation that had come to question the good motives of the monastic reformers.[3]

One might almost claim that Bernard got canonized on the coattails of Thomas à Becket. The latter's phenomenal martyrdom and a wave of defiance against lay people who questioned the role of the clergy and the new orders in contemporary society may have swept aside the last reservations about Bernard's sainthood. But before the dramatic events of the 1170s, there had been years when the legacy of Bernard was in question. As Adriaan Bredero so convincingly has

[2] See Adriaan H. Bredero's illuminating article, 'The Canonization of Bernard of Clairvaux', *Saint Bernard of Clairvaux: Studies Commemorating the Eighth Centenary of his Canonization*, CS 28, ed. M. Basil Pennington (1977) 63–100.

[3] *De nugis curialium: Courtiers' Trifles*, dist i, c. 25, ed. and trans. M.R. James, revised by C.N.L. Brooke and R.A.B. Mynors (Oxford Medieval Texts, 1983) pp 84–113.

demonstrated, Geoffrey of Auxerre, Bernard's secretary and the depository of his tradition, had to scale down some of the criticisms of prominent churchmen in the earliest drafts of the Vita Prima.[4] Geoffrey himself had not been successful as abbot of Clairvaux and had to resign in 1165. His sermon on the tenth anniversary of Bernard's death, in 1163, is probably the most complete statement of his personal bond with Bernard.[5] Here Geoffrey reveals much more about his relationship to Bernard than he does in the later books of the Vita Prima. In these Geoffrey portrayed Bernard as a man of miracles, using all the conventions of the hagiographical genre and leaving the reader only with a sense of distance between Bernard and his surroundings.[6]

This glorification of Bernard was perhaps necessary to reply to some of the rumours circulating at the time, apparently even at the court of Thomas à Becket, that Bernard had occasionally been a flop at performing miracles.[7] Geoffrey had much malicious gossip to counter, but his defence lacks the

[4] Bredero pp 86–90.

[5] S. Lenssen, 'L'abdication du bienheureux Geoffroy comme abbé de Clairvaux', Collectanea O.C.R. 17 (1955) 98–110; Gaudfridi abbatis Claraevallensis, Sermo in anniversario obitus S. Bernardi, PL 185:573–88.

[6] As pointed out by Bredero (p 90), Geoffrey in his later draft of the Vita Prima 'had to take into account the changed information required in the process of canonization'. For Bernard's separation from his surroundings, see Michael Casey, 'Bernard the Observer', Goad and Nail, Studies in Medieval Cistercian History 10, CS 84, ed. E. Rozanne Elder (1985) 1–20, who concludes: 'I, for one, am ready to believe that Bernard did not know that the novitiate was vaulted and didn't care how many windows were in the front of the church.'

[7] Walter Map, De nugis curialium, dist. i, c. 24; pp 79–81: '. . . the madman, on feeling himself freed, began to throw stones at the abbot as hard as he could, chased him through the streets as long as they let him, and,even when the people caught him, still kept his eyes on Bernard, though his hands were held. The archbishop was not pleased with the tale, and said threateningly to John: "These are your miracles, are they?" "Well, says John, "those who were present said it was a very memorable miracle, because the madman was gentle and kind to everyone, and only vicious to humbugs; and it still seems to me that it was a judgment on presumptuousness"'. Also p 81, how Bernard is supposed to have failed to raise a boy from the dead.

warmth and intimacy present in some of the anecdotes found in his earliest draft of the Bernard biography.[8]

The Vita Prima contains in its first book a personal Bernard whom William of Saint Thierry had known, but in the second book provides a political portrait of Bernard, while the final books give us a miracle-making and omni-competent Bernard.[9] Geoffrey of Auxerre leaves the reader only a limited impression of how Bernard functioned within the context of monastery life. Even in William of Saint Thierry's Bernard we gain only a few glimpses of the abbot at Clairvaux with his monks, a far cry from the intimacy displayed, for example, in Walter Daniel's portrait of Aelred together with his monks at Rievaulx. One hears in William of the monastery's golden age, of its phenomenal growth, and how he felt in spending a period of illness in Bernard's domineering company at Clairvaux.[10] But we get only a limited sense of Bernard as father and mother of his monks, able to guide them through everyday spiritual crises and concerned with penetrating into their minds and hearts.

In order to find this more intimate and personal Bernard, we can of course turn to his own writings, especially to his letters. But my concern here is the response of the cistercian community to Bernard: how did he impress its members, and how did they remember him? Here the most recent work of Adriaan Bredero shows how in the 1150s and 1160s there was by no means any general agreement about how to describe Bernard. The first version of the Vita Prima by no means obtained success, and so one cannot claim that the Cistercians remembered Bernard in any clearly defined way.[11] I find, however, that once the process of canonization was

---

[8] 'Les fragmenta de Vita et Miraculis S. Bernardi', ed. Robert Lechat, Analecta Bollandiana 50 (1932) 83–122.

[9] Adriaan H. Bredero, 'Etudes sur la Vita Prima de S. Bernard', ASOC 17 (1961) and 215–60; ASOC 18 (1962) 3–59.

[10] Vita Prima I.38 (PL 185:249), I.59 (PL 185:259), I.62 (PL 185:261).

[11] I am grateful to Adriaan Bredero for sharing with me the text of his contribution to the October 1990 symposium at the Herzog August Bibliothek in Wolfenbüttel: 'Der Heilige Bernhard von Clairvaux im Mittelalter:

over, it was possible for what we might call a more homely version of Bernard to emerge.[12]

This development is evident in the miracle stories and *exemplum* collections that began to appear at Clairvaux in the 1170s. These reveal Bernard to us as a figure of strength and love inside the monastery. The emergence of such a description of Bernard indicates an ongoing cistercian discussion about the identity and role not only of Bernard but also of the Order as a whole.

In these last decades of the twelfth century, the abbot Joachim of Fiore was undergoing a spiritual and intellectual development that eventually took him out of the Cistercian Order.[13] Joachim's evolution is of major concern for the later history of medieval religious orders and for medieval society in general.[14] However divisive Joachim's thought proved to be, he had little influence on cistercian development. The Cistercians had fostered one of Christianity's most influential biblical exegetes and prophets, but the Order remained intact after he separated himself from it. Joachim's emergence

Von der historischen Person zur Kultgestalt' (to be published in the Acta of the 27. Wolfenbütteler Symposion, 'Bernhard von Clairvaux. Rezeption und Wirkung im Mittelalter und Neuzeit', ed. Kaspar Elm). Here Professor Bredero expresses disagreement with my article in *Cistercian Studies*, and I have taken this criticism into account in my revision. I can see now that until the 1170s there was no established cistercian view of Bernard: it is only in this decade that agreement was reached on the portrayal of Bernard.

[12] Here, as so often, I have gained much inspiration from Chrysogonus Waddell, this time in his 'Simplicity and Ordinariness' in the volume of the same name, Studies in Medieval Cistercian History 4, ed. John R. Sommerfeldt, CS 61 (1980) 1–47. Although Father Waddell did not himself include Bernard among the early cistercian figures who reflect these traits, there are moments in our literature about Bernard when Waddell's description of another abbot could be applied to Bernard, as p 37, in describing Abbot Peter of Clairvaux, 1179–86).

[13] Sandra Zimdars-Swartz, 'Joachim of Fiore and the Cistercian Order', *Simplicity and Ordinariness*, 293–309.

[14] As is shown in the work of Marjorie Reeves, *The Influence of Property in the Later Middle Ages* (Oxford, 1969). See especially her, 'Joachim and the Meaning of History' in *Joachim of Fiore and the Prophetic Future* (London, 1976) 1–14.

and the divisions in the church occasioned by debates over poverty among Franciscans are all peripheral issues in cistercian history. The Order remained relatively uninfluenced.

I would like to show here that cistercian self-assuredness that emerged in the 1170s about the legacy of Bernard contributed to a general agreement about the Order's identity and role in the church. This sense of identity kept the Cistercians from the divisions that tore apart the Franciscans. In the late twelfth-century clarification of Bernard's tradition, I find one possible explanation for the ability of the Cistercians to renew themselves without splitting into warring factions. Bernard became a point of reference and a common rallying point not only for the monks of Clairvaux, but for the whole Order. His memory united the monks instead of feeding controversy.

In Bernard the Cistercian Order, as its own writers attest, found a brilliant pillar that gave it support.[15] In our post-freudian consciousness this may be a rather harsh male symbol. But for a very masculine and self-assertive age, it was a necessary assurance that all was well and that the Order's early expansion would not give way to steep decline. As we shall see, the monks of the 1170s and the following decades did much to use the tradition of Bernard to apply early values to contemporary challenges.

The Liber Visionum et Miraculorum (1171–79)

Under Prior John of Clairvaux in the 1170s, the Cistercians made a collection of edificatory and miraculous stories, some of which deal with Bernard. The earliest of these were written down before his canonization, for the word *sanctus* was only later inserted.[16] The collection was probably the result of teamwork at Clairvaux and apparently reflects an interest

---

[15] EM VI.10, p 370: '. . . eiusdem sacri ordinis splendidissimam columnam.'

[16] 'A Lost Clairvaux Exemplum Found: The *Liber visionum et miraculorum* compiled under Prior John of Clairvaux (1171–79)', AC 39 (1983) 27–62.

at the monastery in bringing together stories that had not before appeared in written form.

Stories about Bernard are scattered through the manuscript (Troyes 946). Most of them would be all but unknown today if it were not for the fact that several of them were taken, probably directly from this collection, and included in the section on Bernard in the *Exordium Magnum Cisterciense* (EM), to which we will return. The stories from the *Liber Visionum et Miraculorum* (LVM) in which Bernard is prominent include:

1. A summary of two sermons given by Bernard in chapter, including one in which he claimed that even Judas, if he had repented his crime and become a Cistercian would have been saved (f 3v, used in EM II.2).
2. Bernard telling how a priest celebrating Mass saw Christ on the altar between two angels (f 114v).
3. A story of a brother at Clairvaux who took communion against Bernard's order but could not swallow the host (f 121r-v, going back to *Vita Prima* I.51, PL 185:256).
4. A dead brother released from punishment through the masses and prayers of the Clairvaux brethren (f 132 r-v. Cf. EM II.2).
5. A novice who on Bernard's order did not take communion at Easter and then died without communion because the brothers thought he already had taken it (f 133r-v).
6. Bernard's vision of angels taking down the words of monks who sing the psalms (f 134v. Cf. EM II.3).
7. Bernard's response to the devil when the fiend claimed Bernard was damned (f 134v–135r. Cf. VP I.57, PL 185:258).
8. A miracle performed by Bernard after his death but before his burial (f 174r).

Only two of these stories go back to an earlier written source I can find: that of the lay brother who disobeyed Bernard in taking communion, and that of Bernard who

answered the devil's charges against him. The compilers of
the LVM were interested in stories about Bernard that had
been circulating in the monastery but which had not been
written down. So far as I can tell from the published writings
of Bernard, his sermon about the possible salvation of Judas
if he had been able to convert to the Order does not appear
in earlier cistercian literature. But when Conrad of Eberbach,
the compiler of the *Exordium Magnum Cisterciense*, came across
it, he gave the tale prominence in his collection.

My purpose here is not to trace the development of stories
from one source to another but to look at them in terms of
what they say about Bernard. In this case it is obvious that
except for the final story, all of them concentrate on Bernard
as an abbot who look out for the spiritual welfare of his
monks. Bernard is remembered as having been concerned
about how the monks attended to the liturgy, but he was also
critical of his own actions when he found that a novice had
died without communion because of a misunderstanding.
He was furious with demons for taking this youth, but their
tricks would not prevail because, as he told his monks, 'I am
the one responsible.'[17] The novice was not at fault. Bernard
was, and so he could compensate by asking for the monks'
prayers, 'so we will pursue those thieves.'

Bernard is shown here as knowing what to do to retrieve
a lost member of his community. Here, as elsewhere, his
concern was to see that everyone who came to the monastery
obtained salvation. The monks and even the novices were his
personal responsibility. This attitude is reflected in a similar
story of the brothers being given assurance that one of their
departed brethren had been released from suffering because
of their prayers. 'There is no way to resist the militia of God,'

---

[17] LVM = Troyes MS 946 f 133r: '. . . novicius ille sine viatico transivit
e mundo. tulerunt eum demones et illudunt nobis. sed non prevalebunt.
quia ego sum in causa. quoniam eum sacra communione privavi. Vigilate
ergo et mecum orate. et persequamur latrunculos istos.'

See my article, 'Taking Responsibility: Medieval Cistercian Abbots and
Monks as their Brother's Keepers', *Cîteaux* (1988) 249–69.

Bernard insisted.[18] The graphic descriptions of hell recall the language of visions in the fourth book of Gregory the Great's *Dialogues*. But this place could perhaps be purgatory, for no distinction is made here, Jacques Le Goff's thesis that by now Cistercians had a notion of purgatory notwithstanding.[19] In the cistercian source, the soul of the dead man is not alone, for the powerful arms of a whole community are marshalled in the fight for his salvation.

Bernard knows best. This is hardly surprising, but the stories allow us to see him rallying the community in prayers and making its members aware of the spiritual strength of their way of life. The stories can hardly be called intimate, but they do convey a sense of life in the community with Bernard in charge. We are given an impression of how his words affected the monks, as he once may have spoken them in chapter. Here he provided reassurances about the worth of their cistercian vocation. Later Bernard was seen as the stubborn abbot who refused to be outsmarted by the devil, not only by securing his monks' salvation, but also by defining his own. In perhaps the most striking story in the collection, Bernard was remembered for summing up his own theology of the redemption. The story is an expanded version of what could already be found in William of Saint Thierry's first book of the *Vita Prima*. In returning to this anecdote, our collector showed an interest in William's Bernard as a man who could be tempted:

The saintly man Bernard, when once he was sicker than usual and thought that now he would soon die, was taken up in a rapture to heaven, so that he could obtain the inheritance of the saints on high. But as with Saint

[18] LVM f 133r: 'Non est quod possit huic milicie dei resistere nisi tantum cor impenitens.'

[19] *The Birth of Purgatory* (Chicago, 1984) esp. pp 168 and 364. To be completely fair to Le Goff, however, he does not claim that by the 1170s the concept of purgatory was fully developed among the Cistercians. See my 'Purgatory, the Communion of Saints, and Medieval Change', *Viator* 20 (1989) 63–84.

Martin,[20] so with him, there came to him evil spirits saying with many reasons that he was not worthy ⟨of salvation⟩, since he could not deny that in thought, word and deed he had done many things contrary to the faith and his own profession.

When he was given a chance to defend himself, he responded in this way: 'Indeed I know that I am not worthy. I confess that even though I have sinned, I still have not denied the Lord my God. Nor do I deny that he obtained this inheritance for himself as for me by a twin right. For himself by the right of the Lord, since through him and because of him all things are; for me by right of the servant, for he persevered for my sins, not in just any way, but until death. And if this seems little, the death even of the cross.'

'There is no further way by which he could serve or humble himself. Thus served the servant, the same Lord and my God, taking me up into himself, both enriching himself and his own for me. By this faith then I have in the privilege of his blood, by this confession I have the inheritance of the Father and of the Son and of the Holy Spirit. For me and all who love him, I assert that this is the case for all time and eternity.'

In saying these things Bernard confused his enemies. He showed that for someone who believes there is free entrance into the inheritance of his Lord.[21]

[20] The closest parallel in the *Life* of Saint Martin by Sulpicius Severus I find in ch 22, where the devil claimed that some of Martin's monks had by wrongdoing lost the grace of baptism and so were beyond salvation. See *The Western Fathers*, trans. F. R. Hoare (London: Sheed and Ward 1954, 1980) p 37.

[21] LVM = Troyes MS 946 f 134v: Sanctus vir Bernardus cum aliquando plus solito infirmatus se citius moriturum iam crederet. per *excessum mentis* rapitur ad sublimia, ut hereditatem sortiretur sanctorum in excelsis. Sed sicut sancto martino, ita et ipsi occurrerunt spiritus malignis multis ex causis non esse dignum eum dicentes, quippe qui cogitatione, locutione et opere contra fidem et suam professionem plurima perpetrasse negare non posset.

Quibus data sibi facultate se defendendi, ita respondit: 'Equidem scio me (f 135r) *non esse dignum*. Confiteor autem licet enim peccaverim, tamen dominum deum meum non negavi, nec nego, qui hanc hereditatem tam

One can hardly find elsewhere a more concentrated and straightforward expression of Bernard's faith in salvation and his trust in the redemptive merits of Christ's passion.[22] Devils trying to trick saints and discourage them are a commonplace of hagiographical literature, but here Bernard's response summarizes his theology of the redemptive act. Bernard in these stories is a man of potent words and decisive responses to the spiritual and intellectual challenges of cloister life. He has visions and performs miracles, but in the main these stories reveal him as an abbot looking out for his monks and making sure they get to heaven. His concern and attention allow him no compromises. Here he takes an almost unlimited responsibility on himself.

Herbert of Clairvaux's Liber Miraculorum *and* *Conrad's* Exordium Magnum Cisterciense

In 1178, when the LVM was complete or nearly complete, the monk Herbert at Clairvaux began writing down the stories known as the *Liber Miraculorum* (LM). No adequate edition of

---

sibi quam michi *dupplici iure obtinuit.* Sibi iure domini, nempe per quem et propter quem omnia; michi iure servi servivit enim in peccatis meis, non quomodocunque, sed usque ad mortem. Et si parum videtur, mortem autem crucis (Ph 2:8).

Ultra prorsus non est, quo servire vel humiliari possit. Sic servivit servus, idem dominus et deus meus, me in se suscipiens, et se et sua mihi largiens. Hac igitur fide habeo sanguinis eius privilegio. Hac inquam confessione patris et filii et spiritus sancti hanc hereditatem. michi et omnibus qui diligunt eum etiam ab eterno et usque in eternum confirmo.'

His dictis confusis enim adversariis, liber patuit credenti introitus in hereditatem domini sui.

The italicized words are the same as those in the *Vita Prima.* Both versions emphasize the idea of a double right (*ius dupplex*), but the LVM version is far more specific than is William of Saint Thierry. It is, of course, possible that the compiler of the LVM drew on a written source not available to us.

[22] In Bernard's tract on the Redemption, he concentrated more on the word *iustitia* than on the concept of *ius*, which for him referred to the illegal use of power by the devil. See the *Tractatus contra quaedam capitula errorum Abaelardi*, PL 182:1065–67. This is the same as Bernard's ep 190, to Pope Innocent, SBOp 8:31–32.

this work exists to this day, despite the groundwork laid by Bruno Griesser. For our purposes here it is sufficient to look at the version in the *Patrologia Latina*.[23] Here there are many stories about Bernard, but they are dispersed in a chaotic mass of miracle stories unrelated to each other. Almost all of these stories reappear in Conrad of Eberbach's *Exordium Magnum Cisterciense* (EM) from the end of the century. Instead of searching through Herbert's disorganized work, we will find a more cohesive view of Bernard's place in the Order's consciousness if we turn immediately to the *Exordium Magnum*.[24]

Conrad was not interested in being original, and he gladly took over the bulk of Herbert's stories about Bernard and added some of his own, partly drawing on the LVM, partly on Geoffrey of Auxerre, and partly on sources that neither Griesser in his outstanding edition or I have been able to identify. Once again, however, what is important for our context is not to trace the various versions of the same story but to look upon the whole of the story material about Bernard in terms of what it reveals concerning the monks' use of him.

One notices immediately that in the first twelve of the twenty chapters dedicated to Bernard in the second distinction of Conrad's EM, Bernard is seen inside the monastery of Clairvaux. Thus sixty percent of the stories concern Bernard as abbot, while the remaining forty percent are devoted mainly to Bernard in his dealings outside the monastery. There is some overlapping, however, as in the story of Bernard's visit to the schools of Paris in order to get young men into Clairvaux (ch. 13), or the story of a thief Bernard brought from his place of execution to Clairvaux (ch. 15). If these two stories are included in the list of those that reveal Bernard's abbatial concern for recruitment, we reach the figure of seventy percent of the stories as what might be

[23] PL 185:1273–1384. The best studies on the LM remain those by Bruno Griesser, *Cistercienser Chronik* 54 (Bregenz 1947) 21–39 and 118–48.

[24] For an introduction to the work, my 'Structure and Consciousness in the *Exordium Magnum Cisterciense*: The Clairvaux Cistercians after Bernard', *Cahiers de l'Institut du Moyen-Age Grec et Latin* 30 (Copenhagen, 1979) 33–90.

called 'intra-mural', revelatory of the actions of Bernard as abbot rather than as miracleworker. Finally, the fourteenth chapter concerns a prophecy of Bernard that all the novices in a group which he blessed at Clairvaux would end up as abbots. One of them, Peter of Nydala in Sweden, did so only late in life when a daughter house was founded at Gudvalla on the island of Gotland in 1164. This story concerns both Bernard at Clairvaux and the later development of the Order.

The best way to view the scope of these stories is to provide a brief summary of their contents:

1. A dead brother appeared to Bernard during mass; his salvation was guaranteed (LM II.11 = PL 185:1322).
2. The soul of a dead brother with whom devils played was freed from punishment by the brothers' prayers (= LVM f 132).
3. Bernard saw angels writing down what the monks were singing (= LVM f 134).
4. Bernard saw angels encouraging the brothers to sing the 'Te Deum' with greater eagerness (Source unknown to me).
5. Bernard declared that even Judas would have been saved if he had become a Cistercian (= LVM f 3v).
6. A monk with no faith in the sacrament of the altar is ordered to take communion on the basis of Bernard's own faith (The story is similar to other communion stories in LVM but not quite the same).
7. Monk saw the image on the cross embracing Bernard in prayer (LM II.19 = PL 185:1328).
8. Bernard cured a monk of epilepsy, but only partly (LM II.20 = PL 185:1328).
9. Bernard ordered a dying brother to delay his death so that the brothers' sleep would not be disturbed (LM I.13 = PL 185:1291).
10. Bernard predicted to Lord Guido that because of a fault he would not die at Clairvaux (LM II.11 = PL 185:1324).

11. Bernard, in Italy for three years, thrice visited Clairvaux in the spirit (LM II.14 = PL 185:1324 and 463).

12. Bernard, outside Clairvaux for a long time, returned in spirit to the novices' quarters and consoled one of them (See Geoffrey of Auxerre's *Sermon* on the death of Bernard, PL 185:575).

13. Bernard converted the clerics of Paris (LM II.17 = PL 185:1326).

14. Bernard blessed novices and promised they would one day become abbots. (No written source found. Story may come via oral tradition at Clairvaux from Sweden).

15. A thief was delivered from death by Bernard so he could be brought to Clairvaux and become a monk (LM II.15 = PL 185:1324).

16. Great devotion was shown by lay people on Bernard's trip to Italy (LM II.18 = PL 185:1327).

17. Bernard refuted a heretic in Gascony (LM II.16 = PL 185:1325).

18. A blind man in the same region was given sight through dust where tracks of Bernard showed. (No source found).

19. A dead man was raised by Bernard. (Based on a story in the account of Bernard's miracles in Germany, PL 185:375, 377, 384–85, but as Griesser shows in his notes to the EM edition, the story was not contained in the earliest versions of the EM).

20. The death of Bernard and miracles afterwards. (Sources from Geoffrey of Auxerre and Odo of Morimund. See Griesser's notes to the EM).

Ten of the stories are taken directly and almost verbatim from Herbert of Clairvaux, while three are from the *Liber Visionum et Miraculorum*; the rest come either from known sources, including the writings of Geoffrey of Auxerre, or remain of unknown origin. This review should immediately reveal that Conrad, just as the compilers of the LVM, was mainly concerned with the legacy of Bernard *as abbot at Clair-vaux*. Bernard emerges here as an abbot who did everything possible to look after the needs and interests of his monks. Bernard's involvement is well illustrated by the sixth chapter, where he is seen as having replaced a monk's lack of faith in the Eucharist with his own belief. This he did in order to be able to 'cure' the man and get him to go to communion despite his hesitations. Here, as so often, Bernard is remembered as having known exactly what had to be done in a spiritual crisis. His eagerness to see that every single monk at Clairvaux obtained salvation, and thus to outsmart the devil, is already emphasized in the first story. Here a brother appeared to him when he was in choir and said, 'If you knew how many and what kind of companions you could have in heaven, you would immediately guard yourselves from every form of laxness'.[25] The monk in the vision stated precisely what was so important, the avoidance of *negligentia*, one of the major concerns of the Order in the last decades of the twelfth century, as we can see from the statutes of the General Chapter.[26]

In the very first chapter of the EM's section dedicated to Bernard, he is remembered as having gained an assurance that becomes a major theme of the work's 'intra-mural' stories. 'Yes, they will be saved', he is told about the brothers of Clairvaux. 'And not only they but also all who serve in our Order in obedience and humility will be saved.'[27] Bernard is supposed to have thought immediately about a dead brother

[25] EM II.1 = Griesser, p 98: O si sciretis, quantos et quales socios haberetis in caelis, profecto caveretis vobis ab omni negligentia.

[26] See 'The Cistercian Advance in Retrospect, *The Cistercians in Denmark*, CS 35 (1982) 108–110. A helpful contribution to the debate about decline/change as seen in the statutes of the General Chapter is Robert D. Taylor-Vaisey's, 'The First Century of Cistercian Legislation", *Cîteaux* 27 (1976) 203–25. Also Bennett D. Hill, *English Cistercian Monasteries and their Patrons in the Thirteenth Century* (Urbana: University of Illinois, 1968) 151–52.

[27] EM II.1; Griesser p 98: ' Etiam . . . salvabuntur. Et non solum ipsi, sed et omnes, qui in ordine nostro obedienter et humiliter fuerint conversati, salvabuntur.'

concerning whose salvation he was in doubt, but he was assured, 'Not even to him will the mercy of God be lacking.'[28] Bernard was delighted: *Vehementer gavisus est.*

This message of reassurance about salvation is reinforced by the second chapter, with its story of how a brother who died in sin could be released form sufferings by the monks' prayers. In these stories, angels are everywhere, accompanying, encouraging, and reproving the monks. The brothers were to understand that the angels kept a precise record of their behaviour in the monastery, especially in choir, as the third and fourth chapters show. The assurance of salvation is repeated in the fifth chapter: even Judas would have been saved. This story is related to Bernard's ability to sense his monks' state of mind. During a talk in chapter Bernard realized that he had created such fear of God's judgment in the monks' minds that some of them were beginning to feel that they were beyond hope of salvation.[29] The abbot had to respond to the needs of his monks. He pushed them hard, but not too hard, and so in such a situation he could 'flame up totally in the spirit of fraternal love.'[30]

Bernard as abbot is remembered in the *Exordium Magnum* for his ability to respond and relate to his monks, but he also was seen as considering their situation in terms of community needs. This was the case with a dying monk whom Bernard is supposed to have ordered not to give up his life until the next morning. In this way the brethren would be able to get their night's sleep after a long day. 'I order you', he said to the poor brother, 'that you wait for us until the hour of divine office'. The sick monk agreed, on the condition that he receive Bernard's prayers.[31] Bernard wanted life

[28] Ibid., pp 98–99: 'Nec ipsi deerit misericordia Dei'.

[29] EM II.5; Griesser p 101: '. . . sensit in spiritu quosdam de sedentibus graviter in conscientiis suis turbari et fere in baratrum desperationis prolabi.'

[30] Ibid., 'Tum vero spiritu fraternae caritatis totus flammescens. . . . '

[31] EM II.9; Griesser p 104: '. . . praecipio tibi, quatenus usque ad horam divini officii exspectes nos. Cui aeger respondit: Faciam, domine, libenter, ut imperasti; si tamen voto meo tuis precibus suffrageris.'

to go on at Clairvaux in an orderly manner, so he arranged
even the time of dying, in order to avoid the 'long vigils'
that would have been required if the monk had died at the
beginning of the night.

Bernard knew that Clairvaux was the place where everyone
wanted to die, and so he made sure a man who was otherwise good and religious did not get the privilege of being
buried at Clairvaux because he had prevented his brother
from following Bernard's order and entering Clairvaux. The
story indicates that the nobleman in question, Guido, wanted
to save money and took as his excuse the difficulty of trans-
porting his sick brother from Normandy to Clairvaux (ch. 10).

Clairvaux is described as a magnet that drew the whole
world to itself. Bernard is seen as the source of the magnet's
power. When Bernard was not home at Clairvaux, his monks
are said to have missed him greatly. There are two stories
about the consequences of his absence (ch. 11 and 12). During his three-year stay in Italy he is supposed to have made
a spiritual visit to Clairvaux once a year. His return is thus
likened to the yearly visitation of a father abbot. But the story
also hints that the monks missed Bernard and perhaps were
critical of him for letting them down.

'My sons,' Bernard is to have said in chapter after his italian trip, 'Don't think that I was always absent.'[32] Bernard told
how he had wandered about their workshops and rooms.
'Always uplifted, always consoled, I left, seeing the oneness
and eagerness you had in following the set purpose of your
order.'[33] The story is told to reveal that Bernard was blessed
with the spirit of prophecy, but the elegant literary device

[32] EM II.11; Griesser p 105: 'Et ego quidem, filioli, quamvis per hoc tri-
ennium visus fuerim longe remotus a vobis, non tamen putetis me semper
absentem fuisse.'
[33] Ibid.: 'Sciatis enim, quod tribus vicibus interim reversus sum ad vos
visitans domum istam officinasque perambulans et semper exhilaratus,
semper consolatus abscessi videns unanimitatem atque instantiam vestram in proposito ordinis vestri.'

of 'present in spirit even when absent in body' cannot hide
the hint that the monks sometimes felt Bernard was away for
too long.

This story gains emphasis from the next one in the collection (ch. 12). It tells how Bernard returned in spirit to
the monastery and entered the cell of the novices to find
one of them very distraught. Here Bernard's absence is defended as a necessity: 'Even though most unwilling, he was
forced to leave ⟨Clairvaux⟩.' On his physical return, Bernard
called the troubled novice to him and said, 'I know what is
going on inside of you, and because of fatherly concern, I
have compassion on you.'[34] The wayward novice, identified
with Geoffrey of Auxerre, received great comfort from knowing that Bernard was aware of his state of mind.[35]

Bernard is there even when he is not. He takes care of
his monks and novices and shows special consideration for
those who are discouraged and feel they cannot make the
grade in monastic life. Bernard is seen as penetrating into
the monks' hearts and minds, not only predicting their future lives but involving himself closely with their immediate
states of mind. Just as his anecdote about Judas is said to
have given the monks renewed courage and hope, so too his
attention to Geoffrey's depression, here called *tristitia*, helped
to dissolve it.

Conrad commented on Bernard's ability to speak to the
monks about his own experiences and visions. He claimed it
was a great gift Bernard had, for he could reveal not just to
a few friends, but to all the monks in chapter, the privileges
of insight and prophecy God had given him. He could do so
without jeopardizing his own humility. Conrad here indicates
that Bernard's openness about his visions was unusual, and
he also hints that there might have been criticism of Bernard
for drawing so publicly on his own visions and revelations.

[34] EM II.12; Griesser p 106: 'Scio, fili dilectissime, scio ea, quae circa te
aguntur, et propterea paterno pietatis affectu tibi compatior.'
[35] See Griesser's note 2, p 105 in his EM edition.

'He had a mind so anchored in the fear of God,' Conrad wrote, 'that he was not afraid of being struck by a spirit of vanity.'[36] Bernard's self-assuredness is shown in even more public ways in the stories about how he was received by the common people in Italy or how he effected cures. But Conrad was not content with a presentation of Bernard as a one-dimensional miraclemaker. He puts the saint into the context of the Cistercian Order and the church as a whole. As Conrad says at the end of the eighteenth chapter, which originally was probably the chapter before the one on Bernard's death, 'through him the monastic order regained the ancient strength of holy religion and the Church of God obtained many benefits of divine mercy by means of the apostolic grace given to him.'[37] These remarks are made just after a description of how Bernard's arms had become puffed up like those of a boxer because masses of people tried to kiss them as he passed by. He is presented as a figure that combined popular appeal with the well-being of his monks. Bernard is seen as available for everyone, but the stories concentrate on Bernard as abbot for his monks at Clairvaux, in life as well as in death.

In Bernard's own death, described in chapter 20, his central role for his monks and the Order in general is emphasized. Conrad claims that a great flood of miracles immediately began to take place at Bernard's tomb, even before his burial. The abbot of Cîteaux was concerned that the many healings would bring such a crowd of pilgrims that the brothers would

[36] Ibid.: 'Quid enim in hoc beatissimo patre nostro magis admirer nescio, an quod tantam et tam insolitam gratiam a Domino percipere non semel, sed pluries meruit, seu quod tam excellentem gratiam percipiens non eam apud se servavit teste conscientia, sed nec paucis tantum familiaribus suis eam revelavit, quod certe et ipsum sine periculo vix fieri posse videretur, verum in publico conventu, sicut supra retulimus, coram universitate fratrum eam sibi collatam esse manifestavit et tamen mentem adeo in timore Dei solidatam habuit, ut vanitatis spiritu pulsari nequaquam timeret.
[37] EM II.18; Griesser p 113: '. . . per quem monasticus ordo in antiquum sacrae religionis vigorem refloresceret et ecclesia Dei per apostolicam gratiam ipsi collatam divinae misericordiae beneficia plurima consequeretur.'

not be able to carry out the regular monastic office. Then 'discipline would perish and the fervour of holy religion in that place would grow tepid.'[38] Bernard intervened by stopping the public miracles. In this way, Conrad claims, just as Bernard had been obedient in life to the abbot of Cîteaux as his father abbot, so too he was obedient in death. Miracles for members of the Cistercian Order and a few others did not stop, for the abbot of Cîteaux had forbidden 'only signs that could threaten the discipline of the Order'.[39]

One wonders how the monks, or Bernard, could distinguish one sign from another. Were relatives of monks excepted from the general prohibition? Our source does not tell, but the drying up of miracles may have contributed to claims made by Bernard's detractors, such as Walter Map, that in some cases the powerful abbot was impotent to perform miracles.[40] One of Conrad's anecdotes indicates that according to common knowledge, Bernard did not perform miracles for the laity. This story concerns a devil possessing a woman. When confronted with relics of Bernard's hair and beard, the demon began to rage and spit, saying to the cistercian abbot who had proferred the relics:

> Hey, little abbot, what are you trying to do? What evil are you concocting against me underneath your habit? You are acting vainly and uselessly Keep your little Bernard. He won't help you at all.[41]

The story significantly does not tell whether or not the woman was cured of possession. Its silence hints that the

[38] EM II.20; Griesser p 117: '...ne, si crebrescentibus signis tam intolerabilis illuc populorum turba concurreret, earum improbitate periret ordinis et sanctae religionis fervor in eodem loco tepesceret.'
[39] Ibid.: 'Namque sola illa signa, quae disciplinam ordinis per turbas concurrentium populorum minuerent, domnum Cisterciensem fieri noluisse manifestum est.'
[40] See note 7 above.
[41] EM II.20; Griesser, p 117: 'Eia, inquit abbatule, quid vis facere? Quid modo mali contra me sub illa veste tua machinaris? Frustra niteris, in cassum laboras; serva Bernardulum tuum, nec enim proficies quidquam.'

use of Bernard's relics, in fact, was vain. Conrad here leaves his readers in the dark about the efficacy of Bernard's powers. On the one hand he emphasized Bernard's obedience to his superior, while on the other he hinted that Bernard was remembered as unable or unwilling to cure some of those who turned to him.

In spite of the ambiguity of his last story concerning Bernard's legacy as a popular saint appealed to by common people, the anecdote about stopping his public miracles underlines Bernard's main concern: the monks of Clairvaux and other members of the Cistercian Order. Bernard in the *Exordium Magnum* is invariably seen in terms of the Order as a whole: its organization, structure, and concern for maintaining the highest possible standards. Bernard is depicted as a self-assertive abbot and spiritual leader who was himself obedient to his father abbot. Doing everything possible to spread the Order across Europe, Bernard is also remembered for returning to Clairvaux to read the hearts and minds of his own monks. His love of discipline never went so far that he discouraged his monks. His passion for reform in the Order and in the church as a whole did not isolate him from others but brought him out into the world in contact with common people, priests, cardinals and popes.

Bernard becomes in the *Exordium Magnum* all things to all people, in the favourite cliché for medieval saints taken from Saint Paul (1 Cor 1:19).[42] But he was especially all things to all Cistercians. The chapters about Bernard in the EM are carefully meshed into a presentation of the spiritual heroes and heroic events from the first century of the Order. From the context of hagiography in the *Vita Prima*, Conrad placed Bernard in the context of the Cistercian Order's history. Conrad became the first historian of the Order with a grand vision of its place in church history. His interpretation gives an

---

[42] Alexander Murray has some excellent remarks on the medieval hagiographical use of this phrase, *Reason and Society in the Middle Ages* (Oxford, 1978) 386–89.

enthusiastic account of Bernard without making him into a public figure isolated from his monastic surroundings.

There is no doubt that Conrad was concerned about the state of the Order and wanted to use his account of Bernard's words and deeds to encourage monks in his own time and in the future. Several chapters concern current dangers (*periculis*) in monastic life, and he was aware of restlessness and resentment growing up within groups of laybrothers.[43] At the same time Conrad was acutely concerned about the criticisms of Benedictines, especially in his native Germany, against the Cistercians. They were accused of being an Order whose first monks had broken away from their house at Molesme in order to start the new monastery at Cîteaux.[44] The taint of instability and the slur on the legality of the original cistercian foundation bothered Conrad greatly. It became all the more important to him to exalt the work and role of Bernard to show that the Order had developed through the efforts of such an outstanding man of God.

A closer look at the conclusion of the *Exordium Magnum* reveals Conrad's concern with showing how Bernard provided a central inspiration for the cistercian reform spirit and how that spirit lived on in the present.[45] From Stephen Harding to Bernard and onwards there had been an unbroken surge of reformed monasticism. Conrad pointed to the great number of conversions in Bernard's day but explained that there were never too many monks for the space available at

---

[43] These are found in the fifth distinction: ch. 1, the danger of taking oaths; ch. 2, the danger of property; ch. 3, the danger of dying without one's habit, etc.. The story of the laybrother revolt is in ch. 10, 'De periculo conspirationis'. See J. S. Donnelly, *The Decline of the Medieval Cistercian Laybrotherhood*, Fordham University Studies. History Series 3 (New York, 1949) 34–35.

[44] EM I.10; Griesser p 61: 'Monachi namque nigri ordinis, maxime in provinciis Germaniae degentes, ubicumque vel apud quoscumque possunt, sacro ordini nostro derogare non cessant asserentes sanctos patres nostros cum scandalo et inobedientia contra voluntatem abbatis sui de Molismensi coenobio egressos fuisse.'

[45] EM VI.10; Griesser pp 364–70: 'Recapitulatio finalis eorum, quae in hoc volumine continentur.'

Clairvaux. As soon as they had finished their novitiate, Bernard would send most of the new ones out to found new monasteries. Nothing could deter these brothers from carrying out Bernard's wishes in braving extreme cold or heat to transplant Clairvaux. Conrad tended to place Clairvaux first among all cistercian houses, but he invariably turned to the Order as a whole in order not to make Clairvaux too prominent. He did claim, however, that there was some danger of decline elsewhere (*incuria . . . vel levitas seu dissolutio*), but these symptoms, he insisted, had not managed to penetrate Clairvaux.[46] He recalled his own days there and said that he experienced a tradition unbroken from the time of Bernard to that of his successors in the 1180s and 1190s.[47] Clairvaux apparently remained untouched by the dangers which Conrad saw elsewhere and which caused him 'fear and trembling'. He warned Cistercians outside Clairvaux that they had begun to neglect small matters, but for these there would be great punishments.

Conrad concluded that time, which is able to destroy everything human, could also weaken the fervour of religious life. The *negligentia* of the present generation departed from the standards which Bernard had set and which had been kept in his memory by the seniors of Clairvaux.

The picture Conrad gives of the state of the Cistercian Order at the end of the twelfth century is not a rosy one. He used its history to fight what he considered a decline of standards, even if he was not very specific about the abuses of his day. But Conrad confirms what we find elsewhere: a growing sense of unease about a departure from the spirit of Bernard's times.[48] The memory of Bernard

[46] Ibid., p 367: 'Incuria nempe vel levitas seu dissolutio, quae est ruina ordinis, locum ibi penitus non habebant. . . . '

[47] Ibid., p 368: '. . . usque ad nostram aetatem durantes et exemplum fervoris et devotionis reliquo corpori sanctae illius fraternitatis effecti facile in sua amabili conversatione monstrabant. . . . '

[48] For criticism by Pope Alexander III against the Order, see Jean Leclercq, 'Passage supprimé dans une épître d'Alexandre III', *Revue Bénédictine* 62 (1952) 149–51. See also Leclercq, 'Epître d'Alexander III sur les

provided a necessary element in a constant effort to maintain purity and strictness of life and to warn against any form of complaisance or self-satisfaction. In a world that Conrad thought had grown old and lost its faith, the early years of the Order and the dynamism of Bernard provided hope and a constant reminder of what was necessary for a renewal of monastic life.

The Dialogus Miraculorum *of Caesarius of Heisterbach*

Caesarius of Heisterbach is one of the early thirteenth-century cistercian writers whom most medieval historians know but few take seriously, willing as he was to convey gossip and miraculous tales. In earlier studies I have pointed out how rich a source for the content and attitudes of cistercian life his collection of *exemplum* stories provides.[49] Every time I return to Caesarius, I find his sunny personality and optimism about the growth of the Order a useful reminder that in the Rhineland in the early thirteenth century, new monasteries were carrying on the activities and realizing the ideals of their french twelfth-century predecessors.

In his *Dialogus Miraculorum* (DM), Caesarius preferred, or at least claimed, to use oral sources, and yet when he dealt with traditions about Bernard of Clairvaux, some of his stories were taken from the *Vita Prima*. There are ten chapters of the DM in which Bernard plays a significant role, and of these at least three are taken from the VP. In other cases Caesarius was able to collect several stories which apparently until his time had been in oral circulation but which

---

Cisterciens', R Ben (1954) 68–82. For Gerald of Wales and Walter Map in context, see David Knowles, 'The Critics of the Monks', *The Monastic Order in England* (Cambridge, 1966) 662–67.

[49] 'Written Sources and Cistercian Inspiration in Caesarius of Heisterbach', AC 35 (1979) 227–82. 'Friends and Tales in the Cloister: Oral Sources in Caesarius of Heisterbach's *Dialogus Miraculorum*', AC 36 (1980) 167–247. The *Dialogue on Miracles*, DM, is still most easily available in the reprint of the original 1851 edition by J. P. Strange (Ridgewood, New Jersey; Gregg Press, Inc., 1966).

had not been available in written sources. The accessibility of unpublished stories about Bernard shows how very much alive the tradition of Bernard still was at the time when Caesarius became a monk in about 1200. As he himself tells us, his abbot Gevard had heard some of the 'new' stories at the General Chapter, and others had come to Heisterbach via monks in german houses who had known senior monks from Clairvaux who had been there in Bernard's time.

Here is a summary of the stories about Bernard arranged according to section (*distinctio*) and chapter in the DM:

I.6:   Bernard was remembered as the abbot and preacher who spread the Order. A canon of Liège was converted by him. He wished to join the new monastery at Aulne and Bernard granted his wish.

I.8:   Mascelin, cleric of the bishop of Mainz, was converted to the Order (= VP IV.14; PL 185:330).

I.9:   The false conversion of Master Stephen of Vitry. (See VP I.65; PL 185:263).

I.16:   Henry the cripple joined Clairvaux because of a promise that he would die there.

I.19:   Henry, brother of the king of France, converted to Clairvaux.

II.3:   An apostate monk was made contrite through a miracle of Bernard.

II.16: A knight of Rheims took communion in the presence of Bernard and went away contrite.

III.7: Bernard put an incubus demon to flight at Nantes. (See VP II.35; PL 185:287–88).

IV.1:   Bernard said that remaining faithful in the Order is enough to obtain salvation. (Cf. EM II.5, but also the Vita Quarta of Bernard by John the Hermit, 2.9, PL 185:545).

IV.7:   The devil ridiculed Bernard for polishing his own boots. (See the Vita Quarta 2.16, PL 185:549).

Half of the stories in Caesarius about Bernard appear already in the first *distinctio*, which concerns conversion to the

Cistercian Order. This indicates how well Bernard was re-membered for an ability to bring new recruits to Clairvaux. His travels around Europe were seen primarily in terms of the vocations they harvested.[50] But Caesarius combined the conversion stories with anecdotes about Bernard's closeness to his monks once they had joined. In telling of a canon of Liège who was converted by Bernard's preaching, Caesarius added a story about how Bernard immediately consented to the man's strong desire to be with his fellow monks in founding a new monastery. Bernard looked into the minds of his monks and asked only that they convey their wishes to him. This story is subordinated to the main point of the chapter: that the abbot never should delay confession for a monk who asked for it. Bernard's role and the memory of him are here secondary to a question of monastic discipline. Caesarius could be sufficiently relaxed about the tradition of Bernard not only to introduce a new story about him but also to subordinate Bernard's role to the main point of the chapter.

The story of the conversion of Henry the cripple (I.16), like that about the canon of Liège, contains several episodes and substories. Here we learn not only that Henry joined the Order after he was assured he would die at Clairvaux, but also that Bernard raised the nobleman's servant from the dead after the man had been struck down for blasphemy. A much more detailed version of the story is contained in later versions of the *Exordium Magnum* II.19, but Caesarius does not seem to have borrowed from there. He said he got his story from the former abbot of Heisterbach, Gevard,

---

[50] Jean Leclercq has also noticed the penchant of Caesarius and of later medieval *exemplum* collection to concentrate on Bernard's ability to bring new recruits to the Order. See 'The Image of Saint Bernard in Late Medieval Exempla Literature', *Thought*. Fordham University Quarterly (1979) 291–302, esp pp 293–96. See also my 'A Saint's Afterlife: Bernard in the *Golden Legend* and in Other Medieval Collections', *Bernhardrezeption in Spätmittelalter und Frühneuzeit*, forthcoming as the Acta of a congress held at the Herzog-August-Bibliothek, Wolfenbüttel, October 1990.

who once had spoken with Henry at Cîteaux. The chapter ends with an anecdote about how Henry had once taken a paralytic woman up on his horse so that they could catch up with Bernard and see that she was given a chance to be healed. In this set of stories, Bernard is seen both as a recruiter of monks who attended to the inner needs of his men (their desire to die at Clairvaux) and as a great miracle-worker who attended to the needs of the people (their desire to gain physical health).

Caesarius is often able to project this double vision of Bernard the intimate abbot and the public figure. Another such story shows Bernard staying on a journey at the home of an apostate monk, who had become a parish priest and had a family (DM II.3). Bernard is supposed not to have recognized the fallen-away monk, but when by a miracle he cured the priest's son and gave him the power of speech, the priest was so moved that he confessed to Bernard and promised to return to the monastery. Here there is something for everyone. Bernard performed a miracle that quickly would have become public knowledge (the healing of the boy). At the same time he transformed the interior life of the boy's father, who resolved to return to the monastery he had abandoned. Nothing is said about what might have happened to the boy and his mother, but the man died before Bernard returned from his trip to fetch him the monastery. When Bernard arrived and the tomb was opened, the man was found to be wearing not priestly vestments but the monastic habit. The monk in life had become the monk in death. Everything else was forgiven him.

Caesarius of Heisterbach apparently had no difficulty in presenting a view of Bernard that combined his public achievement with his more intimate bonds with his monks. Miracles and tenderness go together with no tensions, and we even find that one type of 'intra-mural' miracle could be applied to an 'extra-mural' situation. This is the case with a knight who refused to believe in the real presence of Christ in the Eucharist (DM II.16). Bernard insisted he be given communion anyway, and when he received the host, the man regained his faith. This is parallel to the story in the *Exordium Magnum* (II.6) about the monk who refused to take communion but did so when ordered by Bernard. In both stories Bernard's overwhelming faith compensated for the lack of faith in others. His boldness and confidence in the grace of God benefited both a monk and a lay person.

Bernard's belief that membership in the Cistercian Order was a guarantee of salvation is already apparent in the *Exordium Magnum*. Caesarius repeated the same type of stories, but in summary form, such as that about a thief who was to be hung but was retrieved by Bernard so that he could spend his life in punishment as a monk (DM IV.1). Together with this story is an anecdote about how Bernard told a convert to the Order that for his penance he merely had to say an 'Our Father': 'You say just this prayer and keep to the Order, and on the day of judgment I shall render account for your sins.'[51] Caesarius took the phrase from the second chapter of the *Rule* of Saint Benedict about the abbot's responsibility for his monks and used it to show Bernard's conviction that the good Cistercian had nothing to worry about, no matter what the temptation he might encounter.

Bernard is overwhelmingly competent, and not just as a man of miracles. Caesarius included the theme of his responsiveness to his monks. In one incident, Bernard is tempted in an almost banal manner, just as one of his monks might have been: the devil provoked him when he was polishing his own boots as an act of humility (IV.7). He told Bernard he was neglecting the monastery's guests to whom he as abbot should pay more special attention. 'Oh, what an abbot', the demon is supposed to have burst out in ridicule: *Vach qualis abbas*! Bernard provided no theological response as he did in the LVM when the devil attacked him, but he realized what

---

[51] DM IV.1; Strange 1:172: 'Tu tantum hanc oratione dicito, et ordinem custodi, et ego pro peccatis tuis rationem reddam in die iudicii.' See my article 'Taking Responsibility', note 17 above, esp. pp 250–51.

he was dealing with and continued his 'work of humility' so the devil gained nothing.

These ten stories add nothing decisively new to the earlier portraits of Bernard available in the LVM and the EM. Caesarius's stories do, however, show how eager he, like his predecessors, was to draw on both written and oral traditions about Bernard in order to characterize the values of the Cistercian Order: the importance of conversions, the value of confession and of dying in the cistercian habit, and the success of Bernard in casting out devils and securing the faith of the laity in the sacrament of communion. There is nothing subtle or deep about a saint who was remembered for being able to cope with every problem he met. Caesarius's portrait of Bernard is memorable because he as a matter of course integrated stories about Bernard into a larger context: the miracles of recent times showing God's power still being manifested among men, especially in the workings of the Cistercian Order.

In Caesarius's *Dialogus Miraculorum* we experience an easy confidence in the legacy of Bernard. His public and monastic images are effortlessly combined. Caesarius provides no hint of any disputes about the identity or purpose of Bernard's work and life. His devotion to the monks and his outer involvement in the life of the church emerge in a double vision of the saint as abbot and thaumaturge.

Coping with Crisis and Seeking Renewal

If we turn from the omnicompetent Bernard of Caesarius to the invectives of Walter Map against the Cistercian Order, we detect a world shaped quite differently. Confidence in the cistercian mission in the church was replaced by suspicion about cistercian methods and motives. When Walter Map wrote in the 1180s and 1190s, the first laybrother revolts had occurred, and the Cistercians were running into accusations of greediness and rapacity. Walter may well have been a disappointed cleric whose material welfare was undermined by a cistercian house, but his criticism, however, exaggerated, still hits on some areas where we know from elsewhere that the monks were under attack.[52]

Walter pointed out, for example, how the monks sought solitude not simply by cultivating virgin lands but often by razing whole villages and clearing the peasant population off the land. From the studies made by the agricultural historian R. A. Donkin, we know this is correct for some areas of Britain, and in danish studies I have found indications of a similar cistercian policy.[53] The cistercian presence in the countryside must often have been difficult for the peasants and smaller landowners whose holdings lay in their path. The monks had political as well as spiritual weapons to convince unwilling residents to give up their possessions to the monks, as we see in the story of a landowner near Øm abbey in Jutland. After he saw Mary in a dream and she ordered him to surrender to the monks, he the next day, despite his wife's contempt, decided to sell his property to them.[54]

Conrad of Eberbach's final chapter in the *Exordium Magnum* points to increasing cistercian unease at the distance between the simplicity of life among the first monks and the search for property and privileges by their successors. He insisted that Clairvaux was still untainted. It is significant that a few decades later Stephen of Lexington, in his

[52] See the judicious comments in the Introduction to the new edition of *De nugis curialium* (note 3 above), pp xliii–xliv.

[53] R.A. Donkin, *The Cistercians: Studies in the Geography of Medieval England and Wales* (Toronto: Pontifical Institute, 1978), esp. ch. 2, 'Settlements and Estates', with sections on depopulation. See my *Cistercians in Denmark* (CS 35, 1982) 55–6, for the earliest evidence from Esrum abbey near Copenhagen.

[54] Contained in M. Cl. Gertz, *Scriptores Minores Historiae Danicae Medii Aevi* 2 (Copenhagen, 1922, 1970) p 176: '. . . et beatam dei genitricem Mariam audivit celerem mortem sibi minantem, si de coemptione ultra servos suos auderet contristare. Evigilans ergo, magno timore turbatus et intelligens durum esse contra stimulum calcitrare, dissuasionem quoque et verba irrisionis uxoris sue et aliorum, quibus narraverat visionem, parvipendendo despiciens, divini timoris impulsu et reverentia beate Marie, quod prius petebatur, ipse ultro sine mora offerebat.

memorable visitation of the clarevallian houses of Ireland, made the same appeal to the continuing purity of Clarivaux. Stephen saw an order that had 'become not just carnal but the flesh itself, not just terrestrial but engrossed in the things of the earth'. 'Laxity in regard to religious life' and 'eager activity in trading' he saw as threats to the Order's purity.[55]

Stephen was not as sure as Conrad had been that Clairvaux had remained untouched by the impulses of materialism. In three letters he called on the memory of Saint Bernard as an incentive to a discipline in danger of dissolving:

> A house which is so genuine in its religious life and its holiness and so distinguished by its public counsel should take up nothing inadvisedly, inasmuch as it is known to be the foundation, the stimulus and the model of our entire order through the merits and instruction of blessed Bernard. . . . [56]

Stephen saw the process of decline as far advanced: 'Almost everywhere these days greediness and shiftless dissoluteness are pursued in our order.'[57] He saw a crisis in recruitment and believed the only hope for the monks lay in attracting new men 'praiseworthy for their life and for their learning, as it was in the time of blessed Bernard.' But the Order, he insisted, was already 'aging and tottering', so it would be difficult.[58]
Stephen's solution to this development when he himself became abbot of Clairvaux was to try to send its best monks to the schools of Paris. This was by no means an immediate

[55] 'Registrum Epistolarum Stephani de Lexinton abbatis de Stanlegia et de Savigniaco', ed. Bruno Griesser, ASOC 2 (1946) 1–118. I use the excellent translation by Barry W. O'Dwyer, Letters from Ireland, CF 28 (1982) p 60.
[56] Ep 24, whose entire conclusion is a dramatic appeal to the abbot of Clairvaux. O'Dwyer, p 60.
[57] From Ep 26, also to the abbot of Clairvaux. O'Dwyer, p 67.
[58] Ibid., p 69.

success and caused much opposition in the Order.[59] Bernard had been able to go to the schools of Paris and draw clerics away from them, while Stephen almost a century later had to concede that the schools had become the most attractive place in Europe for sensitive and bright young men. If you can't beat 'em, join 'em.

However alarming the reports of Stephen of Lexington, they reveal a continuing awareness that the memory of Bernard was still important in maintaining cistercian ideals. In years of controversy and self-definition, the Nachleben of Bernard remained available not as a static memory but as a source for inner renewal. If Bernard had been all things to all men, then the Cistercian Order could only live up to his tradition by fighting laxity and trying to continue to attract the brightest and best young men of its age. To a certain extent, the Order continued to do just that in many areas, such as the Rhineland and the lowlands of what today is Belgium.[60] At the same time the cistercian expansion towards the East continued, and new monasteries were founded in what today makes up Germany, Poland, and the Baltic States.[61]

Thirteenth-century Cistercians may not have been as dynamic and resourceful in their spirituality as many of their twelfth-century predecessors. But the interior criticism of the state of the Order that came from such men as Stephen of Lexington shows that the monks were still trying to live out the early ideals of austerity and the contemplative life. In this continuing process of self-criticism, combined with the

[59] Werner Rösener, 'Abbot Stephen Lexington and his Efforts for Reform of the Cistercian Order in the Thirteenth Century', *Goad and Nail* (note 6 above) pp 46–55, for an introduction and full bibliography.

[60] Here Caesarius of Heisterbach is a primary, and rather neglected, source for the continuing material and spiritual growth of the Order. See my articles noted above (n 48), and also the indirect evidence for spiritual vitality that can be seen from new bonds between monks and holy women, 'The Cistercians and the Transformation of Monastic Friendships', AC 37 (1981) 1–63.

[61] For an overview and bibliography, see Louis Lekai, *The Cistercians: Ideals and Reality* (Kent State, Ohio, 1977) esp. pp 58–63.

growing voice of dissatisfaction with the Order in the secular church and perhaps also from the new orders, the Cistercians continued to renew themselves. Here the memory of Bernard was a positive and unifying factor, for there were no tensions about what he could be used for. The stories about him, oral and written, were available for use in any attempt to reflect on the meaning of cistercian life and history. As Conrad himself said in closing his *Exordium Magnum*, his own work was not to be exploited as a collection of chronicles for the curious. Conrad defined his purpose as providing materials for edification and reflection.

Bernard lived on in cistercian memory as the abbot who could do practically anything and as God's instrument on earth in spreading the Order and giving it spiritual and material success. He was remembered not only as being potent in his miracles but also as being tender towards individual monks. Obedient to his superior at Cîteaux, Bernard had not founded the Order, but he had made it grow and defined its role in church and society, even after his death.

The doubleness in Bernard's legacy, as public figure and intimate abbot, can perhaps be summarized in four areas where an extra-mural debate about him in the period 1170–1230 was paralleled by an intra-mural discussion. Here views of the church in society are linked to the perceptions of the monks in cloister:

1. An *outer* debate about the *efficaciousness* of Bernard's miracles was paralleled by an *inner* debate about these miracles as a potential *distraction* for the monks. Walter Map questioned whether Bernard could perform all that had been claimed for him, while Conrad of Eberbach indicated that Bernard after his death had to be ordered not to be too free in his miracles, for fear that contemplative life at Clairvaux would be eroded by a stream of pilgrims from all over Europe.
2. An outer debate about cistercian *aggressiveness* and *acquisitiveness* was paralleled by an inner debate about to

what extent monks should *pray* and/or *work* in the fields. Stories abound in the *Exordium Magnum* concerning lay-brothers and their duties. Bernard is remembered for a sermon in which he praised a laybrother who missed the liturgy of Mary in order to carry out his duties at a grange too far from the monastery to allow his return to the church.[62]

3. An outer debate about Bernard as a *church critic* and *reformer* who shocked people was paralleled by an inner debate about Bernard as the *absent abbot* who had to return to monks in visions. Geoffrey of Auxerre had to tone down the *Vita Prima*'s criticism of certain still-living clerics, while Clairvaux monks apparently at times still felt that Bernard had let them down by being away from them for such a long time. Thus Bernard's use of his position as abbot caused *controversy both inside and outside the monastery*.

4. An outer debate about *reform/renewal* in the church was paralleled by an inner debate about *reform/renewal* in the Order. Bernard was remembered as the abbot who had pointed out and defended the legitimate pope and pursued heretics who threatened the church, while at the same time he was looked upon as the depository of the true cistercian tradition. Bernard's role became even more important because the real founder of Cîteaux, Robert of Molesme, had returned to his own house, and so the earliest, pre-bernardine history of the Order was under a cloud.[63]

The memory of Bernard was invoked in the years 1170–1230 át a time of crisis and change in both the church as a whole and the Order in particular. The legacy of Bernard had a positive and not a divisive influence on the further

[62] EM IV.13; Griesser 238–39: 'De converso cuius devotionem sanctus Bernardus per spiritum agnovit.'

[63] See EM 1.15; Griesser p 68, for some harsh remarks about Robert on his return to Molesme.

development of the Order. There was no debate about the fact that Clairvaux had the right to Bernard and had a special obligation to live up to the standards he had set. There was no such thing as an alternative Bernard, as there became an alternative Francis, once the Spirituals began their disputes with the Conventuals.[64] Bernard's versatility proved to work to the advantage of the monks, who could justify their involvement in the world through him and still emphasize the contemplative nature of cistercian life.

Ever since the death of Bernard, the Cistercian Order has continued to debate the content and requirements of monastic life. On a larger scale, the Christian Church has continued to question its own role in the world. In this ongoing discussion, the memorials to the life and works of Saint Bernard provide no clear or one-sided answer. The doubleness of cistercian life, its love of contemplation and involvement in the affairs of the larger church, lives on today. In his twin flair for intimacy and publicity, Bernard defies neat categories, scandalizes new generations of students of medieval religion, and challenges all who care about monastic life and about the church and society.

---

[64] See, for example, John Moorman's review of the various *Lives* of Saint Francis written in the decades after his death and expressing disagreement about his legacy: A *History of the Franciscan Order* (Oxford, 1968) 278–89.

7. Bernard and Mary's Milk

A Northern Contribution[1]

After his death, just as in life, Bernard was full of surprises. As we move into the later Middle Ages, we find new materials added to the tradition of Bernard as a holy man close to God and with enormous influence over other people. Until recently, this growth in the prominence of Bernard has been seen almost as a violation of his true heritage. Scholars since the seventeenth century have been trying to cut away the additions in order to find the real Bernard of the twelfth century.[2] However admirable this project has been, it is significant that the scholar who in this century has done the most to present genuine texts of Saint Bernard, Jean Leclercq, late in life has begun to show an interest in the tradition of Saint Bernard in the later Middle Ages.[3] Like

[1] This chapter is based on a paper given at the Institute of Cistercian Studies, May 1990, as part of the nonacentary celebration of the birth of Saint Bernard.

[2] As the scholar D'Achery, writing in 1651 about the various traditions associated with Saint Bernard, PL 156:1047.

[3] See his 'The Image of St. Bernard in the Late Medieval Exempla Literature', *Thought*, Fordham University Quarterly 54 (1979) 291–302, reissued in slightly altered form as 'Le portrait de saint Bernard dans la littérature

Leclercq, I look upon apocryphal stories about Bernard which cannot be traced back to twelfth century materials as indications of how people in the later period remembered and used a saint. The growth of stories about Bernard indicates that at some point in the thirteenth century he ceased to be the exclusive property, as it were, of the Cistercian Order and became a figure available to new interpretations.

One of the most fascinating and perhaps most provocative stories from this later period tells how Mary appeared to Bernard and gave him milk from her breast.[4] No version of such a story has yet been found in twelfth-century literature about Bernard. Yet by the fourteenth century the so-called lactation had come into fashion in both iconographical and literary treatments of Bernard. It is my purpose here to trace the development of this story and to present in detail one appearance of the story which has been all too little known, an icelandic version from the late thirteenth or early fourteenth century.[5] Already at this point I have to confess that I have not succeeded in achieving what I set out to do when years ago I began research on this question. I have not found what I think of as a missing link, a latin source that could provide an immediate basis for the old norse story. Perhaps, as I shall point out in what follows, we do not need to posit such a link. But it would be enormously helpful if a gifted researcher one day stumbled upon a thirteenth century story in a latin *exemplum* collection which told how Mary nursed Bernard. Until then, I shall have to do with what we know at this time, in the expectation that current

---

des exempla au bas Moyen Age', *Collectanea Cisterciensia* 50 (1988) 256–67.

[4] For a treatment of the development of the image of Mary's milk, see Marina Warner, *Alone of All Her Sex: The Myth and the Cult of the Virgin Mary* (London. Weidenfeld and Nicolson, 1976) 192–205, 'The Milk of Paradise'.

[5] I am greatly indebted to Christopher Sanders, who works at The Arnamagnæan Dictionary of Old Norse Prose at the University of Copenhagen, for invaluable help in translating this source and placing it in its Nordic context. I was originally made aware of the passage source in 1983 by Wilhelm Heizmann, now at the Nordic Institute, Göttingen University, and I look forward to his own contribution on the subject.

interest in precisely this story soon will bring to light further information.

The Pre-Bernardine Lactation Legend

The earliest versions of the lactation go back at least to the twelfth century. Here Mary appears to a sick cleric and rewards him for his devotion to her by nursing him with three drops of milk from her breast.[6] In some of these stories, the sick cleric is named as Fulbert of Chartres, the prominent theologian of the early eleventh century (d 1028). In William of Malmesbury's *De laudibus et miraculis sanctae Mariae*[7] , we have both versions side by side. First Mary appeared to Fulbert and said, 'Don't be afraid. . .I to whom you have offered service for so long a time shall be a mediatrix between you and the Son. And to make you certain about the future, now I shall make you recover from this disease.' At this point, Mary brought forth one of her breasts and placed three drops of 'precious and balsamic liquid on him'.[8] Mary here and in the next story is seen as a doctor who cures those who have been faithful to her.

So far as I can tell, this is the point of departure for later stories about the Virgin's milk. It was thought to have curative powers, and the story of lactation became one of the regular elements in collections of the Miracles of the Virgin so popular in the twelfth century and beyond.[9] The collection

[6] For an overview of the various versions of this story, see Albert Poncelet, 'Miraculorum B. V. Mariae quae seculis vi-xv latine conscripta sunt. Index', *Analecta Bollandiana* 21 (Brussels, 1902) p 359.

[7] J. M. Canal, 'El Libro de Laudibus et Miraculis Sanctae Mariae De Guillermo de Malmesbury', *Claretianum. Commentari Theologica* 8 (Rome, 1968) 146–49: 9. De S. Fulberto Carnotensi, and 10. De monacho aegroto, lacte Virginis sanato.

[8] Ibid.: '"Ne timeas, mi Fulberte, ne timeas, inquam. Ego, cui tanto tempore detulisti obsequium, mediatrix ero inter te et filium: et ut certiorem te faciam de futuro, nunc te probe conualescere faciam ex hoc morbo." Simulque cum dicto, producta e sinu mamilla, pretiosi et balsamici liquoris tres guttas super eum iecit et abiit.'

[9] For an overview of the vexed question concerning the growth of the

of the Miracles of the Virgin commonly called 'Pez' from its eighteenth-century editor, and which probably comes from the late twelfth century, once again emphasized that the sick cleric is restored to health by the milk of the Virgin because of the service he had previously done to Mary.[10] And if we turn to a cistercian collection of Mary miracles from the mid-thirteenth century, we find the familiar story:

> Fulbert bishop of Chartres was devout towards the blessed Virgin and was the first to have her nativity celebrated through all of France. She visited him when he suffered with illness and brought forth her breast and placed three drops of the most blessed milk on his face. He was immediately brought back to health and she ordered him that the nectar was to be placed and kept in a silver vase.[11]

This version summarizes the earlier stories: Mary rewarded Fulbert for his faithfulness, but in curing him she gave him only a few drops of her milk. No physical contact takes place here between Fulbert and Mary. To be more precise: he is not described as having sucked her breast.

---

collections of Mary's miracles, see R. W. Southern, 'The English Origins of the "Miracles of the Virgin"', *Medieval and Renaissance Studies* (London 1958) 176–215, an article to which I am greatly indebted.

[10] *Liber de miraculis Sanctae Dei Genitricis Mariae*, ed. Bernard Pez (Vienna 1731) ch. 30, pp 367–9: 'Hoc, inquiens, nunc habeto ob impensum mihi servitium, possessurus non post multum perenne gaudium'. T. F. Crane reissued Pez as *Liber de miraculis S. Dei Genitricis Mariae* (Ithaca, New York, 1925), a work that has not been available to me in Denmark.

[11] H. Isnard, "Recueil des Miracles de la Vierge du xiiie siècle", *Bulletin de la Société archéologique scientifique et littéraire du Vendomois* 26 (1887) 22–63, 104–227, 282–311, p 54: Fulbertus episcopus carnotensis deuotus erga beatam uirginem prius eius natiuitatem per totam galliam celebrari fecit. Quem in egritudine laborantem uisitauit; et mamillam de sinu producens, lactis beatissimi tres guttas super faciem eius iecit. Qui confestim redditus sanitati, uase argenteo nectar illud recipi et seruari precepit.

The collection is dated after 1230 and was composed at the Northern French abbey of Vaux-Cernay, a daughter of Clairvaux. See Isnard's introduction.

Since this collection has not survived in complete form, we cannot claim that its failure to mention Bernard indicates that he was not yet attached to the lactation story in cistercian circles. But it is likely that if the french cistercian collection had been interested in associating the story with Bernard, it would have done so at this juncture, after telling the older version of the story. The collection has other cistercian materials and is not just a retelling of the classic stories in the Miracles of the Virgin. Like most collections on this theme, it combines recent events with classic stories. But we do not find Bernard among the newer stories.

If we turn from *exemplum* collections of the Miracles of the Virgin and consider the language of theology, we find only a very limited point of departure for the growth of the idea that Mary feeds us—whether spiritually or physically or both—with her milk. Certainly the idea of *mater lactans* is present, but she offers her milk primarily to her son Jesus. In Anselm of Canterbury's magnificent third prayer to Mary, where he summarized all the themes of the previous two prayers and brought together all his themes of Marian devotion, he concluded:

Mother of our lover who carried him in her womb
and was willing to give him milk at her breast —
are you not able or are you unwilling to grant your love
to those who ask it? [12]

Mary's milk here is a sign of her love for Jesus. Because she loved Jesus she can help us to love him. As Anselm wrote a few lines earlier, 'I ask you by the love you have for your Son, that as he truly loves you and you him, you will grant that I may love him truly.'

[12] 'Mater huius amatoris nostri, quae illum in ventre portare et in sinu meruisti lactare, an tu non poteris aut non voles poscenti amorem eius et tuum impetrare.' *Opera Anselmi* 3, ed. F. S. Schmitt (Edinburgh. Thomas Nelson 1946), Oratio 7, p 25. Translated by Benedicta Ward, *The Prayers and Meditations of Saint Anselm* (Harmondsworth. Penguin Classics 1973) 126.

This is impeccable theology, beautifully expressed, and far from the simple story of the sick cleric who gets healed by being given a few drops of Mary's milk. There is a gap here between learned and more popular devotion to Mary, an opposition that we will have to look at later on in order to describe how the expression of religious feeling changed in the course of the later Middle Ages.

If we move to the mid-twelfth-century school of Saint Victor, with Richard's *Explicatio in Cantica Canticorum*, we find a commentary on the passage in the Song of Songs in which the breasts of the bride, celebrated in Song 4, are seen in terms of Mary: 'These breasts can be transferred to the blessed Virgin. For she has two breasts of twin love pouring forth milk, since she seeks forgiveness for the guilty and grace for the just.' [13] Here in a high theological commentary on the Song of Songs, Mary pours forth her milk for sinners in trying to save them. Richard even spoke of her milk as a 'fountain of grace which is extended through the world and lasts until the end of the world'. We are much closer to the lactation miracle story than we were in Anselm, and we can see how within a few decades the image of Mary's milk has become much more available, as it were, for human beings who need Mary's supernatural help. But in his explanation of the image, Richard still distinguished clearly between the material milk which Christ drank from his mother and the spiritual milk of mercy (*lac misericordiae*) which Mary offers us. In a magnificent sentence Richard summarized this distinction, 'Christ sucked in you ⟨your⟩ breasts of flesh, so that through you spiritual things could flow to us.'[14] The *exemplum* idea of the milk of the Virgin that comes directly to us has still not made its entrance into a work of biblical exegesis.

---

[13] PL 196:474: 'Possunt autem haec ubera ad beatam Virginem transferri. Ipsa enim habet duo ubera geminae dilectionis lac fundentia, quia reis impetrat veniam et justis gratiam.'

[14] Ibid. col 475: 'Carnalia in te Christus ubera suxit, ut per te nobis spiritualia fluerent.'

Among the Cistercians, one might expect that Adam of Perseigne, who composed a *Mariale* at the end of the twelfth century, would be the figure to introduce the image of lactation into the vocabulary of theological discourse and to apply it to our reception of help from Mary. But if we look through Adam's formidable *Mariale* of Adam, we find that his sermons do not offer even the physical image of Mary offering of her milk to her Son that we find in Richard of Saint Victor. She is praised as a font of wisdom and mercy, and Adam was careful to point out that Mary has a special place in cistercian life because each monastery of the Order is dedicated to her.[15] She is a symbol of fruitfulness and one of strength to whom we can go in time of need [16] , but Adam did not provide the awareness of Mary's body and its functions that began to find expression in the commentary of Richard of Saint Victor.

Only in one of his letters did Adam of Perseigne use a language of body, milk, and union between us and Mary. Here at last we are allowed to see a direct link between our own spiritual needs and the grace that comes from the milk of the Virgin:

> Those breasts are full from heaven and they refresh with inexhaustible gentleness. They are not emptied by the number of those who drink from them nor does that merciful mother deny herself to those who drink, even though she keeps all her milk for that only one. O inexhaustible fruitfulness! O great multitude of sweetness. How the hunger of the little people sucked the breasts of the Virgin in the flesh. If you wish, it is good that we are here. It is good that we stay longer, and we never can better be anywhere than here. This wondrous novelty is known only to the little people, and the nurse of

[15] PL 211:739. 'Huic fonti irriguo, huic misericordissimae Virgini specialiter deputaverim ego monasteria Cisterciensium: quippe quae omnia et memoriae et meritis ipsius matris devotione debita dedicantur.'

[16] Ibid. col 743: 'Si in tribulatione positus pusillanimitate dejiceris, ex corde refuge ad Mariam, et patientiae fortitudinem impetrabis.'

angels, Wisdom, lowers himself to be nourished by the milk of the Virgin.[17]

If we look at this passage carefully, even though it is ambiguous, we see that Adam apparently meant that the milk of the Virgin was offered primarily to Christ. Through him we can participate in this refreshment. We as little people (*parvuli*), can approach Mary's breasts and try to suckle, but the fact remains that Mary saves her milk for one person, her son Jesus. Here the milk is associated with the idea of Wisdom, for it is Christ, Wisdom himself, who drinks it.

However far we have apparently come in the development of a language celebrating the power and meaning of Mary's milk, we can look upon twelfth-century theological writers as being cautious in extending the benefits of Mary's lactation in a literal, physical manner to anyone other than Christ. Only the *exemplum* stories go this far, and so even at the end of the twelfth century there remained a gap between the realms of story and of theology in the visualisation of this aspect of Mary's activity for the benefit of humankind.

The Entry of Bernard

Until very recently it had been thought that the first versions of the Bernard lactation appeared in iconography and not in *exemplum* literature. Since an important article in 1956, evidence has been collected to indicate that the image of Bernard receiving milk from the Virgin first emerges in the religious art of Catalan territory.[18] But in 1988 the *exemplum*

---

[17] PL 211:636: 'Ubera illa de coelo plena sunt et indeficienti suavitate reficiunt, nec lactentium multitudine vacuantur, sed nec mater illa se misericors negare solet lactentibus, licet totam illi unico se conservet. O ubertas indeficiens! O magna multitudo dulcedinis, quam de viscerosae Virginis uberibus sugit esuries parvulorum! Si vis, bonum est nos hic esse, bonum est nos hic immorari diutius, nusquam alibi melius interim possumus quam hic esse. Mira hic novitas solis nota parvulis, ut angelorum nutrix Sapientia lacte Virginis indigeat enutriri.'

[18] Léon Dewez and Albert van Iterson, 'La lactation de saint Bernard. Legende et iconographie', *Cîteaux in de Nederlanden* 7 (1956) 165–89.

researcher Jacques Berlioz pointed out that an early four-teenth-century old french exemplum collection, the *Ci Nous Dit*, in its section of Bernard stories, has the story of the lactation.[19] The centre of attention has thus shifted from Iberia to Gaul. It does seem logical that Bernard's association with this widely-known legend arose in the geographical area where the memory of him would have been strongest.

In his excellent article, Berlioz has shown how almost all the individual elements in the story contained in the *Ci Nous Dit* can be traced back to twelfth-century descriptions of Saint Bernard. This continuity of story, with the addition of the lactation theme, is in harmony with what we otherwise know about the development of *exemplum* stories: they are traditional in using materials already available but experimental in adding new themes.

In order to describe this evolution, Berlioz uses the French term *contamination*, which should be translated into English not as contamination but as accretion or influence. What is striking about the Bernard lactation in terms of the established tradition of the story is that Bernard is seen receiving milk from the Virgin not because of illness but because the Virgin wanted to give him the ability to preach. So she gave him 'la devine science'. We note here that the entire scene is much more physical than the three drops indefinedly transferred from Mary's breast to the sick cleric or onto Fulbert of Chartres. In the *Ci Nous Dit*, Our Lady 'placed her holy breast in his mouth.'[20] The moment of contact is described in a much more physical way. Perhaps this has something to do with the change of context from latin *exemplum*

[19] 'La lactation de saint Bernard dans un exemplum du "Ci Nous Dit" (début du xive siècle)", *Cîteaux* 39 (1988) 270–284.

[20] 'Lors se mist en oroisons devant Nostre Dame et s'endormi. Et Nostre Dame li mist sa saincte mamelle en la bouche et li aprint la devine science', *Ci Nous Dit. Recueil d'exemples moraux*, publié par Gérard Blangez, t.2 (Paris: Société des anciens textes francais, 1986), ch 705, p 205. I am most grateful to Jacques Berlioz of the Centre National pour les Recherches Scientifiques, Paris, for sending me the text about Bernard.

literature to vernacular. In any case, Bernard comes into bodily contact with Mary in a way that even his devout follower
the cistercian Adam of Perseigne a century earlier apparently did not concede. Adam taught that we get Mary's milk
through her lactation of Jesus. The compiler of the *Ci Nous
Dits* claimed Bernard tasted Mary's milk in the enjoyment of
her breast.

Asking from where the old french collection obtained the
story of Bernard and Mary's milk, Berlioz pointed to a story
which has been attributed to Caesarius of Heisterbach but
which actually comes from a pseudo-Caesarian collection
that is very likely of thirteenth-century cistercian provenance.[21] This concerns 'an unlearned abbot who sucked from
the breasts of holy Mary and was endowed with knowledge.'
The abbot is identified as Henry of Clairvaux (1176–79). When
he was ordered by the pope to preach a crusade, Henry
felt himself incapable of performing the task. Entering the
church of Clairvaux, dedicated of course to Mary, he pros-
trated himself before her altar and with tears asked for her
help. Then

> . . . he saw the most beautiful virgin standing before the
> altar. She called him softly and gently and held forth her
> most sacred breasts to him to suck from them. He with
> the greatest devotion went to her and through that most
> holy fluid, which he sucked, he obtained so great knowl-
> edge of letters that he received the office of cardinal at
> Rome. [22]

[21] Berlioz (note 19 above) p 279, n 32. He cites the collection edited by
A. Meister in 1901, but it was Alfons Hilka in 1937 who showed that the
collection of miracles of the Virgin attributed to the third book of Caesarius' *Libri* VIII *miraculorum* were not Caesarius'own work: *Die Wundergeschichten
des Caesarius von Heisterbach*, Publikationen der Gesellschaft für Rheinische
Geschichtskunde xliii (Bonn 1937) p 164. It should be noted that Berlioz's
point is not dependent on the attribution to Caesarius. What matters is
that the story of the abbot of Clairvaux and the Virgin's milk goes back to
the thirteenth century.

[22] Hilka (note 21 above) p 164: ' . . . vidit pulcherrimam virginem ante
altare stantem, qui eum blande leniterque vocavit et sacratissima ubera

We see immediately here that a latin *exemplum* has the element of sensuality that was missing in its predecessors. The story, written down after 1200, is important for us because the contact between the abbot of Clairvaux and Mary is intimate and physical. The narrative has changed character drastically from that of the healing through three drops. Mary gives no command that her sacred liquor be collected and kept as a relic. This is milk to drink, milk that gives wisdom and the ability to communicate knowledge to others. It is appropriate that the story was attached to one of the Cistercians who preached a crusade and was active outside his own monastery. And when we remember Bernard's own unfortunate involvement in the preaching of the Second Crusade a few decades earlier, we easily understand how this type of preaching would encourage a later moralizing storyteller, the compiler of the *Ci Nous Dits*, to switch the story from a relatively unknown abbot of Clairvaux to the most famous abbot of all.[23]

The development of this lactation story still lacks a final link. So far as we know, there is no latin story from the thirteenth century in which the abbot who receives the lactation is Bernard himself. So long as this story is not found, we cannot say exactly how we get from a latin cistercian milieu to a vernacular clerical context. Despite our 'missing link' I think it important to underline that already before the version in pseudo-Caesarius, we find themes in the latin literature which prepare the way for the attachment of the lactation story to Bernard. In his Sermon on the anniversary of the death of Saint Bernard, for example, his secretary Geoffrey of Auxerre emphasized that Bernard was a born preacher. His

---

sua ad sugendum illi dulciter porrexit. Qui cum maxima devocione ad eam accessit et per illum sanctissimum liquorem, quem suxit, tantam adeptus est scienciam litterarum, ut apud Romam acciperet cardinalem dignitate.'

[23] Berlioz also (note 19 above, pp 281–82) points to a passage in one of the Dominican Stephen of Bourbon's treatises where quotations from Bernard are found next to a story about the lactation of a religious, again an indication of a convergence between the story and Bernard.

mother had a vision of her yet unborn child in her womb as a white dog with red on its back. This story, which appears also in the *Vita Prima*,[24] Geoffrey used as a point of departure for saying that Bernard preached before he drank milk from his mother:

> So indeed our Bernard from the time when he began to live, appeared to be wonderful. For he had not yet been born, and already was being preached about, or more correctly he was already himself preaching, and when he was not yet taking milk, still he appeared praising the Lord. ⟨*nec lactans. . .jam tamen laudans. . . .*⟩[25]

Here in one sentence we have the concept of Bernard who preaches and Bernard who suckles. The juxtaposition of the two activities is intended to contrast them: Bernard in appearing as a barking dog (a story later attached to Dominic) began to praise the Lord before he was even born and could take milk from his mother. But the association of preaching and milk, joined together by the happy coincidence of the latin terms LAUDANS ET LACTANS, perhaps here provided a point of departure for later stories of Bernard who took milk from the Virgin.

Another element in the growth of the image of *Bernardus lactans* comes in the *Vita Prima* itself, where William of Saint Thierry emphasized that Aleth, Bernard's mother, insisted on nursing all her children, including Bernard. She refused to conform to the custom of her social class by procuring a wet nurse.[26] Thus the very first descriptions of Bernard, which would be spread all over Europe with the growth of the

[24] PL 185:227=VP I.2

[25] Gaufridi abbatis claraevallensis iv, *Sermo in anniversario obitus sancti Bernardi*; PL 185:583: 'Sic nimirum Bernardus noster ex quo coepit utcunque vivere, coepit mirabilis apparere. Necdum parturiebatur, et jam praedicabatur, vel magis jam ipse praedicabat: et nec lactans quidem adhuc erat, jam tamen laudans Dominum apparebat.'

[26] PL 185:227= VP I.I: 'Propter quod etiam alienis uberibus nutriendos committere illustris femina refugiebat, quasi cum lacte materno materni quodammodo boni infundens eis naturam.'

Cistercian Order, emphasized his attachment to his mother's breasts—again a possible point of departure for stories of Bernard's being nursed by the mother of God.

Most important of all in the *Vita Prima* for a later association of Bernard and a nursing Mary is William of Saint Thierry's description of a vision Bernard is supposed to have had as a child at Christmastime:

> There came to the boy a revelation of the boy Jesus in his holy Nativity, suggesting the increase of his tender faith, and increasing the mysteries of divine contemplation in him. For it appeared as if the spouse was proceeding from his bed. There appeared to him as if once again before his eyes the infant word being born from the womb of the Virgin mother, beautiful in form beyond the sons of men, and taking on himself the dispositions of the holy boy, dispositions that were hardly boyish. His mind was persuaded, and until now he asserts, that he believed this was the hour of the Nativity of Our Lord.[27]

Bernard's presence at and near-participation in the Nativity William links with his later devotion to the Virgin Mary, for William here mentions how Bernard later wrote praises to her.[28] The vision is unusual in the twelfth-century literature of Bernard because it provides a link of physical intimacy between him and Jesus, something otherwise usually only implied. And in being part of the scene of the nativity, Bernard thus drew close to the presence and body of Mary.

Such a story in itself did not necessarily have to develop into one of Bernard and the milk of Mary. In the course of

---

[27] PL 185:229 = VP I.4: 'Adfuit illico puero suo se revelans pueri Jesu sancta Nativitas, tenerae fidei suggerens incrementa, et divinae in eo inchoans mysteria contemplationis. Apparuit enim velut denuo procedens sponsus e thalamo suo (Ps 18:6). Apparuit ei quasi iterum ante oculos suos nascens ex utero matris Virginis verbum infans, speciosus forma prae filiis hominum, et pueruli sancti in se rapiens minime jam pueriles affectus. Persuasum autem est animo ejus, ut nunc usque fatetur, quod eam credat horam fuisse Dominicae Nativitatis.'

[28] *In laudibus virginis matris*, Sermones I; I. SBOp 4 (Rome 1966) 13–58.

the thirteenth century, the standard literature on saints that grew up outside the Cistercian Order but included Bernard did not refer to any such miracle. The great collection by the Dominican scholar Vincent of Beauvais, the *Speculum historiale*, took all its bernardine materials from the cistercian chronicler of the early thirteenth century, Helinand of Froidmont.[29] Helinand, so far as I can tell, indicated nothing about the lac⁺⁻tion. Likewise the *Legenda aurea* by James of Varaggio (Jacobus de Voragine) from the last decades of the thirteenth century has many stories about Bernard, not all going back to the *Vita Prima*, but the lactation is not present.[30] It would seem that even by the end of the thirteenth century, this story had not yet been attached to descriptions of Bernard of Clairvaux. If it were not for the *Ci Nous Dit* it would still be possible to claim that the motif enters the medieval religious consciousness by way of iconography instead of through *exemplum* literature.

From the first decades of the fourteenth century, however, we have evidence that in Bernard's home territory at the town of Châtillon-sur-Seine in the church of Saint Vorles a statue of the Virgin was treated with reverence as the image of the Virgin that once, when Bernard was praying before it, turned into the real Virgin who offered him her milk to give him the ability to preach. We do not have the original documents from this time, only a notice from 1490 that claims to reproduce the fourteenth-century charters after a fire had destroyed almost all the records of the church.[31] Earlier scholars have been highly sceptical of the authenticity

[29] See *Chronicon*, PL 212:1017–18, for the year 1115.

[30] Ed. Th. Graesse (Leipzig, 1850). *The Golden Legend of Jacobus de Voragine*, trans. by Granger Ryan and Helmut Ripperger (New York. Arno Press, 1969) under 20 August, pp 465–77. For a fuller study, see my 'A Saint's Afterlife: Bernard in the *Golden Legend* and in Other Medieval Collections', *Bernhardrezeption in Spätmittelalter und Frühneuzeit*, forthcoming from the Herzog-August-Bibliothek, Wolfenbüttel.

[31] Contained in L'Abbé Jobin, *Saint Bernard et sa famille* (Poitiers 1891) 648–55. I am most grateful to Chrysogonus Waddell, Gethsemani Abbey, Trappist, Kentucky, who here as so often elsewhere has provided me with

of these documents, and it has been claimed that the 'decisive proof' of their falsity is the fact that an episcopal privilege to the church from 1367 makes no mention of the miracle of lactation, although this 'miracle' was named in a privilege supposed to have been granted by the cistercian pope Benedict XII in 1340.[32] But if we look at the text of the 1367 privilege, it does mention miracles 'made by the glorious Virgin Mother Mary there, while the holy Bernard in her chapel was continually imploring her, to whose person she is said to have shown herself in person, and to have revealed to him many divine mysteries.'[33] Here we have everything except the specific nature of the miracles and the word lactation. I do not think that the failure to describe the miracle in detail in the 1367 document is enough to preclude the authenticity of the 1340 document.

We are nevertheless dependent on a late medieval reproduction of earlier texts, and it is clear that those attached to Saint Vorles in 1490 had an interest in claiming that the miracle of the lactation had already been established in 1340. A further ground for scepticism is the fact that the 1340 privilege asserts the story already was contained in the Life of Saint Bernard.[34] At this point, however, it should be remembered that the literature claimed to be by and about Saint Bernard grew in the later Middle Ages. There was every possibility that some versions of his *Vita* in 1490 did include the miracle of lactation. Nothing can be ruled out. A cautious but necessary conclusion would be that in the fourteenth century there was a cult of Saint Bernard at Saint Vorles where the story of his lactation was remembered and honoured.

---

valuable information and guidance.

[32] L. Dewez and A. Van Iterson (note 18 above), p 166.

[33] *Saint Bernard et sa famille* p 653: '. . . a gloriosa Virgine Matre Maria ibidem factis, dum beatus Bernardus in sua capella eamdem continue exoraret, in cujus persona dicitur eamdem se personaliter demonstrasse, ac eidem plura divina mysteria revelasse.'

[34] Ibid., p 650.

It is no accident that this privilege is from the same period as the *Ci Nous Dit* and about fifty years after the *Golden
Legend* failed to include the story of the lactation. Sometime
between about 1280 and 1340 the story of the lactation of
Bernard by Mary seems to have become common in religious
art, *exemplum* literature, and local cults. With our privilege of
historical retrospective, and with the texts available from the
twelfth century onward, the prominence of Saint Bernard, and
the malleability of the literature of the Miracles of the Virgin,
this development can hardly be surprising. It is indicative of a
culture in which images that can be implied and suggested in
an earlier period later became more concrete and palpable.
The Bernard who was vaguely remembered in wide clerical
circles for his sermons in praise of the Virgin could come to
be very concretely celebrated for the moment when Mary let
him suck milk from her breast.

It is in the later Middle Ages, the fourteenth and fifteenth
centuries, that we find the spread of the term *doctor mellifluus*
to characterise Bernard. As Leclercq has pointed out, 'Saint
Bernard was considered as a model for the masters in the
art of preaching.'[35] Ever since the twelfth century, his gift
of expression had been celebrated and analysed. Now in
the fourteenth century the theme of Bernard the preacher
and Bernard the drinker of Mary's milk were united. Geoffrey of Auxerre's Bernard, who was remembered as praising
the Lord before he drank milk from his mother's breast (*lactans . . . laudans*) became the Bernard who because he drank
milk from Mary's breast obtained a special gift in preaching
and praising the Lord.

Bernard in the *Mariu Saga*

The old norse compilation which its nineteenth century editor, C.R. Unger, gave the title *Mariu Saga*, contains a whole
section devoted to Saint Bernard.[36] This occurs in the part of

---

[35] 'L'eloquence de S. Bernard', AC (1953) p 183.
[36] *Mariu Saga. Legender om Jomfru Maria og hendes Jertegn* (Christiania 1871).

the work called *Mariu Jartegnir*, or Miracles of the Virgin, which occupies the bulk of this huge work, probably the largest collection of Mary miracles we find in medieval literature.[37] In what follows, it is not my intention (and would be beyond my ability) to go into a philological or codicological evaluation of the texts that are concerned with Bernard. But in the light of Berlioz's study of the *Ci Nous Dit*, it is important to see the development of the lactation story in a completely different part of Europe. Most interestingly of all, we will see how the lactation is perceived in a new way, as taking place to satisfy the *physical thirst* of Saint Bernard, and as Mary's demonstration of her appreciation for Bernard's consideration of the needs of his cistercian brothers. The lactation in this version became a celebration of community love and friendship.

In recent years a danish researcher, Ole Widding, formerly chief editor of the Arnamagnæan Dictionary at Copenhagen University, has worked intensely with the *Mariu Saga*, and I am much beholden to his conclusions.[38] Widding points out that after the original saga, which tells the story of the life of Mary taken for the most part from apocryphal sources, the sections in the *Mariu Saga* dealing with the miracles of

---

"Fra Bernardo abota" pp 193–98.

[37] As asserted by Ole Widding, 'Om de norrøne Marialegender', *Bibliotheca Arnamagnæana* 25, ed. Jonna Louis-Jensen, Jón Helgason, Peter Springborg. *Opuscula* 2 (Copenhagen 1961–77) 1–9. I should like to thank Peter Springborg of the Arnamagnæan Institute for pointing out this and other articles to me. Recent work on the Legend being done by the netherlandic researcher Gryt Anne Piebenga, Groningen, has been published only in part. See, for example, her 'Om Marialegenden "Fra hinum heilaga Thomase erkibiskupi"', *Arkiv for Nordisk Filologi* 101 (Lund, Sweden: 1986) 40–49. I am grateful to Gryt Anne Piebenga for presenting some of her results at a seminar held at the Medieval Centre, Copenhagen University, in the spring of 1990.

[38] Besides the article mentioned in note 37, I have benefitted from Widding's article 'Marialegender. Norge og Island', *Kulturhistorisk Leksikon for Nordisk Middelalder* 11 (Copenhagen. Rosenkilde og Bagger, 1981) 401–404. Two fascinating treatments of connections between european and old norse stories are 'St Michele at Gargano. As seen from Iceland', *Analecta Romana Instituti Danici* 13 (1984) 77–83, and 'An Old Norse Version of a Pamphlet on the Papacy of Gregory VI', Ibid. 15 (1986) 51–65.

the Virgin (*Mariu Jartegnir*) can be divided up into three main groups:

1) a classic section, including some of the most familiar and earliest miracles of the Virgin. These come from 'smaller, anonymous collections of legends that were composed in anglo-norman territory in the first period of the miracle collections, which means from about 1050 to 1200'.[39]

2) an historical section, which has indications of an arrangement of the legends according to the rank of the persons involved, whether bishops, priests, or abbots. Here the main manuscript in the Unger edition Widding called MarS, and he places it in the first quarter of the fourteenth century. It is in this section that we find stories dealing with 'Abbot Bernard'. They are preceded by tales concerning Abbot Hugh of Cluny (1049–1109) and followed by a section on archbishop Thomas Becket. Widding says that the stories in this part of the Miracles of the Virgin for the most part are not 'rewritten or dressed-up legends but independent translations'.[40] The style is known in Danish as 'florissant', a rich and complex style difficult to translate into modern English.

3) later translations based on the works of named latin compilers, especially Vincent of Beauvais. Here we can see that the compiler/translator remained very close to the latin text.

The dating of different parts in the *Mariu Saga* cannot be established with great certainty. The materials in the narrative, according to one expert, indicate that it cannot be older than about 1250.[41] But our central manuscript for the Bernard section, MarS, Widding places in the first quarter of the fourteenth century.[42] There is a theoretical possibility that the

---

[39] Widding, 'Om de nørrøne', p 4.

[40] Ibid. p 7.

[41] Finnur Jónsson, *Den Oldnorske og Oldislandske Litteraturs Historie* 2 (Copenhagen 1923).

[42] Widding, 'Om de norrøne',p 5. The Bernard narrative is also in manuscript E, dated by Stefan Karlsson to the second half of the fifteenth

Legend existed in Old Norse in a lost version from before 1300, but we are forced to make do with what we have. The story of Bernard and the lactation can be seen as appearing in old norse literature in the early fourteenth century.

It should be noted that the section on Bernard is repeated later in our old norse text.[43] This second version is taken in part from other manuscripts, but their content is very close to the initial text, which we will follow here. One problem we will not consider, and which remains to be worked out by the linguistic experts, is how the collection published by Unger as *Mariu Saga* was put together in the first place. We will have to be content with asserting that our old norse compiler has provided us with stories about Bernard that deal with his devotion to Mary and her attention to him.

In what follows I shall provide a summary of the narrative, thanks to the guidance provided by Christopher Sanders at the Arnamagnæan Dictionary in Copenhagen.

1. In a castle in Burgundy called Castello was an important lord called Olezin. He had a noble wife called Elerin. They were good people, serving God. When Madame Elerin was pregnant, she had a dream that a barking dog was inside her. He was all white except for some red on his back. An angel explained that the child would make a great noise against God's enemies. His white was for true chastity, his red was for patience. (cf VP I.2; PL 185:227–8)

2. Elerin gave birth to a beautiful boy, who was baptized and called Bernard. He was put to school under a famous master in the castle named. He was obedient to his parents and from the first he feared God and loved Mary with all his heart. (cf VP I.3; PL 185:228)

---

century (KLNM 15:692). Interestingly enough, E deletes many of the personal and intimate details in the Bernard story contained in the earlier MS. I should like to thank my faithful guide, Christopher Sanders, for pointing out this variance to me.

[43] *Mariu Saga* pp 489–93.

3. When Bernard was a teenager, his mother became deathly sick. Priests were called to give her the last rites. When the psalms were finished and the verse, 'Per passionem et crucem tuam libera eam, domine' was said, she lifted her right arm and made the sign of the cross, dying at that moment, so that her hand remained in mid-air, not pointing down at the body but showing which way the spirit had gone out of the flesh. (cf VP I.5; PL 185:230)

4. Bernard received proof that his mother was with God because one night she appeared to him and said, 'You, Bernard, are getting into books of worldly wisdom, and you are not in the same school as in childhood. . . . If I had known that you would develop in this way, then I would never have fed you at my breasts.' (cf VP I.9; PL 185:231)

5. After this vision Bernard turned to spiritual concerns, rejecting the world, losing interest in school, and thirsting to serve God. When he decided to become a monk, more than thirty companions wanted to follow him. Among them was Hugh of Macon, who later founded the house at Pontigny and ended as bishop of Auxerre. All of these companions entered the noviciate of the Cistercian Order. (cf VP I.13; PL 185:234–5 for Hugh of Macon. Note that the old norse text here uses a latin phrase: Noviciatum cisterciensis ordinis.

6. Bernard was twenty-two years old when he rejected the world and within six years he had founded the cloister of Clairvaux and become its leader. At 28 he was ordained abbot of Clairvaux with great honour and dignity by the bishop of Châlons. (cf VP I.3l; PL 185:245). Clairvaux took on the leadership of the other monasteries because of its founder. For that reason, blessed Bernard often visited subordinate houses as a true father from the mother house.

7. One day when Bernard had left the monastery and was going on visitation together with two of his brothers,

he and they became very thirsty because of the heat of the sun. They had only a tiny cask full of wine, which was not more than enough for one person. Because of their mutual love, none of them was willing to drink of the cask (and thus deprive the others of something to drink).

Bernard wanted the brothers to drink what there was, but they could not let him do without. When they were all almost exhausted, the abbot told the brothers to sit down and rest for a while as they drank from the casket. He went aside, fell on his knees, and suddenly a great light came over him. Mary appeared to him, gentle in countenance towards her beloved Bernard (*moti Bernardo sinum elskara*). She said to him that she had seen how his tongue, which daily sounded her praise, suffered from the heat. So now he should come and taste of the breast from which her son Jesus once drank.Bernard drank of the breast like a child from its mother. The other monks saw the apparition, and Bernard ordered them not to reveal it during his lifetime.

8. After this vision, Bernard profited from Mary's blessing by being able to speak beautifully and convincingly, especially when he was praising Our Lady. He speaks in one place of Jesus the living son of God who was born among lilies. As it says in the Gospel, "Wherever two or three are gathered together in my name, I am among them"(Matt 18:20). Jesus loves to be in the middle of things. We must plant beautiful lilies over our hearts. Christian man, whatever you intend to offer to God, you put into the hands of Mary and ask her to bring it forward. No sooner does the lover of purity see so beautiful an agent working on behalf of you, than he will receive (the offering) because of his love for his mother.

9. Bernard from then on did everything to please God and Mary. They continued to reward him with visions.

One Christmas night through the Holy Spirit he saw
the Queen of heaven and earth as she was when she
gave birth to her son with joy and without sorrow.
The beautiful Jesus went from the room of his mother
as David said in his book, 'In the sun he placed his
tabernacle and he was as it were the spouse coming
from the bed.' (The quotation is given in Latin: *In sole
posuit tabernaculum suum et ipse tanquam sponsus procedens
de thalamo*, Ps 18:6. Cf VP I.4; PL 185:229).

10. Bernard did not get puffed up because of such gifts.
One night Bernard saw a beautiful boy standing by
him in a light. The boy told him that from now on he
would speak with complete confidence all that God
had appointed. After this vision Bernard as abbot was
so self-assured in speaking out against injustice that
he became a mouth of brilliance and a hammer of
punishment. So he showed something more like the
behaviour of a bishop rather than of an abbot ⟨*likara
byskupligri framferd enn abotaligri*⟩. this is to such an extent that all future abbots of Clairvaux were in his
shadow.

11. Later another Bernard was a holy man and very famous
who in the course of time became pope at Rome. There
were also Gerard and Peter Monoculus. This Peter was
of noble family but chose to turn away from worldly
ambition.

Origins of the Bernard Narrative

If we look at the story as a whole, we realize immediately
that most of it is deeply indebted to the *Vita Prima*'s first
book and its story of Bernard's youth compiled by William of
Saint Thierry. William got much of his account from the frag-
mentary compilation made by Geoffrey of Auxerre.[44] Thus
the hound of heaven is a familiar motif, and we find also

[44] Robert Lechat, 'Les Fragmenta de Vita et Miraculis S. Bernardi par
Geoffroy d'Auxerre', *Analecta Bollandiana* 50 (1932) 83–122.

the description of the death of Bernard's mother, with her hand pointing up to heaven. Our compiler, however, has not included materials that were immensely popular in later medieval *exemplum* literature about Bernard. Absent are, for example, stories about how Bernard resisted temptations to his chastity from women trying to win his favours.[45] This deletion may be due to a nordic lack of interest in the virtue of celibacy among the clergy, but it just as well may have been a result of the compiler's desire to stick to stories that for the most part dealt with Mary. The result is indeed not a biography of Saint Bernard but a selection of stories that reveal his close bond to Mary and her affection for him.

One part of the story which I cannot find in the twelfth-century *Vita Prima*, however, is the admonition made by Bernard's mother that she had not nursed him at her breast so he could grow up to become interested in secular studies. This remark reminds us, of course, of William of Saint Thierry's statement that Aleth nursed her children at her own breast. It also recalls the story that Bernard's decision to become a monk was prompted by his vision of the image of his mother reproaching him for not choosing the monastic life: 'for she had not educated him to hold on to this type of trifles and had not brought him up in this hope.'[46] In this parting line is the essence of the mother's statement in the old norse narrative that it was not for this purpose that she had nursed him. The mother's education of Bernard in William's version becomes her nursing of Bernard in our narrative, a small but significant alteration. William's description of the event is turned into what Ole Widding would call a dramatization.

[45] VP I.6–7; PL 185:230–31. This was probably the most popular of the late medieval tales of Bernard, as can be seen from the number of references in Frederic Tubach, *Index Exemplorum*, FF Communications 204 (Helsinki 1969) nr 598: 'St. Bernard gets rid of a temptress by shouting "thieves"'.

[46] VP I.9; PL 185:232: '. . . sed matris sanctae memoria importune animo ejus instabat, ita ut saepius sibi occurrentem videre videretur, conquerentem et improperantem, quia non ad hujusmodi nugacitatem tam tenere educaverat, non in hac spe erudierat eum.'

Indirect speech is turned into a direct quotation. The use of dialogue makes the story more memorable.

In practically all respects, except for the story of the lactation, the narrative of Bernard in the old norse *Mariu Saga* can be traced back to earlier materials. We find in William of Saint Thierry mention of Hugh of Macon, his foundation of Pontigny and his end as bishop of Auxerre. Even the assertion that Bernard was born at Châtillon (here called Castello) can be traced back to some of the earliest manuscripts of the *Vita Prima*, even though most versions point to his birth at Fontaines and his education at Châtillon.[47] The old norse narrative was thus following a relatively respectable tradition in centering everything at Châtillon. In entering Cîteaux, Bernard is said to have had "more than thirty companions", almost a direct quotation from William of Saint Thierry.[48]

Only in a few places do we run into mistakes in factual matters. The names of Bernard's parents are of course far from the Latin originals (Aleth and Tescelin), but this linguistic development does not in itself say anything clear about relative fidelity to the source. A clear departure from historical records, however, appears in the assertion that Bernard became abbot of Clairvaux within six years of his entrance to Cîteaux. In point of fact this happened within three years, but since this is not made clear in the *Vita Prima*, it is easy to understand that the compiler could have latched onto another tradition or made a guess.

If we turn to the lactation scene, it appears at first to be completely outside the two traditions of Mary's milk we have considered: the healing by Mary of a sick cleric, and the endowment of an abbot with the knowledge and ability to preach. In the *Mariu Saga* Mary simply takes care of Bernard's thirst. Her love for him is expressed in terms of his love for the brothers with him. He preferred to go thirsty so he could

---

[47] For a discussion of the two traditions, see Watkin Williams, *Saint Bernard of Clairvaux* (Westminster, Maryland. The Newman Press. 1952) 1–2.
[48] VP I.19; PL 185:237: '. . . cum sociis amplius quam triginta. . . . '

let them drink, an indication that Christ really is with him and his brothers, in their midst.

Behind this unexpected and very physical story, we find more familiar themes. Mary says she wants to look after the tongue which was now parched and which earlier had sung her praises. Bernard is described in a very tender way as drinking like a child from its mother's breast (thus returning us to the theme of Bernard's closeness to his biological mother). Finally and most importantly, the story is completed by a mini-homily on how Bernard because of Mary's milk became a great preacher. This sermon, couched in a language difficult to penetrate, clearly builds on the language of Bernard's *Sermones in Canticis*, where he described the lily among thorns.[49] But our old norse version, so far as I can tell, interprets and simplifies the original latin sermon rather than providing a translation of it. What Bernard had implied about Mary now became very specific.

In this section of the *Mariu Saga*, we return to the familiar theme that through Mary's milk Bernard gained a gift of speaking out and spreading theological wisdom. The old norse version of the story is thus in line with what we find in France, even if it is much fuller and by no means dependent on the old french version. We have here a wealth of reflections that could have been used in a sermon to a lay, not monastic, audience. The 'christian man' addressed in the compiler's commentary could be anyone. The point is that the Virgin's gift to Bernard is available to all of us: we must go to Mary when we want something from Christ. She will take care of us.

Just at this point in the narrative, when one would think that our compiler has exhausted his images, he returns to William of Saint Thierry and an anecdote from Bernard's youth. This is the Christmas vision, which William concentrates on Bernard's perception of the birth of Christ, while our

[49] See SBOp I:67. SC Sermo 48, commenting on the passage in the Song of Songs 2:2, 'Sicut lilium inter spinas, sic amica mea . . . . '

source places Mary at the centre.[50] The old norse
anecdote emphasizes her birth as being without sorrow. The
role of Mary in the vision described by William of Saint
Thierry is clarified and glorified, in accord with the whole
direction of the narrative, concentrating on the miracles of
Mary.

This vision of Bernard is followed by another not explicitly in William of Saint Thierry but which may ultimately
have been derived from the same nativity vision: Bernard
saw a beautiful boy telling him that henceforth he would be
able to speak out with total confidence. In a way this anecdote seems superfluous here: it is not about Mary and it
repeats the point already made that Bernard preached and
influenced people because of his knowledge and power of
delivery. But this vision prepares the way for a further com-
ment on Bernard: he was an active man in the church, so
much so that he seemed more like a bishop than an abbot.
The contrast harmonizes with a late medieval view of Bernard
as the outstanding preacher who usually got his way.

The 'other Bernard' mentioned at the end of our passage
could only be Bernard Paganelli, a cistercian abbot who became pope Eugenius III (1145–53), and whom Bernard did
his best to advise and guide. The other abbots mentioned,
Gerard (ll70–75) and Peter Monoculus (ll79–86) are both well
known to us as abbots of Clairvaux after Bernard. The naming
of them here is especially appropriate in the second version
of the Bernard story in the *Mariu Saga*, where this section is
followed by one on Peter Monoculus.[51]

---

[50] Note that in William's narrative of the Nativity vision, Mary is only
mentioned once by name: 'Apparuit ei quasi iterum ante oculos suos
nascens ex utero matris Virginis verbum infans. . . . ' (VP I.4; PL 185:229).
But at the end of the passage, Bernard's sermons in praise of the Virgin are
named, and so she is brought into the centre of the scene. This could have
been a point of departure for a later growth of this story in concentrating
on Mary's role.

[51] Unger, 493–9. I hope at some point to return to this narrative and to
compare it with european latin materials.

The Compiler and his European Source

Are we dealing with an original story about Bernard in the lactation scene or are we witnessing here the translation into Old Norse of a latin source still unknown to us? If we are cautious, it would probably be best to see the entire narrative as dependent on a latin source which remains to be identified. But this is by no means a foregone conclusion. The story could have gotten into this collection by oral as well as by written influences. This at least can be seen as happening elsewhere in the *Mariu Saga*, when we are told how a clerk of the norwegian king got the story of the five salutations of Mary, which he originally found in a book that belonged to 'Nicholas monk of the rule of Cluny'. Unfortunately our clerk did not have the time (or presence of mind?) to write it all down. When he returned to Norway he was asked by the abbot of the cistercian house Lyse, as well as by his brothers and by God-fearing laymen, to reproduce the story. He could only do so by memory.[52]

This description of how a marian story came to Norway is doubly fascinating for us. First, in a section of the *Mariu Saga* close to the Bernard narrative, we are told how the nordic compiler got legendary material without copying it down. Secondly, we find the Cistercians of Lyse near Bergen involved in the process, encouraging the cleric to record the story. But the interests of the Cistercians are said to coincide with those of good laymen. This particular part of the *Miracles of the Virgin* in Old Norse, then, comes not from a cistercian but from a cluniac source. This borrowing is in harmony with the fact that the monks of Cluny and its associates are named at many places in the historical section of our old norse *Miracles of the Virgin*.

[52] Unger pp 230–31: 'sa ek fordvm a bok Nicholai mvnks af Klvniacensis reglv.' In MS E, the abbot of Lyse is called Guido. James France, whose forthcoming book *The Cistercians in Scandinavia* includes an abbot list for Lyse, has an abbot Gunner who is mentioned in 1310 and 1312. I am grateful to him for this reference.

There would thus seem to be alternative explanations for the provenance of the Bernard narrative here: either it was written down by a nordic cleric from memory and could thus easily have been dramatized and expanded, or else it was translated more or less faithfully from a latin source on Bernard that had been compiled from earlier materials. To this latin source, the inevitable X, the lactation narrative had already been added before the story ever got to the North. Only further discoveries will clarify the progression of the story from France to Norway. I am inclined to think that our nordic compiler was drawing on a complete latin source, but for now the main point remains that we have here a wonderful instance of the popularity of stories about Bernard and Mary one and a half centuries after his death.

The Sensualisation of Religious Experience

A useful way to penetrate further into the origins of the Bernard narrative in the *Mariu Saga* would be to compare it with other monastic materials in the same source and to see to what extent they are beholden to known latin monastic sources. A related story about Mary has already been carefully investigated: Mary at the judgment of a wicked benedictine abbot bared her breast to her son Jesus, asking for mercy for him because in life he had shown devotion to her.[53] In the old norse version of the story the abbot is called Vallterus, and he is said to have been a Cistercian but got the approval of bishop Henry of Winchester to become a Benedictine. Eventually he was elected abbot at Tavistock in Devonshire. This story was compared with a similar exemplum contained in a British Library manuscript where Mary also bared her breast to save a rich benedictine abbot. But here the historical information found in the old norse version

[53] Ole Widding and Hans Bekker-Nielsen, "The Virgin bares her Breast. An Icelandic Version of a Miracle of the Blessed Virgin", *Bibliotheca Arnamagnæana* 25, Opuscula (1961–77) 76–9. The text is in Unger pp 789–90.

is lacking.[54] The editors of the article appealed to those who had a further knowledge of european latin sources to provide a more immediate source.

In reviewing a Paris MS (BN 15912) about which I have written on an earlier occasion, I have found the same story in the section 'De veneratione Virginis Marie".[55] But this version, just as that from the British Library, only says that the abbot was a Benedictine from England.[56] Thus at this early point when the BL and Paris MSS were composed (about the year 1200), the story had already lost some of the specific information that somehow was preserved in the old norse version! The cistercian monastery of Beaupré, which probably drew up the Paris MS in the early thirteenth century, could thus not have been the source of the old norse version, at least on the basis of the manuscript we have. The Paris MS contains

---

[54] British Library Add. 15723 f 87v and Harley 2851 f 82r, described in H.L.D. Ward, *Catalogue of Romances in the Department of Manuscripts in the British Museum* 2 (London 1893) pp 635,670. It is the first MS which is particularly interesting, for it dates to the late twelfth or early thirteenth century.

[55] 'The Cistercians and the Rise of the Exemplum in early thirteenth-century France: A Reevaluation of Paris BN MS lat. 15912', *Classica et Mediaevalia* 34 (Copenhagen. Museum Tusculanum, 1983) 211–67, esp. p 228. Jacques Berlioz of the CNRS, Paris, has informed me that he and a team of researchers are in the process of editing this important MS for the history of the exemplum collection.

[56] I quote from part of MS Paris BN lat 15912, ff 84–5, to give a sense of the story: 'Fuit in anglie partibus abbas quidam nigri ordinis deliciis multis et divitiis affluens, sed anime sue periculo minus caute providens, cure carnis in desideriis faciende operam nimiam impendebat. Hic gravi preventus egritudine ad extreme pervenit . . . . (The scene of his judgment before God) Ubi cum aliquamdiu ut sibi in summa necessitate adesse dignaretur orasset, piissima dei genitrix humili prece permota, et ad filium conversa sit, ait. "Audi, domine, quam pie quam obnixe homo iste in necessitate sui me requirit defensionis auxilium." . . . . After Jesus at first refused to listen, Mary bared her breasts and placed them on the knees of the Judge! Ad hec clementissima dei genitrix solio regali descendens, super scabellum tribunalis iudicis genua devote flectebat, et ubera sua protrahens super iudicis genus deponebat, tali cum prece sollicitans: "Fili dulcissime, rex glorie sempiterne, ecce pectus et ubera, ecce venter et viscera que homo iste in sua necessitate mihi commemorat. Attende quid tam humilis invocatio mereatur."' At this point Jesus has to give in, 'Behold I leave the culprit to your judgment, mother!'

a story which is said to have come from Norway, and some kind of link between Beaupré and nordic compilers cannot be excluded.[57] For the time being, however, we cannot get much further than the Arnamagnæan Dictionary in asserting the likelihood of an unknown european latin source for the story of Mary's appeal for mercy.

In spite of our philological frustrations, a pattern in cultural history emerges that is worth considering. The old norse Bernard narrative shows how Bernard had physical needs and how Mary satisfied them. In a more traditional passage from hagiography he would have been seen as not satisfying his thirst, thus remaining faithful to the image of the desert father. But here, in late thirteenth or early fourteenth century Northern Europe, Mary took care of Bernard. We have come a long way from twelfth- century hagiography, where visions normally mean seeing, not touching, tasting or feeling. We are in the midst of a european religious culture where the cult of the Eucharist had grown to enormous proportions. The presence and availability of the host were virtually a matter of life or death for many religious women.[58]

There may be a cultural link between the old norse Bernard of the fourteenth century with his rich, sensual experience of lactation, and some of the female cistercian visionaries from the Low Countries in the thirteenth century. In both cases saintly people through physical deprivation obtained an experience of the spiritual world and its blessings. Thus

[57] This story tells of an abbot from Norway who visited the cistercian house and told how his monastery had been given a property on which there was a church placed next to the sea and dedicated to Saints Margaret and Agnes. An ill-behaved weaponer, who threatened the church, was punished with a terrible vision in which two girls placed burning candles in his face. (Paris MS 15912, f 88). The vision is especially interesting because it shows contact between norwegian and french monasteries and indicates the moralizing tales they would have exchanged with each other.
[58] See for example some of the stories in pseudo-Caesarius (Hilka, note 21 above) and the treatment by Caroline Walker Bynum, *Holy Feast and Holy Fast* (Berkeley, 1987).

the physical Bernard, needing to be looked after by real milk from Mary (and not just a few symbolic drops), belongs to the same development in western consciousness that can be seen in the lives of female saints such as Ida of Nivelles and Lutgarde of Aywières. The object of these women was not Mary but Jesus. One can almost hear in their experiences the words 'Taste and see', for they are united to the object of their affection just as Bernard in the old norse story gained the Virgin Mary as his loved one.

In the *Life* of Ida of Nivelles, written by a cistercian monk probably soon after her death in 1231, we find how she was presented with the physical enjoyment of the divinity. A stunning man, dressed in purest white, transferred from his mouth a liquid that was white and is described as manna. He said to her:

> You have desired so violently, my dearest one, to know and to taste, even though you are inexperienced, the ineffable knowledge of my divinity. I want the strongest desire of your soul be fulfilled with the honeycomb of my divinity which is more delicious than anything else.[59]

Here the liquid from the mouth of the beautiful man is said to have 'dripped' into Ida's mouth. The physical contact of one mouth on another is not described. The latin phrase *stillavit in os meum* is given no further detail, but this is a sensuous scene in which the power and attractiveness of God are transmitted in a very physical way.

The experience of Lutgarde of Aywières, who died in 1268 and had her life written by the Dominican Thomas of Cantimpré, was just as immediate. In going into church one

---

[59] 'Tu desiderasti vehementer, o carissima mea, cognoscere et sapere, inexperta licet, ineffabilem meae divinitatis notitiam, et ego libentissime, ut ardentissimum animas tuae desiderium adimpleatur, super omnia sapidissimum divinitatis meae favum cordi tuo ad cumulum instillabo.' Text in Chr. Henriquez, *Quinque Prudentes Virgines* (Antwerp 1630) p 255. I am preparing an introduction to three cistercian lives, including that of Ida, in a new translation made by Martinus Cawley of Guadalupe Abbey, Oregon.

day, she met the crucified Christ, who lowered one of his arms which had been fastened to the cross:

> He brought her mouth to the wound of his right side. There she drank so much sweetness that from then on she became all the more vigorous and eager in the service of God.[60]

Here, as in the experience of Bernard in the *Mariu Saga*, the saint obtained strength through the liquid given him/her. The transference of this power takes place in a direct, physical way that leaves little to the imagination. One can see Christ hugging Lutgarde and pushing her face down to his wound. Another generation would have emphasized the freudian aspect of such a vision. Recently even so astute an historian as Aron Gurevich has repeated traditional judgments and has written of the sexual hysteria of such women.[61] And yet the experience is on the same level as that imagined with Saint Bernard: in getting physical sustenance, spiritual enlightenment comes to the saint, so that he or she better can carry out the work that needs to be done.

This great hunger for the godhead and for sharing with the saints characterized the entire later medieval period and has given many an historian a chance to condemn the extremities which thought and feeling reached at the time. Ever since Johan Huizinga described the later Middle Ages in autumnal terms,[62] we have been encouraged to consider it decadent that late medieval people tried to make spiritual symbols

---

[60] 'In ipso ostio ecclesiae ei Christus cruci affixus cruentatus occurrit: deponensque brachium cruci affixum, amplexatus est occurentem, et os ejus vulneri dextri lateris applicavit. Ubi tantum dulcedinis hausit, quod semper ex tunc in dei servitio robustior et alacrior fuit.' The text is to be found in the *Acta Sanctorum Junii* 4. Book I, ch. 13, p 239.

[61] 'The mystic ecstasies of visionary religious women (and nuns) often imply the barely disguised sexual experience of their "marriage to Christ"',*Medieval Popular Culture: Problems of Belief and Perception*, trans. Janos M. Bak and Paul A. Hollingsworth (Cambridge University Press 1988) p 240, n 67.

[62] *The Waning of the Middle Ages* (first published in English in 1924. Harmondsworth. Penguin 1955 and later).

into physical realities and to realize their spiritual values by experiencing them in physical ways. This prudish sensitivity has had its day. We can accept the graphic display of religious feeling in such narratives as something intensely felt and inherently therapeutic. The religious experiences of female cistercian saints, far from driving them away from the rest of the community, created a greater bond between individual and community.

In the old norse story of Bernard and the lactation, Mary united herself closely with Bernard and thus allowed him to take care of the brothers whom he loved and who loved him. At the same time as physical experience links the saint to the spiritual world, he or she comes closer to fellow human beings in community. Leaving behind the three drops of Mary's milk, preserved as a relic, we get a whole mouthful taken directly from her breast and swallowed to quench thirst. The vision and drink of milk provided a point of departure for a lifetime of preaching and politics, activities our northern compiler seemed to accept and appreciate.

Relations between Popular and Learned Culture

In a recent collection of articles, the russian historian Aron Gurevich has addressed the question of popular culture and its relationship to the learned culture of the church. He claims in his 'Foreword' that the church in its official culture drove the culture of the *'common people'* (his italics) 'back to the periphery of spiritual life'.[63] Gurevich insisted that the folkloric tradition among the common people was only partly integrated into the culture of the church, and so he sets out to glean from figures like Gregory the Great and Caesarius of Heisterbach remnants or clues to popular culture. However admirable this quest may be, and however much in harmony with the approach of the french Annales school and its champions Jacques Le Goff and Georges Duby, I find

---

[63] *Medieval Popular Culture* (note 61 above) p xviii.

that Gurevich constantly faces a methodological problem. How does one distinguish the popular from the learned in any clear and consistent manner? At the end of his book he practically abandons the concept of popular culture, and one wonders whether this 'Afterword' is not chronologically at a great distance from the 'Foreword'.[64] The latter hints at the old marxist doctrine of class conflict, while the after-word, with its openness and questioning, suggests the era of *perestroika* and *glasnost*, when old dogmas have lost their validity.

It is particularly appropriate to consider Gurevich and his theories on popular culture when we look at the lactation of Bernard in terms of old norse material. Gurevich claimed that there was a fundamental difference between nordic culture and that of latin Europe: 'The mythopoetic tradition in nordic culture was a highly productive organic whole combining archaism with refinement.' [65] Not so with latin culture, where there is a gap between the culture of a people, 'driven back to the periphery of spiritual life' and the official culture of the church.

I find no such gap in the Miracles of the Virgin. Here the nordic version is very much in contact with the latin ecclesiastical tradition. We see one translation or adaptation after another, and we find our neglectful cleric who did not bring anything home in writing having to respond to the needs both of monks and of lay people. Perhaps fourteenth-century nordic culture is outside of the period with which Gurevich deals, but his distinction between latin and nordic worlds can only lead us astray in trying to understand the bonds between the original Miracles of the Virgin and their nordic

---

[64] At a lecture given by Professor Gurevich at Copenhagen University in April of 1990 I was able to ask him if he had changed his views on popular-learned culture in the course of writing his book. He replied that this in fact was the case. I detected a great openness in him towards a restructuring of his own views concerning the cultural role of the medieval church.
[65] Ibid. pp xvii-xviii

version. One sees cooperation and continuity in both worlds, Latin and Norse.

If we think in terms of Gurevich's 'productive organic whole' in which 'archaism' is combined with 'refinement', we use as a point of reference the *Miracles of the Virgin* in their development from the eleventh to the fourteenth centuries. The refined and gentle Mary who in the old norse version rewarded Bernard is derived from the much less physical mother of God found in the early latin stories. The archaism that we detect in the continuity of Mary's power is combined with a refinement in her increasing gentleness and accessibility as a human being. Here the development of the latin and old norse stories cannot be differentiated: Nordic culture in the same way as latin experienced a growing emphasis on the physicality of spiritual experience. In the end both high theology and popular narrative teach the same lesson. Indeed the two are intimately combined in the old norse narrative, for it says that if we, like Bernard, are devoted to Mary, she will take care of us.

In the *Mariu Saga* the mother of God becomes accessible to many the way she was available only to few in the prayer of Anselm of Canterbury to Mary. But the change is by no means exclusively nordic. It is part of the movement of medieval religion towards an palpable grasp of the spiritual dimension in order to secure the salvation of the individual human being. In this process the church still played a central role but was willing to go far in conceding the validity of visionary experience for the religious or even the lay person.

And what has happened to Bernard? He has become in the late Middle Ages a popular saint with his own rich tradition. The growth of this tradition became a problem only for post-medieval clerics who found the lactation story repulsive and apocryphal. They imposed their own view within a counter-reformation religion that felt obliged to cut back on physical manifestations of spiritual power. Even in our own time, monks can find great difficulty in relating to precisely this story.

In the vernacular stories of the later Middle Ages Bernard became more than ever a saint for ordinary people. Cistercian literature became available to an ever-wider public, as we can see in the translation of the second half of Caesarius of Heisterbach's *Dialogus Miraclorum* into German in the fifteenth century.[66] We are just beginning to pay attention to the importance of a development in the tradition of saints' lives in trying to understand the way late medieval people lived their christian religion. We have hardly begun to approach the rich material waiting for exploration and analysis in the North, where the latin and old norse traditions met. Here we find Bernard being remembered as a lover of fellow monks and a lover of Mary. The bonds of friendship, the duties of the abbot, the links with a world of permanence and beauty, all are summarized in the physical act by which Saint Bernard took Mary's breast into his mouth and sucked freely from her. In a cold northern clime, the hot and dusty roads of Burgundy were remembered in a moment when physical and spiritual worlds met in total harmony:

> It thus once happened when the blessed ⟨Bernard⟩ left his cloister, he made his way with two brothers through a wood in great heat of the sun to visit his subordinates and to strengthen the word of God. He was extremely thirsty and likewise the brothers, both from the excessive heat of the sun and the walk. But they had no more wine to consume than a tiny cask-full. There was not more than enough for one person.
>
> They went on walking for a long time, since none of them was prepared to drink from the casket because of the warmth of their love. The abbot wanted them to drink what there was. But the brothers were pained that the abbot should go without.
>
> So when they were all on the verge of exhaustion, the abbot told the brothers to sit down and rest a while as they drank from the casket. But he turned aside into a

[66] Karl Drescher, *Johann Hartliebs Übersetzung des Dialogus Miraculorum von Caesarius von Heisterbach*, Deutsche Texte des Mittelalters 33 (Berlin, 1929).

clearing away from them, humbly falling on his knees in prayer. Shortly afterwards a great light came over him. In this light there appeared to him the beatific and blessed queen of heaven, the noble begetter of God, maid and mother, the mildest virgin Sancta Maria. She was especially gentle in countenance towards her beloved Bernard, saying to him with heavenly sweetness of words:

'My dear Bernard! I have seen what heavy heat that tongue which has daily sung my praise today has suffered. Therefore come to me, your mother, tasting of the breast from which my beloved son Jesus Christ formerly drank, the King of Heaven and redeemer of creation.'

After these words she, the blessed, bared her most sublime breast, presenting it to Bernard's lips. And God Almighty gave him, a mortal man, so much daring that he opened his mouth. He drank of the lady's breast like a child from its mother.

Everyone is capable of the words to describe the scent and sweetness and heat of love that filled this man, Bernard the abbot, at so great a feast, receiving here at parting with words of sweetness a blessing from the queen. God Almighty and the Blessed Mary allowed those who had accompanied Bernard the abbot to see full clearly all of this vision. And when he, having returned to them, was aware that they were amazed at the sight, hardly daring to look towards him, he commanded them by virtue of obedience that they should tell no one of these things so long as Bernard the abbot was in the flesh. [67]

---

[67] I am grateful to Christopher Sanders for this translation. I have changed the historical present of the Old Norse into the past tense, and I have divided a few sentences to make the passage more readable.

8. Bernard and the Embrace of Christ

Renewal in Late Medieval
Monastic Life and Devotion

Bernard grew in the last medieval centuries. From about 1350 to 1550 came a great surge of manuscripts and then books containing his works or writings attributed to him. His corpus expanded to an extent matched by that of only one other medieval author, Saint Anselm. It was not until our own century that the genuine writings of Bernard, as those of Anselm, were restored to us.[1] The clearing away of accretions has made us much more precise in locating the twelfth-century Bernard. It is nevertheless worthwhile to consider the late medieval tradition of Bernard in order to see what he might have meant to Cistercians and other religious of that period.

Such an excursion into an apparently obscure corner of medieval literary history can involve more than a pleasant exercise. It brings us to a question historians need to debate: to what extent can late medieval monastic spirituality be

[1] See the introductions provided by Jean Leclercq and Henri Rochais in SBOp 1–8. Also Leclercq, *Recueil d'Etudes sur Saint Bernard et ses écrits* 1–3 (Rome. Editioni di Storia et Letteratura, 1962–68). For Anselm, S. *Anselmi Opera Omnia* 1–6, ed. F. S. Schmitt (London: Thomas Nelson, 1938–61).

227

looked upon as a recasting of themes already presented in the twelfth century? To put the question more bluntly: are fifteenth-century spiritual writings for a great part nothing more than recycled twelfth-century materials?

Since the appearance in 1971 of two seminal articles by Giles Constable, late medieval spirituality has been seen in terms of the creativity and fruitfulness of the twelfth century.[2] Constable has shown to what extent the number of manuscripts containing twelfth-century spiritual writings increased in the later Middle Ages and how writers of this period drew on the ideas and language of their predecessors. According to Constable, three forms of spiritual activity dominate and bridge the two periods: devotion to the humanity of Christ, a search for the inner life and self-knowledge, and an attempt to combine active with contemplative life. For Constable the thirteenth century appears as a pause between two periods of christian spiritual writings.

This interpretation of the medieval centuries in their intellectual and emotional orientation provided welcome relief from the view favoured by Etienne Gilson that twelfth-century theological endeavour leads towards the synthesis of the thirteenth century and especially of Thomas Aquinas. In Gilson's eyes, what comes after Thomas's death signals a sad departure from the most fruitful development of medieval thought. Constable's reevaluation of the medieval synthesis builds on the work of such earlier editors and historians as André Wilmart, Jean Leclercq and R. W. Southern.[3]

---

[2] 'Twelfth-Century Spirituality and the Late Middle Ages', *Medieval and Renaissance Studies* 5, ed. O.B. Hardison Jr. (Chapel Hill: University of North Carolina Press, 1971) 27–60; and 'The Popularity of Twelfth-Century Spiritual Writers in the Late Middle Ages', *Renaissance Studies in Honor of Hans Baron*, ed. Anthony Molho and John A. Tedeschi (Dekalb: Northern Illinois University Press, 1971) 5–28.

[3] Wilmart, *Auteurs spirituels et textes dévots du moyen-âge latin* (Paris, 1932); Southern, *The Making of the Middle Ages* (New Haven, 1953 and later), especially the final chapter, 'From Epic to Romance'.

Leclercq's major contribution in this area came, of course, with his *The Love of Learning and the Desire for God* (first published in Paris in 1957

Constable's achievement has been to extend these scholars' findings into the later medieval period.

The influence of Constable's interpretation of later medieval spirituality as essentially a continuation of twelfth-century themes and concerns can be seen in the writings of his outstanding pupil, Caroline Walker Bynum. In her recent work she makes little or no distinction between twelfth- and fifteenth-century female visionaries.[4] Bynum sees in every medieval century from the twelfth onwards women using food to exercise spiritual power over themselves and their contemporaries. With a thematic structure rather than one based on periodization, Bynum's book is concerned with one important change in the medieval approach to spiritual food, as we see in her heading, 'From Bread of Heaven to the Body Broken'. Here she shows how the Eucharist in the Early Middle Ages provided an opportunity for churchgoers to partake of a common spiritual meal. Later, however, concentration on the individual's participation in the sufferings of Christ became more important than any sharing in a heavenly feast.

Bynum's relative lack of distinction between the twelfth and fifteenth centuries indicates the great success Constable has had in establishing a static and derived element in later medieval mentalities. In his concentration on the twelfth century, Constable has deepened the appreciation of the period that originally appeared with Charles Homer Haskins at Harvard in the 1920s.[5] The Haskins thesis received new attention in an excellent collection of studies which Constable and Robert Benson edited in the early 1980s.[6] This concentration

and in New York in 1961. Now Fordham University Press 1982). Leclercq's distinction between monastic and scholastic theology was a boon to the serious study of monastic texts. But today the distinction needs to be considered anew. I hope elsewhere to return to this question.

[4] *Holy Feast and Holy Fast: The Religious Significance of Food to Medieval Women* (Berkeley: University of California Press 1987).

[5] *The Renaissance of the Twelfth Century* (Cambridge, Massachusetts, 1927).

[6] *Renaissance and Renewal in the Twelfth Century* (Oxford: Clarendon Press, 1982).

on the twelfth-century content of fifteenth-century spirituality has shown itself in a new interest for one of the distinctive
movements in late medieval religion, the *devotio moderna*. The
twelfth-century roots of this movement have now been investigated by Otto Gründler, who sees parallels between early
carthusian writings and the literature of the Brethren of the
Common Life.[7]

It is important for historians to realize that this shift in
our understanding of what happened in the medieval centuries in terms of religion has not altered a more popular
view of the later Middle Ages. For many non-specialists, the
dominant theme remains that of decline, as can be seen
in the 1970s with the success of Barbara Tuchman's *A Distant Mirror*.[8] Even though medieval historians may regard the
book as amateurish, its immediate appeal to a larger audience shows that it touched a perennial modern undercurrent
of disdain for the later Middle Ages. Tuchman's success was
overshadowed in the 1980s by that of Umberto Eco's *The
Name of the Rose*, a cleverer book and a novel instead of an
historical narrative. Again triumphed a view of the period that
emphasized violence, social unrest, and the collapse of religious faith and institutions.[9] Eco had an understanding for
religion and medievalists' debates about religion, qualities

---

[7] 'Devotio moderna', *Christian Spirituality: High Middle Ages and Reformation*,
ed. Jill Raitt (New York: Crossroad, 1987) 176–93 and esp. '*Devotio moderna
atque antiqua*: The Modern Devotion and Carthusian Spirituality', *The Spirituality of Western Christendom* 2: The Roots of the Modern Christian Tradition,
CS 55, ed. Rozanne Elder (1984) 27–45.

[8] First published in 1977 and reissued in paperback several times from
1978 onwards. The book has been translated into many languages, including Danish. The popular and able danish historian Palle Lauring has on
several occasions praised Tuchman's treatment as one of the very best
narratives of the later Middle Ages.

[9] First published in Italian in 1981 and translated into dozens of languages, this book became popular not only in Europe and North America
but also in Asian countries. In the autumn of 1985, after the danish translation was published, I participated in a series of lectures on the book held
at the Folkeuniversitet in Copenhagen. The lectures had to be doubled,
for more than two hundred and fifty people attended.

Tuchman acknowledged she lacked. Even so, both writers ended up repeating and confirming the pessimistic view of late medieval culture found in our century's perhaps most brilliant study of the period, Johan Huizinga's The Waning of the Middle Ages.[10]

Huizinga's influence has surpassed that of any other interpreter of the period because he gave the impression of providing a total understanding of the currents of the age. At the same time he wrote in beautiful, cadenced prose. His dutch style translated well into English. To this day Huizinga remains a pleasure to read, even if he chronicled unpleasant events. In Huizinga sensuous prose and surprising images, together with his intimate knowledge of both written and pictorial contemporary sources, have provided a point of departure for an understanding of fifteenth-century Europe as one world dying while another waited to be born.

Concentration on the decline and collapse of the medieval synthesis is sometimes associated with yet a third interpretation of the fourteenth and fifteenth centuries. Here medieval intellectual and religious figures have been looked upon as 'forerunners of the Reformation'. The thought and expression of the day are valued as a point of departure for what was to come. The Tübingen historian Heiko Oberman provides a sophisticated presentation of this view of the fifteenth century.[11] In both this and the decadence theory, the age is seen in terms of what came before or after. Decadence

---

[10] First published in Dutch in 1919, translated into English in 1924. This edition and subsequent ones in English have a special preface by Huizinga, in which he spoke of the new version as one of 'adaptation, reduction and consolidation under the author's directions'. In 1979 I edited a series of essays about the question of late medieval social crisis and cultural flowering. The contributors paid special attention to the popularity of the Huizinga-Tuchman interpretation (Kulturblomstring og samfundskrise i 1300-tallet (Center for Europæiske Middelalderstudier, Københavns Universitet, 1979, 1985)).

[11] Forerunners of the Reformation: The Shape of Late Medieval Thought (New York: Holt, Rinehart and Winston, 1966). See also the even more seminal work, The Harvest of Medieval Theology: Gabriel Biel and Late Medieval Nominalism (Cambridge, Mass.: Harvard University Press, 1963).

emphasizes the achievements of the High Middle Ages, while the forerunner view narrows the concerns and integrity of fifteenth-century people to extract what might have been relevant for sixteenth-century reformers.

There are thus problems with all three interpretations of the later Middle Ages: decadence, forerunners, or recycling.[12] In my view, Constable has done best in looking at the actual content of late medieval spirituality. However viable Constable's approach, it nevertheless emphasizes continuity at the expense of change. In concentrating on the repetition of literary themes and spiritual concerns, Constable has provided a portrait of medieval religion that by itself allows for little or no development between the twelfth and the fifteenth centuries. One easily returns to twelfth-century writings as 'the real thing', while fifteenth-century tracts appear for the most part as secondary and derivative. They can become curiosities, anchored in their tradition, but symptomatic of a church and religious orders mulling over the same old themes.

Constable's learning and acuity are a legend among generations of medieval scholars. His reorientation has been a boon to medieval studies. In what follows, my purpose is to emphasize the possibility of change within the continuity of spiritual language and themes. A competent presentation of this point of view would require the same comprehensive treatment of the subject that Constable gave. I will try here only to make a beginning, providing a few suggestions on how a different approach to later medieval spirituality might provide alternative insights. My guide will be the Cistercians, who can offer an example of broader developments.[13]

[12] For a solid attempt to consider the later medieval church as a whole, see Francis Oakley, *The Western Church in the Later Middle Ages* (Ithaca and London: Cornell University Press, 1979).

[13] It is my hope during the next years to provide a larger study of the spiritual life of the later Middle Ages, concentrating on developments within old and new religious orders, especially the Cistercians, the Carthusians and the Brigittines. Thanks especially to the guidance and inspiration of James Hogg in Salzburg, carthusian studies have been given new life. A similar flowering of studies is now happening in Scandinavia with the

Late Medieval Cistercian Areas of Vitality

In his already classic history of the Cistercian Order, Louis Lekai looked upon the last medieval centuries in terms of 'The End of Prosperity'.[14] In economic terms, he is correct. Abbeys suffered terribly under the Black Death, the Hundred Years' War, and other political and social pressures. Cistercian houses were no longer looked upon as desirable foundations by the aristocracy, and the number of new houses declined drastically. In the fourteenth and also in the fifteenth centuries, the central government of the Cistercian Order, its General Chapter at Cîteaux, at times failed to function. Individual monasteries became more provincial or more national in their orientation than they had been in the High Middle Ages. The great international order of the twelfth century can hardly be recognized in its now splintered and squabbling regional groups.[15]

All the developments are neatly reviewed in Lekai's easy prose and skilful review of the documents. Other sources, however, provide a more nuanced view of the changes that were coming about. A treatment of cistercian taxation of the individual houses shows resistance to the General Chapter, but also its insistence in maintaining the system despite social and economic problems.[16]

Some houses seem to have countered economic decline by opening themselves to currents of lay piety that could have provided an income. Heisterbach in the early fourteenth century, for example, received the permission of the General Chapter to allow women into the church on the feast of its

---

Brigittines, with recent seminars headed by Tore Nyberg, Odense and Alf Härdelin, Uppsala.

[14] *The Cistercians: Ideals and Reality* (Kent State University Press: Ohio, 1977) 91–108.

[15] For the situation in one country, see my *Cistercians in Denmark* CS 35 (1982) esp. 156–66, 'The decline of dependence on international structures'. which I saw as beginning already by the end of the thirteenth century.

[16] Peter King, *The Finances of the Cistercian Order in the Fourteenth Century*, CS 85 (1985) esp. 203–205.

dedication. These women, described as 'noble and powerful', had in past years been forcing their way into the church. Now the Chapter said it was acceptable that one day a year, the women could come in order to obtain indulgences by participation in the feast.[17] One wonders whether women had been as violent in demanding access to the church as the source claims, or if this was the monks' excuse for letting them in. Whatever the case, the monks of Heisterbach accepted an income and a form of devotion that would have seemed foreign to their twelfth-century predecessors and even to their tolerant thirteenth-century storyteller, Caesarius. In his stories lay people and monks talked freely to each other, but the monastery precinct and the monks' church remained off-limits to the laity and especially to women. Now the Cistercians opened their doors to women and even encouraged them to come.

This alliance between lay devotional practices and cistercian needs helps also to explain the presence of Saint Bridget of Sweden at a male cistercian house, Alvastra, for three years in the 1340s.[18] Bridget, a member of the royal family of

[17] *Urkundenbuch der Abtei Heisterbach*, nr 238, ed. Ferdinand Schmitz, Urkundenbücher der Geistlichen Stiftungen des Niederrheins 2 (Bonn 1908) p 316, dated to 1317: '. . .ad festum dedicationis ecclesie vestre annuum frequentiam esse innumerabilis utriusque sexus populi et concursum, nec vos aliqualiter posse prohibere vel resistere quin mulieres nobiles et potentes eodem tempore ob magne devocionis affectuum causa indulgenciarum a sede apostolica ac diversis archiepiscopis et episcopis predicti festivitatis dedicationis vestre largiflue concessarum ecclesiam vestra et septa monasterii contra vestram prohibicionem et ordinis instituta introeant violenter. . . . cupientes benivole precare devocionem quoque populi et frequentiam ad dictum festum non minuere. . . . ' For further examples of cistercian encouragement of lay devotion in the period, as the bavarian abbey Langheim's shrine of Vierzehnheiligen, see Lekai (note 14 above) 388–89.

[18] See my 'Spiritual Life and Material Life in the Late Middle Ages: A Contradiction?', *Mensch und Objekt im Mittelalter und in der Frühen Neuzeit* (Veröffentlichungen des Instituts für Realienkunde des Mittelalters und der Frühe Neuzeit 13: Vienna 1990), 285–313. I am grateful to Gerhard Jaritz, Institut für mittelalterliche Realienkunde Österreichs, for inviting me to prepare this paper for the conference 'Mensch und Objekt im Mittelalter. Leben-Alltag-Kultur' held at Krems in September 1988.

Sweden, had lost her husband and had not yet determined what type of life she would lead. The Alvastra years provided an important transition before her public career as visionary and reformer of the church. Bridget managed to ally herself with the monks at Alvastra, who came to believe in her devotion and did not find any contradiction between her presence in the immediate vicinity of the monastery and the requirements of male monastic life.

Thanks to Bridget's stay, the spiritual landscape of Alvastra is illuminated. The sources about her reveal that she was but one of a number of visionaries leading an intensely devotional life there. Stories about Bridget necessarily described spiritual monks who had visions confirming the legitimacy of her presence among them. A monastery in a land distant from power centres of cistercian administration emerges in a new light. One wonders how many other houses would reveal similarly devout monks and nuns if their activities had been better publicized or the sources better preserved. The case of Bridget warns us not to allow the lack of sources to deny the pervasiveness of deep religious feeling in cistercian monasteries at the end of the Middle Ages.

By the last years of the fifteenth century, the drastic drop in recruitment which had characterized the fourteenth century was being replaced by a modest new wave of monks. The english houses dissolved in the 1530s were by no means empty, and some of the monks there ended their lives by dying for their faith.[19] In Denmark dissolution was gentler, and the persistence of cistercian life into the 1580s, a half-century after the Reformation, indicates something of its strength in spite of the changes the church had undergone.

In the later Middle Ages it is important to distinguish between developments in France, where the Order really was in trouble because of social unrest or the intervention of kings or nobles, and Northern Europe, where the Cistercians in

---

[19] Lekai pp 91, 119–20.

some areas continued to flourish.[20] Around the monastery of Villers in Brabant, new houses of nuns were founded and old ones revived, just as they had been in the thirteenth century. The abbot of Villers did his best to visit these houses and maintain control, but as Roger de Ganck has shown, the nuns had a great degree of self-determination.[21] In Germany, the Low Countries, and Scandinavia, to say nothing of Eastern Europe, cistercian monasteries at the end of the Middle Ages were beginning to grow again in numbers and wealth.

In renaissance Italy, where one would hardly expect to find an old agrarian Order keeping apace of social change, the monks accepted urbanization and adapted themselves to the new times. At Florence, Alison Luchs has shown the outlines of a building programme that transformed a decrepit church into a monument of renaissance architecture and renewed cistercian life in an urban setting.[22] The Cistercians of the fifteenth century could show a keen ability to adapt and to adjust to the currents of life around them.

One monastery that seemed to hold its own and even revive, despite being plundered by the Hussites in 1433, was Oliva, today in Poland near Gdansk, in the Middle Ages an outpost of german cistercian life.[23] Oliva has left us a fifteenth-century manuscript bought by Gethsemani Abbey, Kentucky, in the 1920s and now at the Cistercian Institute at

[20] The Cistercians in Denmark 251–59. William J. Telesca, 'The Cistercian Dilemma at the Close of the Middle Ages: Gallicanism or Rome', Studies in Medieval Cistercian History, CS 13 (1971) 163–85, and 'The Cistercian Abbey in Fifteenth-Century France: A Victim of Competing Jurisdictions of Sovereignty, Suzerainty and Primacy', Cistercians in the Late Middle Ages. Studies in Medieval Cistercian History 6, CS 64, ed. E. Rozanne Elder (1981).

[21] 'De Reformatie-Beweging bij de Zuid-Nederlandske Cisterciënserinnen in de 15de Eeuw', Cîteaux 32 (1981) 75–86.

[22] 'Alive and Well in Florence: Thriving Cistercians in Renaissance Italy', Cîteaux 30 (1979) 109–24. Also the more complete, Cestello. A Cistercian church of the Florentine Renaissance (New York: Garland, 1977).

[23] J. C. Kretzschmer, Die Cisterzienser Abtei Oliva, Geschichte und Beschreibung der Klöster in Pomerellen (Danzig, 1847). For connections between Oliva and pomeranian monasteries such as Colbatz, H. Hoogeweg, Die Stifter und Klöster der Provinz Pommern 1 (Stettin, 1924) 254–56.

Kalamazoo (MS 25). There is no proof that the manuscript was composed in Oliva, for the library catalogue marking from Oliva is in a seventeenth-century hand. But the manuscript's contents (several cistercian works as well as a german poem about how to be a good monk) point strongly to Oliva or at least to a northeastern german cistercian house.[24]

After a few pen trials and verses, the manuscript starts with the Rule of Saint Benedict and then (ff 31r–32r) contains the cistercian form of visitation, a treatise on the three monastic vows (ff 32v–42v), a treatise (not by Bernard) on the twelve degrees of humility (43r–61r), a De *professione monachorum* attributed to Thomas Aquinas (62r–92r), Thomas's genuine De *perfectione vite spiritualis* (92v–106v), composed during the controversy between mendicant and secular masters at the university of Paris, then a treatise attributed to Saint Bernard, De *disciplina monachorum* (107r–120r), a *Formula pulchra vivendi* (120r–130r), various sermons (130r–160v), liturgical notices and an anonymous liturgical treatise (170r–191v), various blessings, an alphabetical index in a sixteenth-century hand not covering the actual contents of the manuscript (195r–210v), the Rule of lay brothers, Usus *conversorum* (211r–217v), and finally a letter of Bernard of Clairvaux.

I have listed the contents of the manuscript because they reveal something about the interests of a late medieval cistercian house. The manuscript is a real miscellany, and its various segments, while they may have been assembled only after the medieval period, were for the most part written down in the fifteenth century. There is attention to texts

---

[24] Kalamazoo MS 25, f 170v: 'Mutwille, unkeusch unde eygenschaft/ Swechet orden unn klosters kraft,/ Wer dy drey wol meyden kan,/ Der yss eyn guth klosterman./ Cleyder auss, cleder an,/ Essen, trinken, slofen gan,/ Singen, lesen, fru off stand,/ Das yss daz leben dass wir han . . . . '

In the german description of the manuscript, in typescript from the 1920s, perhaps drawn up in connection with the sale of the work, it is noted that this poem is associated with a fifteenth-century 'Spottverse' against the German Order of Knights which operated in the area of Oliva:

'Kleider aus, kleider an,/ Essen, trinken schlofen gan/ Iss das Leben, das die teutschen Herren han.'

that provide a foundation for monastic life: the Rule of Saint Benedict itself, and various cistercian statutes and other monastic treatises. Of greatest interest for us is the pseudo-bernardine De disciplina monachorum, which a german scholar of the manuscript in the 1920s correctly recognized as two treatises by a thirteenth-century Franciscan, David of Augsburg, his Formula honestae vitae and Tractatus super Ad quid venis.[25] Both works are contained in volume 184 of the Patrologia Latina, itself a miscellany of medieval texts ascribed to Bernard and now conceded to others.[26]

Attribution to Bernard must have given the work greater authority in late medieval cistercian circles. Both treatises are brief, practical guides for the monk (or friar) about how to live in harmony in community. There are no spiritual heights, just solid, sober advice. Such guides to monastic discipline might seem to indicate a departure from the twelfth-century spirit of Saint Bernard, which emphasized interiority and reflection. But in reality the provisions found here are close to the spirit of General Chapters held at the end of the twelfth century. Here Bernard's successors looked for clear formulae about how monks could maintain community.

The Anthidotarius Anime

At Oliva as elsewhere in the later Middle Ages, texts were being attributed to Bernard that he could never have written. Spiritual language and images gained authority by using his name. In this development we can look at a compilation attributed to a medical doctor, Nicolas Salicetus, who became a Cistercian and abbot of Baumgarten near Strasbourg. His Liber meditationum devotarum qui Anthidotarius anime dicitur was first published in 1489.[27] It became an instant success, with

[25] For David of Augsburg, see the Dictionnaire de Spiritualité 3 (1957) 42–44.
[26] PL 184:1167–98.
[27] See the Dictionnaire des auteurs cisterciens, Documentation cistercienne 5, ed Emile Brouette and Eugene Manning (Rochefort, Belgium, 1978) col. 527. The incunabulum collection at the Cistercian Library in Kalamazoo contains two copies of the work, one dated Strasbourg 1491, whose pagina-

editions in French as late as a century afterwards.[28] Nicolas was a collector of other people's wisdom. His work abounds with prayers attributed to Augustine, Anselm, Bernard, Bridget of Sweden, and Jean Gerson. A closer study of the work's contents needs to be made, but an overview is sufficient to conclude that Nicolas combined a sense of the liturgical year with a talent for finding texts which, in the words of Chrysogonus Waddell, are 'shot through with evident trinitarian and christological concerns'.[29] Although several prayers are dedicated to Mary, there is a great amount of material concentrating on Christ and the Redemption. Even in the prayers addressed to the saints, Nicolas took care to relate them and their activities to the central mysteries of christian revelation. This is no pious textbook of derivative religious feeling. It is a compilation and summation of centuries of devotional literature. Its purpose, as Nicolas pointed out in his conclusion, was to provide material for meditation as a cure for the ills of the soul.[30]

Saint Bernard appears at several junctures in the compilation, but I will concentrate on two prayers. The first is meant

---

tion I follow in my references, the other, which is shorter, dated Haguenau (near Strasbourg) 1494. I am in great debt to Father Chrysogonus Waddell, Gethsemani Abbey, for pointing out the bernardine content of this prayer book and for providing much-needed guidance in this difficult and unfamiliar area of cistercian spirituality. Thanks are due also to Beatrice Beech, librarian at the Institute, for her ready help.

[28] Professor David Bell of the Memorial University of Newfoundland has kindly informed me that the *Anthidotarius* was a companionpiece to the *Anthidotarius Nicholai*, a medical treatise attributed to Nicholas of Farnham. See his forthcoming work, *An Index of Authors and Works in Cistercian Libraries of Great Britain* (CS 130). He has also referred me to Lynn Thorndike and Pearl Kibre, *A Catalogue of Incipits of Mediaeval Scientific Writings in Latin* (Cambridge, Mass. and London, 1963), Index under 'Antidotarii'. See also Robert Gottfried, *Doctors and Medicine in Medieval England 1340–1530* (Princeton, 1986).

[29] Letter to me dated 15 March 1989, which I quote with permission.

[30] *Antidotarius anime* (1491 edition) p cxlvi: 'Animarum christi fidelium anthidotarium salutiferiis quo etiam egrotantes ad optatam sanitatem restitui et sane in ipsa sanitate conservari valeant hic finem sumpsisse cerneres, o lector devotissime deo.'

to be said to him, 'Oratio de sancto Bernardo clarevallensi et doctore egregio',[31] while the second is supposed to be by him: 'Oratio devotissima beati bernardi abbatis clarevallensis, quam cum semel dicteret ante imaginem crucifixi, ipsa imago de cruce se inclinans eum amplexata est' (Most devout prayer of blessed Bernard abbot of Clairvaux, which when he once said it before the image of the crucified, that image bending down from the cross embraced him).[32]

What is remarkable about the first prayer is its relative restraint. The anonymous composer asks Bernard for the grace of tears as a sign of compunction and mentions the sins of his youth. He remembers Bernard for the embrace Jesus gave him from the cross. Images do not pile up, and the language remains relatively uncrowded:

> He who loved you with such charity that he deigned to embrace you with the arms of his passion and his precious death. May I deserve to praise and venerate you worthily and be able through inner sweetness by meditating, loving, seeking, to obtain forever the joys of eternal life.[33]

There is a brief litany to Bernard as *oliva fructifera, sanctarum virtutum vas, preciosum cor,* language that recalls some of the terms used in the cistercian liturgy for the feast of Saint Bernard.[34] The central point made here is that Bernard, mindful of the sinner, can bring him to union with the Christ who once expressed his union with Bernard. The prayer is brief and to the point in the way that the liturgy commemorating a

---

[31] Ibid. p. cxl (p cxxiv in 1494 edition).

[32] Ibid. p. lxxii (p lxv in 1494 edition).

[33] Ibid. p. cxl: 'Qui tanta caritate dilexit te ut brachiis sue passionis et preciose mortis te amplectere dignatus est. Teque digne laudare et venerari merear et interna dulcedine gaudia eterne vite valeam meditando amando sectando in perpetuum adipisci.'

[34] Compare the *Antidotarius* ('Tu oliva fructifera in domo dei') with the phrase in Bernard's proper office, 'O oliva fructifera in domo dei'. See *Breviarium Cisterciense Reformatum. Pars Aestivalis* (Westmalle 1951) p 589.

saint on his feast day often can be, in using striking incidents and images from the saint's life and work.

Simplicity and directness here recall the language of Bernard himself. We find themes which Constable rightly pointed out as belonging to twelfth-century spirituality: concentration on the humanity of Christ and emphasis on the interior life, so that attitudes and feelings become of primary importance. In this sense Constable was quite correct in showing how fifteenth-century spiritual writers followed the interests of their predecessors.

But if we turn to the second, longer prayer, we find much more elaborate language and images. We can call this prayer Bernard's *Salutatio*, his embrace of the body of Christ, who in the *Exordium Magnum Cisterciense* is remembered for reaching out and enfolding him.[35] We notice first of all that the prayer is literarily much more ambitious than its predecessors in the collection. It has both internal rhymes and end rhymes, which give it a beat and a cadence that flow along in lithe eight-syllable segments, despite latin words that can be long and difficult.[36] Here is a sequence from the first section, the 'Salutatio ad pedes', Bernard's greeting to Christ's feet:

> O amator peccatorum/ reparator confractorum/
> O dulcis pater pauperum/ Quidquid est in me confractum/
> dissipatum aut distractum,
> Dulcis iesu, totum sana/ tu restaura, tu complana/
> Tam pio medicamine./
> Te in tua cruce quero/ prout queo corde mero./
> Me sanabis, hic ut spero./ Sana me et sanus ero/
> In tuo lavans sanguine.[37]

> O lover of sinners, repairer of the broken
> O sweet father of the poor, Whatever is in me broken
> disturbed or distraught.

[35] EM II.7. See my chapter above, 'The First Cistercian Renewal'.

[36] As Rozanne Elder has pointed out to me, the metre is close to that of 'Stabat mater dolorosa'.

[37] *Antidotarius* p. lxxii.

Sweet Jesus, heal the whole, restore, smooth out,
By so kind a medicine.
You in your cross I seek. As I can in bitter heart.
You will heal me, here as I hope. Heal me and I will
     be well,
washing in your blood.

The rhyme endings are on the pattern aabb, but then a c
ending links up the same ending at the end of the next four-
line stanza. One does not have to be an expert in medieval
poetry to realize the effect such language could have. Read
aloud to others or half aloud to oneself in a quiet corner, this
prayer-poetry encouraged almost a form of private incanta-
tion which would provide a point of departure for meditation
on the truths involved.

The prayer is divided up into various greetings that Bernard makes to parts of the body of Jesus: to his feet, his
knees, his hands, side, breasts, heart, face, and so on. In the
final *salutatio*, the various events of the Passion are recalled,
while in the earlier greetings, the historical details of the
Passion are set aside in order to concentrate on a meeting
between the sinner and the beloved body of Christ. Here the
poetry provided a multiplicity of images in order to describe
this contact.

In such a prayer we leave behind twelfth-century bernardine spirituality. Bernard built up his texts with biblical al-
lusions and reminiscences. As the new edition of his work
shows by its capitalizations, almost every sentence in his
writings has a biblical passage either on the surface or just
below it. This is not at all the case with the *Salutationes*. It uses
language not to suggest the biblical background of Christ's
actions but to provide a direct *physical* meeting with Christ.
Twelfth-century cistercian spirituality at its most corporeal
had concentrated on the face of Christ or the kiss of the
lover in the *Song of Songs*, while now the whole body of Christ
becomes an object of veneration.

Touching and handling each part of Christ's body, the sinner emphasizes how he uses this body as a necessary point of departure for spiritual union: 'Whoever here has come to you/ he has touched these feet with his heart.// Sick man has left well/ Leaving behind all he has done and kissing the wounds.'[38]

Kissing, feeling, touching, exploring, embracing: all these verbs are used at different places in the prayer to describe what the sinner wants to do with Christ's body. There is a desire for intimate personal contact that becomes so intense that the only solution is for the sinner to enter into the very wounds of Christ. There are words that describe blood and gore, and yet there is not enough graphic description to let one charge the author with anything bordering on necrophilia. The Christ described here is a living physical being, a man who suffers greatly, and a man who loves greatly: 'Holy hands, I embrace you, and weeping I rejoice in you./ I thank you for so many hammer strikes and harsh blows with bleeding,/ and I add tears to my kiss.'[39]

Physical contact between the sinner and Christ knows almost no bounds here. The author speaks of licking, as well as of tasting Christ (*te ardenti corde lingo*). This union with the body of Christ is necessary because only his physical body can provide the sinner with the refuge he seeks: *In hac fossa me reconde/ intra meum cor profunde* (In this cleavage hide me/ enter my heart deeply). At the same time as one enters the wounds, Christ enters into one's heart. Physical and spiritual union coincide.

It is easy to image how Huizinga would have interpreted this prayer. His ascetic sensibility could not have tolerated such ornateness of language and heaviness of images. But if we look at this prayer as an expression of devotion to

---

[38] Ibid. p. lxxii: 'Quisquis huc ad te accessit/ Hosque pedes corde pressit/ Eger sanus hinc abscessit/ hinc relinquens quicquid gessit/ dans osculum vulneribus.'

[39] Ibid. p. lxxii: 'Manus sancte vos complector et gemendo condelector./ grates ago plagis tantis clavis diris gutis ictis./ dans lachrymas cum osculo.'

Christ and an attempt to bridge the gap between everyday life and yearning for permanence, union and love, its language contains conviction, discipline, and imagination.

Such an interpretation has to take into consideration the place of such a prayer in terms of medieval spiritual expression. If we turn to the original cistercian description of how Jesus embraced Bernard, we can compare the imagery of the prayer with its point of departure. This is found in Herbert of Clairvaux's *Liber Miraculorum* from the late 1170s, and was repeated in the *Exordium Magnum* of the 1190s:

> ⟨There was a monk⟩ who once found Bernard the abbot in the church praying alone. When he was prostrate before the altar, there appeared a cross to him with its crucified, on the floor set in front of Bernard. He devoutly adored and kissed it. Then that Majesty took its arms from the branches of the cross and seemed to embrace and draw the servant of God to himself.[40]

The story as told here is simple and brief. Jesus on the cross appears to Bernard, unlike the depiction of the event in religious art and in the prayer to Saint Bernard in our collection, where it is the figure of the crucified above the altar which comes alive.

We can compare the original twelfth-century narrative to a panel from the 1496 altar at Esrum abbey in Denmark. Here Bernard actively embraces Christ, assumedly responding to Bernard's action of venerating the cross. In Herbert of Clairvaux, Jesus embraces Bernard, who remains a passive receiver of Jesus' affection. In the Esrum altar Bernard grips a Christ figure that seems almost to be falling onto him.

I once described the Esrum Bernard panel as indicative of a continuity in cistercian themes from twelfth-century french literature to late fifteenth-century danish ecclesiastical art.[41] I would today qualify this statement, considering the Esrum

---

[40] Herbert LM 2.19; PL 185:1328. EM II.7, ed. Bruno Griesser pp 102–103.
[41] *Cistercians in Denmark*, pp 255–57. The Esrum altar should more properly be spoken of as northern european art, for its type of crowded Golgo-

altar in terms of the *Salutatio* prayer, and would point out how later versions of the embrace of Christ embellish the basic story and give it further dimensions. A spiritual vision, something which happened entirely in the mind of the observing monk, became a physical event. The late medieval prayer takes every single aspect of the event under investigation and describes it in the greatest possible detail. This results in a dialogue between the one who prays and the Christ who is embraced, a dialogue that lasts for several hundred lines as the devout monk asks to enter into Jesus and begs him not to resist: 'Behold how he is so taken towards you, desiring ardently to feel, desiring powerfully to enter. Please, do not resist. You ought to consent to him.'[42]

Of medieval authors of prayers who communicate themselves with passion and intensity, only Anselm in the earlier period comes close to this form. But Anselm hardly dealt so directly with the physical body of Christ as a refuge for the sinner.[43] We cannot turn to any twelfth-century prayers genuinely by Bernard, but if we look at the *Meditations* of his good friend and confidant William of Saint Thierry, we find a language of prayer emphasizing the passion of Christ but without the same wealth of detail and concentration on Christ's body. Nor does William consider the body of the sinner and its union with Jesus. It is the soul alone which enjoys contact with the dying Jesus:

> So too with crucifixion; it is not my body which is crucified, but my wretched soul that is put to greater inward

---

tha scene and accompanying panel representations was usually made in Northern Germany.

[42] *Antidotarius* p. lxxiii: 'Ecce tam post te movetur te ardenter vult sentire. Vult potenter introire. noli contraire. Debes ei consentire.'

[43] Anselm in his 'Prayer to Christ' did speak of wanting to have 'kissed the place of the wounds where the nails pierced', but most of his physical images concern his own emotions in desiring Christ: 'My Lord and my Creator,....I thirst for you, I hunger for you, I desire you, I sigh for you, I covet you.' Benedicta Ward, *The Prayers and Meditations of Saint Anselm* (Harmondsworth 1973, 1986) pp 94, 96.

agony than that of any cross. Yet I am crucified with you, Lord Jesus, at least upon the cross of my profession. By your gift of grace daily and constantly I offer it to you. These are your gifts, your presents. But when from my own pleasant cross I look at the cross of your passion, the nails of fear of you pierce me. I am confounded and all my spirit quails, not from the pain of my cross (which by your grace is nothing to me now) but because of the pain of my heart. I consider your work revived in the midst of the years. . . . [44]

When we compare the measured theological yet personal considerations of William with the physical language of the *Salutatio* prayer, we detect both change and continuity in spiritual literature from the twelfth century to the fifteenth. One striking image, the appearance of the crucified Christ to Bernard, is preserved and expanded in cistercian literature through the entire period. This image takes on new layers of meaning in cistercian meditations on the sufferings of Christ.

Cistercian devotional literature is here associated with similar developments in what is inadequately called popular religion, where there was a great desire to exemplify and concretize every mystery of faith, every story of Jesus, and every recorded or imagined deed of the saints.[45] When the

[44] *Meditativae orationes* 5.3: 'Nec invenit corpus meum crucem in qua crucifigatur, sed infelix anima mea super omnem crucis dolorem in seipsa cruciatur. Crucifixus tamen tibi sum, Domine Jesu, utcumque in cruce professionis, quam de munere tuo quotidie et jugiter tibi offero, quia munera tua, data tua, sed de meae crucis deliciis contemplans passionem tuae crucis, clavis timoris tui confixus, confundor et totus contabesco, non ex dolore crucis meae, qui ex gratia tua jam mihi nullus est, sed ex dolore cordis, quo considero opus tuum in medio annorum vivificatum.' *Guillaume de S. Thierry, Oraisons ineditées*, Pain de Cîteaux 21, trans. P. Robert Thomas (1964) 90–92. English trans. by Sister Penelope, *On Contemplating God, Prayer and Meditations*, CF 3 (1971).

[45] There has been renewed sensitivity in recent years to the importance of lay forms of religious devotion in the period. Francis Rapp led the way in this area, *L'église et la vie religieuse en occident à la fin du moyen âge* (Paris: Press Universitaires de France, 1971). More recently the work of Richard Kieckhefer has been of significance, as summarized in his important essay, 'Major Currents in Late Medieval Devotion', in *Christian Spirituality* (note 7 above)

cistercian writer asked Jesus to place his head in his arms (*caput tuum hic reclina. in meis pausa brachiis*),[46] he was asking for the same intimate contact with Jesus that had become important to lay persons, especially women, in the cult of the eucharist, in stories about eucharistic miracles, and in religious art, where the theme of the *pietà* became a leading motif.

One can look upon this form of spiritual literature as derivative and even as vulgar, for it clearly tried to manipulate the emotions of the devout by sensationalizing phrases and images. But one cannot underestimate the power of such language at a time when words had a durability they have lost in our own age. The fifteenth-century prayer of *Salutatio* to the body and sufferings of Christ, with its extreme statements of physicality, is far from the classic cistercian language to be found in Bernard, William of Saint Thierry, or even Aelred of Rievaulx. Such a prayer, however, provides stunning witness to the vitality of cistercian spirituality. It could draw on an image emerging from twelfth-century stories about Bernard. Even if we know little about the book's audience, we can assume from the several printings it experienced that it was popular and responded to a widespread desire for meditation on the mysteries of faith through rumination on images arising from monks' *lectio* or holy readings.

75–108. A good general survey is Rosalind and Christopher Brooke, *Popular Religion in the Middle Ages* (London: Thames and Hudson, 1984), but this stops in 1300. I am grateful to Daniel Bornstein, University of California at San Diego, for sending me his article, 'The Shrine of Santa Maria a Cigoli: Female visionaries and clerical promoters', *Mélanges de l'école française de Rome* 98 (1986) 219–28. Recent publications on late medieval english spirituality are of great interest in this area: Jonathan Hughes, *Pastors and Visionaries: Religion and Secular Life in Late Medieval Yorkshire* (Woodbridge, Suffolk: The Boydell Press, 1988), and *De Cella in Seculum: Religious and Secular Life and Devotion in Late Medieval England*, ed. Michael G. Sargent (Cambridge: D.S. Brewer,1989). The manifold publications in *Analecta Carthusiana*, published by James Hogg, Salzburg, shed much new light on the period. What characterizes all these works is that they consider the late medieval period on its own terms and not primarily as a preview or a decline.

[46] *Antidotarius*, p. lxxiiii.

A Jesus We Can Touch

In the original *Exordium Magnum* story, Jesus on the cross touched Bernard. There is no indication that Bernard in return embraced Jesus. In our fifteenth-century cistercian prayer ascribed to Bernard, we touch and feel and get inside of Jesus. There is an erotic quality in the prayer which goes beyond twelfth-century expression. We can rightly ask what has happened to Bernard. He was immensely important to our author, who at one point could claim that a prayer was only said to be from Bernard.[47] We have seen how Nicolas included a prayer close to the cistercian liturgy for the feast of Saint Bernard. But in the *Salutatio* prayer, our compiler went far beyond the historical Bernard and his writings. Twelfth-century spiritual texts had been intense and had sought to stir up emotion, but they were not as physical in their language as this prayer. In its passion for rhyme and concentrated imagery it is reminiscent of Anselm's prayers, but it is more than a bad imitation of earlier prayers.

The author of the *Salutatio* was not interested in manipulating biblical language to provide spiritual references. He wanted to use prayer–poetry in order to convey personal experience. The eleventh- and twelfth-century origins of such a literature are clear, but the spirituality and mode of expression have developed in new directions, with a more tangible content and more accessibility for the average monk.

Although such writings cannot be called popular, since they were in Latin and thus limited to a relatively small part of the population, they should be seen as part of a late medieval effort to make christian spirituality available to new audiences. The writings of Bernard, with all their tricks of language and hidden meanings, demanded a learned audience in a way that the prayers in Nicolas' collection did not. To return to Constable, it is clear that fourteenth- and

---

[47] *Antidotarius* p. lxviii: 'Item alia brevis de quinque gaudiis beate marie et beati bernardi abbatis clarevallis ut dicitur.'

fifteenth-century humanists understood and used twelfth-century texts, but average monks required something different. In the *Salutatio* we find what they could use: a prayer that almost lilts off the tongue and at the same time provides the monk with powerful material for meditation on the love of Jesus for us. The result is an almost physical experience that involves the entire being.

A still common picture of late medieval Cistercians as well-nourished gentlemen living off the fat of the land may have some truth to it, for most houses did seek material comfort.[48] But the prayerbook of Nicolas and its pseudo-bernardine passages remind us that behind a well-heeled facade we can find men and women who looked for an accessible, human Jesus. Like their twelfth-century forbearers, the Cistercians of the Late Middle Ages accepted the physical on the way to the spiritual. In embracing the human Christ, they expected to make their way to God. Like their predecessors, these monks and nuns looked for viable ways of making this journey of hearts, minds and bodies.

[48] In Denmark, for example, cistercian abbeys are still called 'herre-klostre', to indicate that their monks were 'lords' over the surrounding area, a conception that concentrates exclusively on the aristocratic and privileged nature of cistercian life in the later Middle Ages.

9. Saint Bernard In the USA Today

The Growth of Cistercian Studies[1]

Until the 1960s Bernard of Clairvaux drew the attention usually of monks or nuns who made use of him within their own religious devotion or of scholars who tried to penetrate the meaning of his theology. The Bernard of piety familiar to our age resulted in large measure from seventeenth-century trappist spirituality combined with a nineteenth-century concentration on personal piety.[2] The Bernard of theology

[1] In what follows I am indebted to the cistercian monks and nuns who over the years have shared with me aspects of the most recent history of their Order. I am especially grateful to Dr. E. Rozanne Elder at Kalamazoo for her help in correcting some of my misconceptions about the history of the last twenty years and providing me with exact references.

It should be pointed out already here that at the end of the nineteenth century the Cistercian Order was formally reorganized into two separate orders, the Order of Cistercians (O.Cist. for *Ordo Cisterciensis* today, formerly S.O.Cist. for *Sacer Ordo Cisterciensis*) and the Order of the Cistercians of the Strict Observance (O.C.S.O. for *Ordo Cisterciensis Strictioris Observantiae*), popularly known as the Trappists.

[2] Only in recent years has the cult of Saint Bernard begun to draw the attention it deserves, and so I cannot refer the reader to any body of literature on the subject. Jacques Berlioz, *Saint Bernard en Bourgogne: Lieux et mémoire* (Paris: Les éditions du bien public, 1990) has some useful

emerged from the seminal study of Etienne Gilson from 1934 and brought a new interest in Bernard and his contribution to the theological vocabulary of the High Middle Ages.[3] Bernard the theologian became better known through the publications that marked the eight-hundredth anniversary of his death in 1953,[4] and especially through the work, both scholarly and popular, of the benedictine monk Jean Leclercq.[5]

Although Gilson's book was translated into English in 1940, most work on Bernard's theology and his contribution to monastic life was done in French or German, while the English-speaking world concentrated on Bernard in terms of his political role in the history of the twelfth century.[6] One

---

materials. Louis Lekai, *The Cistercians: Ideals and Reality* (Kent State University Press, Ohio: 1977) says in his 'bibliographical notes' to chapter 14, 'Much of what has been published on 19th-century Trappists is colored by excessive piety' (p 422).

[3] *The Mystical Theology of Saint Bernard* (London: Sheed and Ward, 1990; Cistercian Publications 1990), now with an important preface by Jean Leclercq in which he evaluates the significance of Gilson's work on Bernard.

[4] *Bernard de Clairvaux.* Commission d'histoire de l'Ordre de Cîteaux, VIIIème centenaire de la mort de Saint-Bernard (Aiguebelle-Paris, 1953) as well as *Mélanges Saint Bernard.* XXIVème Congrès de l'Association bourguignonne des Sociétés Savantes: Dijon 1953). Also *Bernard von Clairvaux, Mönch und Mystiker* , ed Joseph Lortz. Internationaler Bernhardkongress, Veröffentlichungen des Instituts für europaïsche Geschichte Mainz 6 (Wiesbaden: Franz Steiner Verlag, 1955).

[5] An invaluable collection of Leclercq's research results is *Recueil d'études sur Saint Bernard et ses écrits* 1–3 (Rome 1962–69). Leclercq's attractive *Saint Bernard et l'espirit cistercien* (Paris. Editions du Seuil, 1966) appeared as *Bernard of Clairvaux and the Cistercian Spirit* in Cistercian Publications in 1976. See also Leclercq's *Bernard de Clairvaux* (Paris: Desclée de Brouwer, 1989).

[6] Here the dry and factual biography by Watkin Williams, *Saint Bernard of Clairvaux* (Westminster, Maryland: The Newman Press, 1952) seems to have discouraged interest in Bernard, while the much lighter and more attractive work of Bruno Scott James, such as his *Saint Bernard of Clairvaux: An Essay in Biography* (London: Hodder and Stoughton, 1957) seems not to have gained much attention in the United States. One of the problems in american interest in Bernard may well have been the fact that american academics are notoriously reluctant to read works in other languages, even in French and German. A work has to be available in a good english translation in order really 'to exist' for the greater segment of the academic public.

of the few bridges between the French and English speaking world in the 1940s and 1950s was the monk of Gethsemani, Father Louis, better known as Thomas Merton. His *The Seven Storey Mountain* from 1948 made the american Cistercians of the Strict Observance, also called Trappists, much better known than ever before in their history in the New World. But in his everyday life in his crowded monastery in Kentucky, Father Louis spent much of his time reading in the original latin the twelfth-century cistercian fathers, especially Bernard of Clairvaux. I have had the opportunity to see some of his original manuscripts and his notes at Gethsemani, and they give one the impression of a scholar who worked carefully and methodically.[7] From Merton's correspondence, in French as in English, one can also see that he respected the lead of french scholarship in bernardian studies.

Merton's great contribution, here as elsewhere, was not so much his formulation of revolutionary ideas as his ability to make his subject accessible to a broad english-speaking public.[8] Merton's work pointed to the relevance of Bernard's life and thought for the contemporary debate on the directions monasticism was taking: the question of personal piety and community liturgy, the desire of many monks to live for shorter or longer periods as hermits, the problem of authority and the decision-making process in the monastery, and the dilemma of the bonds between the monastery and the world. Merton wanted to understand Bernard as a person who summed up in his life the aspirations of his age but who could also speak to other ages. At a time when trappist-cistercian vocations were booming and new foundations were

[7] I owe a debt of gratitude to Brother Patrick Hart, former secretary of Thomas Merton, for many good conversations on the subject of Merton, and for making it possible for me to see, for example, Merton's original typescript of a then (1986) unpublished book on Aelred of Rievaulx. I had always thought of Merton as a spiritual writer, not as an historian of christian spirituality, and I was delighted to discover his Aelred work, now published in segments in *Cistercian Studies* 20–24 (1985–89).

[8] The most convenient collection for Merton's use of Bernard is *Thomas Merton on St Bernard*, CS 9 (1980).

springing up from the mother houses in New England, Kentucky, and Iowa, Thomas Merton emerged as what we in retrospect might call the first well-known american cistercian scholar. To his reading public he was known as a Trappist, a member of a strict, apparently post-medieval order whose members never, or almost never, talked. Trappist silence enabled Merton to spend time with the very talkative monks of the twelfth century: Bernard and his band of friends became Merton's friends and helped him rediscover the medieval sources of his monastic life and the cistercian roots beneath its trappist surface.

It was not the Trappists (O.C.S.O), however, but the Cistercians of the Common Observance (O.Cist.) who underwrote the publication of a critical latin edition of the works of Bernard. The first volume appeared in 1957 and confirmed the promise of the 1953 congresses and the books which emerged from them. Bernard now became available in a standard edition that eventually replaced the problematic volumes in Migne's *Patrologia Latina*.[9] Bernard studies could rest on a solid foundation, all the more important in the 1960s, when the Second Vatican Council called for the reevaluation of all institutions within Roman Catholic Christianity, including monasticism. Debates on the role of the church in society affected the question of how monks and nuns contribute to the life of the church. It was only natural for scholars, monastic and secular, to turn to the works of Saint Bernard and to see what he had said on such matters.

In America community discussions became commonplace in monasteries where once silence had reigned. In the course of the 1960s the rule of absolute silence was replaced by more and more periods in the monastic day when talking

---

[9] *Sancti Bernardi Opera* 1: *Sermones super Cantica Canticorum* 1–35, edd. Jean Leclercq, C.H. Talbot, Henri M. Rochais. The series was completed in 1977 with Volume 8, dedicated to the Letters of Bernard. In the later volumes, C.H.Talbot does not appear as editor.

was acceptable, even desirable.[10] For the first time many monks and nuns had to face their brethren as social beings instead of maintaining a silent distance from them. Resulting encounters, and the restlessness of the times, meant that many Cistercians, especially men who had been trained for priesthood in a curriculum designed for pastors, left the monastery. Some returned later, but even today in the folk memory of many communities, the end of the 1960s and the early 1970s is recalled with some bitterness.[11] It was a time of difficult adjustment. Communities had to face a shrinkage that often exceeded fifty percent. Sometimes even abbots resigned and departed, leaving their communities with a sense of personal loss and bewilderment.

The tragic accidental death of Merton at a conference on monasticism east and west in Bangkok in 1968 may well have intensified this sense of the collapse of the hopes and dreams of the Council period of the mid–60s. But for us who are privileged to look at events from a certain chronological distance, the Bangkok conference should also be seen as a positive turning point. One of its participants, Jean Leclercq, here made contacts with american monks and arrangements were made for him to visit their houses. In the furious debate about the meaning of monasticism and in the prevailing, sometimes superficial admiration for everything eastern, there emerged a cosmopolitan monk who drank from the sources of the twelfth century and knew Bernard so well that he could easily deepen the scholarly side of Merton's work and at the same time address the importance of Bernard in terms of contemporary monasticism. In the hurricane of change there remained a peaceful centre where monks could find guidance and meaning.

[10] James Jaksa and Ernest L. Stech, *Voices from Silence: The Trappists Speak* (Toronto: Griffin House, 1980).

[11] This assertion is based on talks with abbots and monks during visits to cistercian houses in the United States in the 1980s.

The Founding of Cistercian Publications

In the context of this monastic revolution of the late 1960s, trappist cistercian abbots charged with the formation of young monks and nuns seem to have realized that it was essential to their region that monks and nuns consider the origins and foundation of their order in order to anchor their lives in something solid. To do so, they could do nothing better than read Bernard. Strange as it may now seem, few monks and nuns in their formation training until then had been encouraged to read Bernard. Many of them had never even heard of other twelfth-century cistercian figures such as William of Saint Thierry and Aelred of Rievaulx.

The opening to medieval cistercian theology and history, however, came at the same time as the change to the vernacular. New recruits were no longer always required to learn latin, for the liturgy at most houses abandoned latin.[12] It was thus important to make Bernard available in English. Much of his work had already been translated, but in large tomes and in a flowery style.[13] In 1969 Cistercian Publications was founded. Its chief editor was Basil Pennington, monk of Saint Joseph's Abbey, Spencer, Massachusetts. The very first lines of his 'editor's note' show the orientation of his efforts: 'This series is sponsored by the cistercian communities of America primarily to provide cistercian monks and nuns with good english translations of the Fathers of the Order'.[14] One notices immediately that the word 'trappist'

---

[12] In this connection there is the story of how one monk in an american house was shocked when in praying the psalms for the first time in English, he discovered how aggressive some of the texts are. He had 'understood' the psalms in latin in his own way, but the new translation forced him to confront an aspect of the Psalms that previously had been hidden from him.

[13] Still used in monasteries and revered by an older generation of monks are the irish trappist Ailbe John Luddy's translations, *Saint Bernard's Sermons on the Canticle of Canticles* 1–2 (Dublin: Browne and Noland, 1920) and *Saint Bernard's Sermons for the Seasons and the Principal Festivals of the Year* 1–3 (Dublin: 1921–25).

[14] *The Works of Bernard of Clairvaux* 1: *Treatises* 1 (Shannon: Irish University Press, 1970) p ix. Dr. E. Rozanne Elder has, however, kindly pointed out

was not used. From now on, 'cistercian' would stand for the two Orders that traced their roots back to the twelfth century and which found their greatest writer and representative in Bernard of Clairvaux. The monks of Spencer (OCSO) thus stretched out a hand to the american Cistercians (O.Cist.), especially to a learned group of hungarian emigré monks that staffed a university at Dallas, Texas, and was intellectually led by the outstanding historian of monastic life, Louis Lekai.

At the same time, however, there was nothing in Basil Pennington's declaration about any secular audience. While scholars and students slowly discovered the books, he pointed out that the new translations were directly aimed at the contemporary cistercian debate. The four texts in the first volume of Cistercian Publications, Pennington wrote, 'have a very special relevance to the present time when we are intent upon monastic renewal. Renewal in its fullest sense was one of the basic thrusts of the cistercian spirit'. In defining the cistercian life, Pennington and his co-editors chose Bernard's *Apology* to his friend William of Saint Thierry, with its criticism of lax monastic practices. As background for discussions about authority, Bernard *On Precept and Dispensation* was appropriate. And in the pivotal debate about changes in the liturgy and the office, Pennington took the prologue to the Cistercian Antiphonary and Bernard's Office of Saint Victor. Together with the texts themselves, as important today as they were in 1970, the translators and commentators can be seen as central persons in the growth of cistercian studies: the versatile and pivotal Jean Leclercq; Chrysogonus Waddell, monk of Gethsemani, expert on liturgical chant and history and friend of Merton; Michael Casey, monk of Tarrawarra in Australia and future Bernard expert; as well as Conrad Greenia, monk of Mepkin in South Carolina and astute translator;

----

to me that Father Basil Pennington involved secular scholars from the outset of Cistercian Publications. They were few but made up an editorial committee.

and Martinus Cawley, an Australian who had joined a daughter house of Spencer which in 1955 moved from New Mexico to Oregon, Our Lady of Guadalupe. Cawley, like many other monk priests of this generation, had been trained in Rome and learned Latin almost as a second language. He developed a love of language that persists in his later work. All these monks have been important in the growth of cistercian studies in the last two decades and fortunately are still with us today, as is Basil Pennington himself. Their traditional knowledge of Latin, flair for language, and ability to translate into fluent English, all these qualities were necessary to make the new series attractive to a new generation of monks and nuns.

Ambition and fiscal reality can conflict with each other in our time as they did in the twelfth century. The first handsome volumes of Cistercian Publications were printed in Ireland and distributed from Spencer. Repeated strikes and price rises in Ireland led the publications to locate new printers in the United States. The project proved to be more time-consuming than a single monk could handle. At the same time the individual cistercian houses in the United States were experiencing a financial crunch. In the early 1970s the traditional source of income at american monasteries, farming, was no longer paying its way, and monasteries had to look for new ways of making a living. It was difficult in these circumstances, with a slowdown in new vocations and an increase in critical voices about the monastic life in general, to find support for the impressive but limited-circulation volumes not only of translations but also of critical studies, often from symposia for a few select monk scholars.[15]

[15] As is the case with *The Cistercian Spirit: A Symposium. In Memory of Thomas Merton*, ed. Basil Pennington (Washington, D.C.: Consortium Press, 1973). This is very much of an 'in house' work in which the monastic participants in the seminar (all male) felt obliged to work towards conclusions on the connection between the intentions of Cîteaux's founders and contemporary cistercian life.

The Appearance of the Cistercian Scholar

Just at the time Cistercian Publications needed a new and broader foundation, something of a modern miracle began to happen. Of all places, it came about in the oddly-named city of Kalamazoo, tucked away in Michigan halfway between Detroit and Chicago.[16] Here a group of dynamic young professors, headed by professor of history John Sommerfeldt, had in 1962 begun holding a biennial medieval studies conference. The original purpose was to invite colleagues and high school teachers from the area to come and learn more about the Middle Ages.[17] Forty-five attended that first very regional meeting. But in the heady days of the late 1960s, when anything seemed possible in America, the Medieval Conference at Western Michigan University became an annual event which began to attract medieval scholars from all over the country. Its special quality was its informality and openness. Graduate students who had never before delivered a paper to an academic forum were welcome to come and try out, as it were, at Kalamazoo.

Since John Sommerfeldt was especially interested in Bernard of Clairvaux, it was only natural that he invited both religious and secular scholars to give papers on cistercian

---

[16] Kalamazoo is, of course, an Indian name, but in America is perhaps best known for the popular song 'I've got a girl in Kalamazoo'. At the Medieval Congress one year, buttons were distributed with the logo, 'Yes, there really is a Kalamazoo.'

[17] To my knowledge there is no written account of the history of the Medieval Congress at Western Michigan University, but Professor Cornelius Loew is at work on this much-needed narrative. My description of its early development is based on talks in the spring of 1989 with Professor George Beech of the Department of History and the Medieval Institute. George Beech worked together with Otto Gründler (now head of the Medieval Institute), John Sommerfeldt (now professor of history at Dallas University), and Rozanne Elder (now head of the Institute for Cistercian Studies). Other colleagues at Western Michigan University also contributed, but my sources inform me that John Sommerfeldt and his wife Pat were the central figures in the planning and execution of the first congresses. 'They did the lion's share.'

life and spirituality in the Middle Ages.[18] The early success of the conference was accompanied by the setting up at Western Michigan University of a Medieval Institute.[19] Contact between Cistercian Publications and the new Institute came as a result of its Director's scholarly orientation. In the early–1970s, when Cistercian Publications at Spencer was in need of a new home, Kalamazoo provided the best possible alternative. The Publications and Western Michigan University collaborated in establishing a twin Institute of Cistercian Studies. Gethsemani Abbey in Kentucky contributed to the new Institute by placing on permanent loan its Obrecht Collection of rare books and manuscripts relevant to medieval and post-medieval cistercian history. The new Cistercian Institute library gave the University a resource that began to attract scholars first from elsewhere in the United States and eventually from all over the world. The Medieval Congress, which soon became annual, the Medieval Institute, and the Institute of Cistercian Studies and its library, put Kalamazoo and Western Michigan University on the academic map of the world. At prestigious academic congresses in Europe and in centuries-old universities where medieval studies flourished, Kalamazoo became a 'household word'.[20]

[18] This development is described by John Sommerfeldt himself in his 'Introduction' to *Studies in Medieval Cistercian History* 2, CS 24 (1976) pp xi-xii. In September 1970 about fifty scholars met at St. Joseph's Abbey in Spencer 'sponsored by Cistercian Publications' whose 'primary purpose was to foster studies of cistercian life and thought'. A second meeting took place in October 1972 at the cistercian house near Dallas. Subsequently the first Cistercian Studies Conference took place at Kalamazoo on May 16 to 19. 'Two sessions were held at which eleven fine papers were presented', as part of the Conference on Medieval Studies.

[19] Western Michigan University grew out of a State Teachers' College founded in the early years of the twentieth century. In the 1950s it attained university status and distinguished itself as being one of the few secular universities in the United States which had a department of Religion.

[20] As I had the privilege of experiencing at a Congress on Bernard of Clairvaux at the Herzog August Bibliothek in Wolfenbüttel, Germany, in October 1990. Here several speakers referred to papers given in the spring of 1990 at Kalamazoo.

In moving to Kalamazoo, Cistercian Publications, as it were, changed its audience and redefined its role. From aiming principally at english-reading monks and nuns, the publications now aspired to reach a broader audience, offering academics texts on monastic life in past and present and students with good, relatively inexpensive translations of monastic texts.

The move to Kalamazoo confirmed a new orientation that had already been in the making. At an orthodox-cistercian symposium held under Publications sponsorship at Oxford in 1973, 'One Yet Two: Monastic Tradition East and West', many participants were non-monks. One of them, Professor Bernard Hamilton of the University of Nottingham, provided an assessment of the conference that today seems prophetic in terms of the new alliance between scholarship and spirituality, monks and lay persons:

> I am a Roman Catholic layman and a medieval historian and accepted the invitation to attend the Symposium chiefly because I wanted the opportunity to meet and talk with scholars from other countries working in the same field as myself. This I was able to do, which was helpful in many ways. But what distinguished this conference from similar academic gatherings was that all the matters discussed, even problems of detailed textual criticism, were approached primarily as aspects of the spiritual life. I found this specially valuable because it has helped me to set my own work more firmly in its religious context as part of the christian life.[21]

In retrospect it becomes apparent that this combination of love of learning and desire for God, to borrow from the title of Leclercq's seminal book, was consciously intended at Oxford or at Kalamazoo in early 1970s. The meeting of learned monks and nuns with secular scholars brought about

[21] *One Yet Two: Monastic Tradition East and West.* Orthodox - Cistercian Symposium, Oxford University 26 August–1 September 1973, ed. Basil Pennington, CS 29 (Kalamazoo, 1976) p 4, note 6.

a fruitful milieu for discussing the history of christianity in terms of monastic developments, without the requirement that the results of such discussion confirm any sectarian views. Scholars could deal with Bernard without feeling obliged to bow to Rome and declare him a saint. Yet the presence of monks and nuns made it impossible to overlook the impact his life and teaching could have on people's lives. The very lack of any compulsion to piety probably contributed more than any other factor to making it possible for the contributors to the cistercian conferences to grow into a community of scholars deeply involved with spirituality and crossing barriers not only between disciplines but also between ways of life.

One of the contributors to the 1973 Oxford conference was E. Rozanne Elder, a recent Toronto Ph.D. who had written a thesis on the Christology of William of Saint Thierry and was the newly-appointed Editorial Director of Cistercian Publications. When John Sommerfeldt left Kalamazoo in the summer of 1978 to take over a position at the University of Dallas, she assumed leadership of the Cistercian Institute as well as Cistercian Publications. Rozanne Elder sums up the special combination of ecumenism, spirituality and scholarship that has become the cistercian studies trademark. She is an active Anglican but has gained full acceptance in Roman Catholic monastic circles. A scholar in her own right, Dr. Elder continues to produce work on William of St Thierry. She is an organizer not only in terms of editing books but also in making Kalamazoo a centre for contacts between cistercian scholars and cistercian monasteries in North America. Rozanne Elder accepted from the start the drudgery of practical chores connected with conferences and editing, as well as business managing. She opened her home to the new people that began appearing in Kalamazoo, just as John Sommerfeldt and his wife Pat had done, and made them feel more than welcome.

It is probably at Kalamazoo that the concept of the 'cistercian scholar' was invented. It has been clear from the

mid–1970s that such a person, male or female, is not necessarily a monk or nun but is someone who studies monks
and nuns, in history or in their life today. Almost ironically,
it has been fortunate for Bernard studies that Rozanne Elder's specialty is not Bernard. She has been able to look at
new work on him from a certain distance and to require that
Bernard not be seen in isolation in close textual studies, but
also in terms of his relationships to other monastic figures,
both in his own time and in later periods. Since 1978 the
study of Saint Bernard has continued to be the foundation
of cistercian studies, but also a point of departure for many
other approaches to the history of christian spirituality and
spiritual life.

The Growth of Bernard Studies and the Cistercian Conference

The Medieval Conference at Kalamazoo used to commit
one very narrow room to the Cistercian Studies group. When
I first attended the Conference in 1978, the Cistercians had
seven sessions, in which twenty-two papers were given.[22] Of
these sessions, one was dedicated to Bernard, another to
'other fathers', one on Merton, one on the Cistercians in the
seventeenth century, one on the cistercian impact, and two
on cistercian art. This distribution of interests has been fairly
standard ever since: there are almost always three to five
papers on Bernard, while Merton has frequently been given
his own special sessions at the conference.

What surprised me most at that very first session at 1 pm
on Thursday 4 May 1978 in Room 105, was the congenial-
ity of the atmosphere at the Cistercian Studies Conference.
Obviously, many of the participants knew each other from
earlier meetings, but there was no sense of an 'old boys'

[22] I base these statistics on the Conference program, issued by the
Medieval Institute usually in January. When the conference takes place in
May, there are often many changes. The papers I mention I can remember
being given, while the statistics on the number of papers actually given
might need to be adjusted slightly.

club that looked after its own people. The first speaker was a protestant theologian who presented eloquently 'Ethical Theory in the Sermons on the Canticle'. I was taken aback to find that a teacher at a protestant seminary would deal with Bernard at all.[23] In the ensuing discussion all contributions were welcome. During the next few days I discovered how monks and scholars met each other in a friendly and open way. When Edward McCorkell, then abbot of Berryville in Virginia, invited me to come to his monastery and speak to his novices about my work on Caesarius of Heisterbach, I was amazed. What could I tell young american men about the thirteenth century that would help them in their attempt to discern the meaning of the call they felt?

Whatever my doubts and hesitations, I saw from the first day that the Cistercian Studies Conference provided a congenial atmosphere of scholarship and friendship. In the background was the liturgy, a daily early mass whose existence I did not even discover until the next time I came to Kalamazoo. No one asked if one were a Catholic or not: the passport to the cistercian group was an interest in things cistercian. There was no question of showing loyalty or dissent. I could say the most awful things about Bernard of Clairvaux and still be understood. Later I realized that my seemingly drastic statements paled by comparison with what some monks could say! They knew the life from the inside, and they had been spending years in an inner dialogue with Bernard's writings, using some, discarding others.

There are other groups at Kalamazoo that have formed in the course of the years where there is similar dialogue

[23] This was William Paulsell, then of Atlantic Christian College, now President of the Lexington (Kentucky) Theological Seminary (Disciples of Christ). Rozanne Elder has in a letter (8 October 1990) aptly commented on my reaction: 'Your amazement at Bill Paulsell's paper in 1978 really tells more about your situation than about the american scene. We were fairly used to Protestants, Anglicans, and Catholics all studying things medieval, including theology and spirituality, together. Coming from a Reformation environment, you found it more startling than we did.'

between religious and seculars, such as Dominican studies, canons regular, Franciscans, and the *Vox Benedictina* group led by Margot King of Toronto, with its concern for women and mysticism. But the Cistercian Studies Conference has continued to show scholarship combined with spirituality without descending into sermonizing or sectarianism. One of the yearly highlights for the Cistercian Studies group is the paper given by Chrysogonus Waddell of Gethsemani, with his source studies on the origins of the cistercian liturgy or of the background for Cîteaux's reform. In 1978 I unwittingly missed a sparkling joust between Waddell and Louis Lekai about the cistercian reforms of the seventeenth century. Here the trappist tradition was pitted against that of the 'common observance' cistercians in a fraternal argument, with no holds barred. Louis Lekai's disabling illness from the early 80s has ended his participation at Kalamazoo, but his brethren from Dallas continue to attend and to make their contribution to the ongoing redefinition of cistercian history.

Monks and nuns who normally went to bed by eight or nine in the evening showed a great capacity for enjoying food, drink and conversation late into the evening. Somehow they managed to get to the early mass, and this combination of partying and praying perhaps provided a necessary support for the solid scholarly results of the annual conferences. As I have looked back over the programmes of the Medieval Congress, organized skilfully by the Medieval Institute under Otto Gründler, and the concurrent Cistercian Studies Conference of the Cistercian Institute, I can see that papers on Bernard have by no means been dominant. And yet Bernard has been a constant point of reference for a great number of presentations. In 1986, there were two sessions on Bernard out of eight cistercian sessions, and here we find scholars such as Denis Farkasfalvy, now abbot of Dallas, Francis Kline, then of Gethsemani, now abbot of Mepkin, Sister Kilian Hufgard, an Ursuline whose many studies of Bernard

and art now have led to a book on the topic[24] , and Thomas
Renna, a layman who in the course of the years has approached Bernard from many different perspectives . Several
of the papers dedicated to Bernard would take a small part
of his literary production and look at it intensively in order
to understand its meaning. But such lectures would almost
never end in academic overspecialization and aridity: the audience would inevitably expect some broader theme which
perhaps could be applied to spiritual life today, whether implicitly or explicitly. At the same time the many papers on
cistercian art and architecture, about two sessions per year,
organized faithfully by Meredith Lillith of Syracuse University, would succeed in getting a new audience for Bernard
and unexpected attention to the role of the Cistercians in
their so-called golden age.

At times I would find a presentation to be more a rew. rd-
ing of the text than a rethinking of the material at hand.
Since Bernard writes so well, speakers can delight in quoting him at length. Sometimes talks in the Cistercian Studies
group, especially on Bernard, have been more homilies than
lectures. In recent years, as more and more cistercian nuns
have gained an opportunity to attend the conference, I have
noticed that many of them, though bright and insightful students, lack basic training in academic research and methods.
Their papers have been inspiring rather than investigative.
Despite centuries-long efforts from Rome to shut the nuns
off from the world, it is my hope that educational opportunities available to monks will also be extended to nuns. A
process of enlightenment has begun in America that ecclesiastical male chauvinism will not be able to stop. The onrush
of studies on Bernard will make it easier for nuns as well
as monks to draw on the wealth of knowledge now available
to them through Cistercian Publications and the increasing

[24] *Saint Bernard of Clairvaux. A Theory of Art Formulated from his Writings
and Illustrated in Twelfth-Century Works of Art*. Mediaeval Studies 2 (Lewis-
ton/Queenston/Lampeter: The Edwin Mellen Press, 1989).

number of contacts within the Order and with secular scholars. There is a fine line between scholarship and homily, one that can be established only if the student can place his or her work in the context of a research tradition and can engage in a dialogue with other scholars.

This has been the Kalamazoo miracle. Through the 1980s, in an increasingly polarized American Catholic church, the Cistercian Studies Conference has continued to provide discussion and academic foment for scholars unafraid to admit the role of spirituality in history. One of the *agents provocateurs* in this process is the formidable David N. Bell, whose ironic smile, seemingly harsh tongue but gentle eyes I first met at the 1978 conference. Oxford-trained and professor of religion at the Memorial University of Newfoundland, Bell has made use of the Kalamazoo conference and of Cistercian Publications to focus his work on the sources of William of Saint Thierry and on the cistercian intellectual tradition, especially in England, in the later Middle Ages.[25] At the same time as he works on latin monastic sources, Bell has published widely in the field of Coptic studies. His vast knowledge of eastern religions and languages has been available to oppose many of the modish comparisons between East and West that plagued medieval and religious scholarship in the 1970s and early 1980s. But behind his bearish facade Bell has revealed himself as a generous and responsive scholar greatly appreciated and even loved.

Another scholar who has contributed greatly to the congenial atmosphere of the conference has been Luke Anderson, prior of a 'common observance' Cistercian monastery in Pennsylvania. In recent years he has taught theology at the Divinity School in Princeton and is a rare Roman Catholic clerical figure at gatherings of Calvin experts. His warmth and humour are infectious, just as his presentations are

---

[25] David N. Bell's diversity of interests is indicated by his latest book, A Cloud of Witnesses: An Introductory History of the Development of Christian Doctrine, CS 109 (1989).

original and surprising in the way they show the importance of Bernard's theology to scholastic and Reformation writers.

Delightful though I would find it, I have no intention here of providing a catalogue of the personalities involved at the Cistercian Studies Conference. The scholars who came during the 1970s and 1980s were gathered once again for the great conference held in May of 1990 in conjunction with the Medieval Congress and celebrating the nine-hundredth anniversary of Bernard's birth. Here John Sommerfeldt, assisted by the Cistercian Institute, organized twenty-seven sessions, of which twenty were directly concerned with Bernard. There were ninety papers planned, and most of them were given. The Cistercian Studies Conference had already moved in the early 1980s into a much larger conference room. For this occasion it completely left the core area of the Medieval Conference and went up the hill to the ascetic basement of the Episcopal-Lutheran chaplaincy, Saint Aidan's Chapel, and to the plush air-conditioned Fetzer Business Center. In 1990 the Cistercian Studies group held two and sometimes three concurrent sessions at once. The International Centre for Medieval Art, as well as the Society for the Study of the Crusades and the Latin East, also held sessions centred on Bernard. At times it was impossible to make a fair choice between all the possibilities available. The Cistercian conference had become a reflection of the giant Medieval Congress itself: an embarrassment of riches and a consumer's dream . . . or nightmare.

Only the forthcoming publications from the Conference will reveal the quality of these presentations, but for me the 1990 conference confirmed the increasing commitment of the Cistercian Order to the idea of cistercian scholarship open to all thoughtful comers. A quiet but deeply constructive presence at many of the sessions was the Abbot General of the Strict Observance, Dom Ambrose Southey, who seemed to enjoy the discussions immensely. More Europeans than ever gave cistercian papers this year, even a few Danes who managed to find their way across oceans of academic separation.

This infusion of european research traditions provides american scholars with a standard of comparison for their work. The great Jean Leclercq was unable to attend to give his paper 'In Search of the Real Bernard'. Fortunately he was aptly replaced by the australian Michael Casey, whose Athirst for God: Spiritual Desire in Bernard of Clairvaux's Sermons on the Song of Songs (CS 77) published in 1987, has provided a new impulse to Bernard scholarship.

In his writings as well as in his Kalamazoo presentation, Casey has attempted to make Bernard available to an audience that has difficulty in reading and understanding him. Casey does not expect his listeners or readers to like Bernard, at least not at the beginning. His point of departure is the fundamental difference between Bernard's way of life and mode of expression and our own. In the talk, given in a plenary session of the Medieval Congress, Casey even defined Bernard's character in terms of the Briggs-Meyers personality categories. Such an approach displeased at least one distinguished american medievalist, who later told me that he had considered walking out in the middle of the lecture. But many listeners found, perhaps for the first time, that Bernard had been presented in a way that made him understandable in terms of networks of friendship and social background.

Michael Casey's belief in an approachable Bernard is undermined by his assertion that no modern translation can fairly convey the content of Bernard's message. At the same time as Casey, who himself translates Bernard, makes the difficult saint accessible to larger audiences, he creates a distance. Perhaps this is necessary in order to maintain scholarly integrity, but it reveals a schizophrenia that can be found in a larger reaction to the success of cistercian studies. Academics have often told me how they admire the success of the Cistercian Conference and the ability of Cistercian Publications to provide new translations and studies. But they also express reservations, only sometimes justified, about the quality of the work being presented. Behind the seeming welcome of a scholarly initiative lie old prejudices and forms of snobbery. Such a contradictory attitude is difficult to document and can only be asserted here as an impression one gains from academic shoptalk. But it is clear that any such initiative will always be looked upon with suspicion for combining popular appeal and accessibility on the one hand with solid scholarship on the other.

Saint Bernard on the Cistercian Circuit

At the Kalamazoo conference in 1980 the abbot of New Clairvaux at Vina, Thomas Davis, invited me to come to his monastery and share some of my research with his monks. I took the invitation to a cistercian house more seriously than I had done in 1978, perhaps partly because of a growing curiosity about modern monks, and perhaps because of the very name 'New Clairvaux'. How could any community of men, I wondered, four hours away from the places where I had grown up in the San Francisco Bay Area, take on the name of Bernard's own monastery and consider itself to be his successor?

It was not until 1982 that I came, with danish wife and then two year old korean son, to this lush grove and former Stanford estate in the great Central Valley of a California that I hardly knew. This new encounter was like 1978 and the Kalamazoo conference all over again, but even more complete an experience. I would go from choir, where I was guided through the office, to chapter house, where I took the abbot's place in conveying the meaning of the cistercian life. As an historian, I had a distance to my subject, but as a twentieth-century person among sceptical, challenging monks, I had an audience I never before had met.

In 1986 Rozanne Elder arranged for me to go on what she has named 'the cistercian circuit', a speaking tour of a number of monasteries where I would lecture as I had done at New Clairvaux. That spring, on the way to Kalamazoo, I crisscrossed the United States and visited six houses for men. It was an overwhelming experience, an immersion in the monastic life I had never before had, and a unique chance to try out the results of my research with a sensitive and responsive audience. Even though (especially at evening lectures) monks would be fighting sleep (and some would succumb, just as monks do in medieval *exemplum* stories), I found their questions and comments far more exciting than the response I often got in lecturing at universities. There I inevitably came in the middle of a busy term and received apologies from medievalists who could not make it to my lecture and wanted a copy. For the select audience that did show up, I would give my performance, get some polite questions, and then be dismissed.

For me the cistercian experience was much more complete, for it gave an opportunity to live for a few days with the members of my audience, and to get their reactions at leisure either after the lectures or when they came to see me individually. Inevitably some of the personal interviews turned into the beginnings of friendships that since 1984 have grown and developed, as I have returned time and again to the american cistercian houses.

Where is Bernard in all this? I am just one of a number of cistercian scholars who in the past years has made the cistercian circuit. We are a privileged group that can reflect on the experience of the twelfth century in order to get a response from twentieth-century men and women for whom the foundation of the Order, the role of Bernard, and its development after his death are of vital interest. We meet men and women who regularly read Bernard or who have decided NOT to read him, because they had him forcefed when they were novices and did not like the experience. For those who read him, Bernard can be part of *lectio*, their meditation on a spiritual text, often done in the dark hours of the early morning after vigils when the monk or nun is particularly open and responsive to the few outside impulses that are allowed to penetrate. For such people, Bernard is part of a living experience, as one monk once wrote me:

So why do I read Bernard? I think my interest in him began because I realized early on in my monastic life (some ten years ago) that it was important that I be in touch with some of the outstanding spiritual leaders of our tradition if I were going to be able at all to understand what it meant to be a cistercian. I don't think tradition needs to be an inhibiting or binding factor, but that it can give a sense of direction, a sense of where we have come from and what avenues might be open for us for the future within a particular lineage. I have come to understand the concept of teaching lineage within the eastern traditions and think it has something to offer those of us in the West. Too often we seem more than willing to submit ourselves to the teaching of another tradition rather than to explore the rich heritage that is ours by right.[26]

These eloquent lines perhaps sum up what happened to the study of Bernard in many monasteries in the 1980s. While the Cistercians for generations had looked to other schools of spirituality in which to establish their inner lives, monks and nuns in the 1980s began turning to the tradition of their own Order. The practice of apophatic meditation and an interest in eastern mysticism introduced in the 1970s has continued in several monasteries, but the texts now more and more abundantly available in Cistercian Publications are also being read and used. The advantage of reading Bernard is the sense, expressed above, of his being 'ours by right'. Entitlement could bring curiosity about the development of the cistercian tradition. Monks—and now nuns too—are asking what happened to cistercian life and spirituality after the death of Bernard. What, if anything, went wrong? Why did an older generation of monks and nuns prefer such devotional tracts as writings about Thérèse of Lisieux or *The Imitation of Christ*? What role do affective bonds have in monastic life?

[26] From a monk of Snowmass, Colorado, a monastery to which I have returned time and again and where I find openness, joy and courage in a meeting between the cistercian tradition and the contemporary world.

What could the experience of the twelfth century say about friendship and sexuality? As one monk wrote to me:

> Although the nuns surrender more of their freedom to the abbess, in return she becomes a real mother-figure, especially for the younger nuns, and gives them the affection they need. But in monasteries of monks, the abbot (and generally all monks) keep a certain affective distance, especially from the younger ones. This is a situation that needs to be addressed openly, putting aside or laying bare all homophobic, homosexual and homogenital fears. God will *not* supply human affectivity. Only the community can (and *must*) do that.[27]

Such dilemmas monks and nuns have posed to me, and I in turn have often been able to refer them to writings of Bernard or of other Cistercian Fathers. In studying the literature and practice of friendship in monastic life in the early 1980s, I realized that good friendships normally are to be found in the twelfth century in good and loving communities. I saw how the bonds monks had with each other found expression within thriving monasteries, where economic success, spiritual depth, and human relations all mattered. Before I began looking at the sources themselves, I had thought of friendship as something stolen from the community, for I took my point of departure in the post-tridentine fear of 'particular friendships' that undermine community life. In the twelfth century I found networks of friendship among monks and nuns of different communities. I could visit twentieth-century monasteries and talk about how friendship can contribute to the growth of community.

In my talks, I have perhaps allowed myself to sermonize too much and have not been careful about the distance an historian must have in order to deal with his subject from all possible aspects. But monks and nuns themselves have encouraged enquiries into the perennial problems of celibate

[27] Letter of 10 September 1989.

community life. The very openness of monks about themselves, their self-doubt, their fears, all this for me has been very much in the spirit of twelfth-century monastic life, where letters of friendship concerned such matters. I have felt especially privileged to be able to speak to some abbots about their ways of experiencing their roles in the monastery. Here I often find the same combination of self-confidence and humility that I think characterized Bernard's approach to his position.

This accessibility of monks and nuns to a modern secular scholar parallels the relative openness of the Cistercian Studies Conference itself and the very spirit of twelfth-century christian humanism, rooted in belief in the ability of the human being to reach truth that can deepen a personal bond to the spiritual universe. Here knowledge counts, but not for itself, for it is but a step on the way to God. The thirst for God is summed up in the desire for human understanding through collegial relationships and genuine friendships.

For those who know better, this portrait of cistercian studies and the cistercian monasteries today in the light of Saint Bernard may seem like a naive glorification. Certainly for those who are involved in editing texts, writing new studies, or living the cistercian life itself, hard work is involved. There can be serious doubts and questioning about the meaning of it all. But on a visit to several monasteries in the spring of 1990, before the great Bernard conference at Kalamazoo, I was impressed by the way that several houses had arranged to make it possible for all members of the community to get to know and use Bernard better. At Wrentham in Massachusetts, for example, every member of the community belonged to a study group, whose theme was determined by the areas to be covered by a Bernard conference sponsored by both Orders in Rome in September of 1990. From Bernard on angels to Bernard and conversion to the cistercian life, the nuns of Wrentham have covered the writings of Bernard with a methodicalness and care characteristic of the women's houses in their response to cistercian life. At

Wrentham, where enclosure is interpreted with a strictness which exceeds anything visible in the mens' houses, individual nuns visited my temporary 'office' off the cloister to tell me how they were celebrating Bernard's birthday and what aspect of his writings was their special concern.

The Future of Cistercian Studies

Cistercian Publications has in its twenty-one year existence put out more than a hundred and fifty titles. By the end of 1991 it is planned that all the works of Bernard will be available in translation. At the same time a twelfth-century Cistercian Father like Aelred of Rievaulx, who was influenced by Bernard, is now available for the first time in a complete translation of his central theological work, The Mirror of Charity. New studies continue to appear on Bernard: Michael Casey's biography of Bernard is anticipated with great interest. Just as exciting are new studies on cistercian and other monastic women. Thanks to the editing of Sister Lillian Shank of Our Lady of Mississippi Abbey and to John A. Nichols of Slippery Rock University in Pennsylvania, a new generation interested in women's history has been able to make use of Cistercian Studies.[28] Here Jean Leclercq's work has, as in so much else, made an important contribution.[29] But what is most encouraging is the participation of women—both nuns and seculars—in the ongoing interpretation of Saint Bernard and his heritage.

Where do we go from here? The provocative David Bell holds the theory that the number of academic studies in the medieval field is directly proportional to the availability of translations in any given area. By this logic the number of new studies on Bernard should increase greatly in coming

---

[28] Medieval Religious Women 1: Distant Echoes, CS 71 (1984) and 2: Peace Weavers, CS 72 (1987), while 3: The Cistercian Monastic Woman: Hidden Springs is forthcoming.

[29] La femme et les femmes dans l'oeuvre de Saint Bernard (Paris: Editions Pierre Tequi, 1982), trans. as Women and Saint Bernard of Clairvaux, CS 104 (1989).

years, even though numbers are no guarantee of quality. Here it is perhaps a loss that the series 'Studies in Cistercian History', which reached eleven volumes, has been discontinued. These volumes contain some of the best papers of the Cistercian Studies Conference from the mid–1970s to the mid–1980s. It is only here, for example, that one gets an idea of the contributions of the literary historian Marsha Dutton, whose many studies of Cistercian Fathers, especially Aelred, have created controversy at many a cistercian session. Now cistercian scholars are encouraged to turn over the results of their research to cistercian journals, such as *Cistercian Studies* edited at Gethsemani (and from 1991 at Vina) or *Cîteaux: Commentarii Cistercienses*, published at Achel in Belgium and since 1986 at Cîteaux in France. In my view both of these journals have become far more international and interesting in recent years, to a certain degree thanks to the Kalamazoo papers that have been appearing in them.

One can fear that, as the number of scholars working on cistercian topics grows, the number of studies that are not properly vetted may also increase. Certainly it was easier to gain an overview in the 1970s when cistercian scholars had their own comfortable niche at Kalamazoo. But in this very success I can only sense a contemporary need for milieux where spirituality and scholarship combine, where scholars do not have to hide the fact that they believe in something, and where believers are expected to convey their ideas in terms of scholarship.

I hope that Kalamazoo will be able to continue the miracle of the 1970s, both in terms of publications and of contacts made at the congress and on the cistercian circuit. At times during cutbacks at Western Michigan University in the early 1980s, the very existence of the Cistercian Institute was threatened. The present unsettled situation in the world, especially in the Middle East, can easily bring a new assault on this centre for study and spirituality. If this happens, one can assume that scholars from all over the world will publicize the importance of having such a place at a secular university where there is room for religious studies and where people of all different backgrounds and commitments come together to study monasticism.

Would Bernard turn over in his grave (if he had one today!) at the sight of all this interest and, as Americans say, hype? I claim no direct line to him, but I can cite one of his letters, probably to William of Saint Thierry, in which Bernard reassured his audience that it could trust that he means what he says, but also that we must be prepared for all he is not yet ready to hand over to us:

> As I drew myself in my letter to you, so I really am; except that I could not express on paper all that I felt in my heart. You have not and never have had any reason at all to fear me.... I am not worthy of holy leisure, I am not privy to the holy peace of contemplation. But because you deem me worthy of yourself, I am yours and shall be yours as long as I live.
> The sermons you ask for are not yet ready, but they shall be got ready and you shall have them.[30]

Cistercian scholars will in coming years discuss to what extent Bernard meant what he said. They will continue to question his affective relationships, also with women. The pioneering work of Gilson and Leclercq will be supplemented by new interpretations of Bernard the theologian. The Atlantic Ocean will provide less and less of a barrier for cistercian scholars, many of whom in the Bernard year travelled both to Michigan and to european conferences in Dijon, Rome, Himmerod, Wolfenbüttel, or elsewhere. Bernard will probably remain a chimaera of his age and of our own, at one moment a central figure, at the next seemingly overrated and overextended beyond his just deserts.[31] I can only think

[30] Ep 506; SBOp 8:464, trans. James pp 128–29.

[31] Here the healthy scepticism of Pascal Phillips of Guadalupe Abbey was a refreshing alternative at the 1990 conference to the general tendency to put Bernard at the centre of twelfth-century life. I look forward to the publication of his paper, 'The Presence—and Absence—of Bernard

of his smiling at all this commotion, as America teaches, Europe learns, and new cistercian monks, nuns and scholars in the rest of the world also begin to involve themselves in a debate that involves both scholarship and spiritual life.[32]

in Medieval Chronicles', which he kindly let me read.

[32] I borrow the phrase *America docet* from Jean Leclercq, who in 1974 provided a valuable overview of bernardian studies, 'Saint Bernard in Our Times', *Saint Bernard of Clairvaux. Studies Commemorating the Eighth Centenary of his Canonization*, ed. Basil Pennington, CS 28 (1977) 1–26.

Epilogue

From Twelfth-Century Cistercians to Twentieth-Century Americans: Myths of 'The Valley of Fruitfulness' and 'The City on the Hill'

In the preceding pages I have looked at many aspects of the life and influence of Saint Bernard. I have tried to show that to a certain extent we can approach him as a human being within the context of his time. In his own age Bernard created controversy and through the centuries has remained at the centre of debates about monastic life, christian ideals, and involvement in the world. If Bernard remains for the reader a 'difficult saint', one whose inner life I have failed to capture, then I am not surprised or disappointed. For me Bernard remains accessible not in terms of who he 'really' was but through the impact he had on his surroundings and his successors. This approach explains why four of the nine preceding essays have limited themselves to Bernard after his death: the historical Bernard, what he really said or did or meant, will always to a certain extent remain submerged in the Bernard of the cistercian tradition. This Bernard for centuries slumbered at Clairvaux. His bones were scattered at the French Revolution, but today he in many ways has returned to us. Most importantly, in my mind, Bernard shows himself in the living witness of the two monastic orders which call themselves Cistercians and which continue to manifest the perennial vitality of Saint Bernard.

For me this enduring strength became visible in 1990 at the numerous congresses dedicated to Bernard. Originally I had felt that the nine-hundredth anniversary of Bernard's birth was a bad excuse for studying him, but in the course of the year I became aware of some of the new interpretations being offered of his place in medieval and modern history. At a congress on Bernard's*Rezeptionsgeschichte* at the great Herzog August Bibliothek in Wolfenbüttel, I expected to hear a number of boring papers from stuffy german professors. Instead I discovered an academic milieu, under the able leadership of Kaspar Elm of Berlin, in which Bernard came alive. It was as if something of the twelfth-century cistercian spirit managed to penetrate this outpost of Reformation Lutheranism and to reveal Bernard's presence behind many a reformation theologian. In the midst of a Bernard who, in the words of Christopher Holdsworth was 'everywhere and nowhere' in the twelfth and later centuries, I sensed the privilege of being a medieval historian who can deal with questions of historical origins and influence.

Myths of Origins

After two brief decades of writing history, I do not believe in anything resembling 'human nature' or 'innate' human characteristics. If the study of history teaches anything, it is that human behaviour here finds expression in many different varieties. In historical experience I see indications of how human communities and articulate individuals have tried to define themselves by accounting for their origins.

These explanations may conveniently be called myths.[1] Myths are not necessarily false. Whether or not they correspond to events that actually took place, they are stories

[1] For redefining myth in a positive manner, the work of Joseph Campbell deserves great credit. See his *The Masks of God* 1–4 (Harmondsworth 1976 for 1–2 and London Souvenir Press 1974 for 3–4) and *The Hero with a Thousand*

that not only deal with past events but which also influence present attitudes and behaviour. Myths are stories that refuse to become dated because they use the past to interpret the present. In this way myths shape the futures of the individuals and communities which make use of such stories. A myth can become what many cultural critics in the 1960s looked for: usable history, a history that makes a difference.[2] Such a form of history writing matters to people because it creates more than a collection of dusty artifacts and memories. The historian has to deal with such myths in the past, to see how they themselves change and how they shape human activities.

In his own day, Bernard drew on myth. When Bernard wrote to his fellow monks, he expressed a myth of cistercian devotion to the Rule of Saint Benedict. He encouraged his brethren by reminding them that he was with them in their sense of growth and renewal. Here Bernard contributed to the twelfth-century cistercian myth that the Order was a phenomenal success. As he wrote in the late 1130s to the monks of Grâce-Dieu:

> 'Who will give me the wings of a dove that I may fly away' (Ps 54:7) and see the good zeal of my sons, their progress, peace, order, and discipline? I want to see the new inhabitants in their new site, how they observe their Rule among strangers, how they 'sing the song of the Lord in a strange land' (Ps 136:4). Already I have flown to you in imagination and am with you in spirit, but, according to the words of the Lord, 'the spirit indeed is willing, but the flesh is weak' (Mt 26:41), and cannot just now follow the spirit. . . . [3]

Faces (Bollingen Series 12: Princeton 1972). Also Robert A. Segal, *Joseph A. Campbell. An Introduction* (New York and London: Garland, 1987).

[2] A book that heralded the requirement of the 1960s for a usable past was Raymond Williams, *Culture and Society* 1780–1950 (New York: Columbia University Press, 1958, reprinted as a Harper Torchbook by Harper and Row, 1966).

[3] SBOp 8:465, translated Bruno Scott James, p. 245. James rightly takes

Here we are in the midst of the cistercian expansion. It might be worthwhile to go back to the very beginning, before Bernard's arrival, to see how it all might have begun and what myths were formed and grew out of the Order's origins.

In what follows I intend to look at myth in a positive manner as a way of understanding the cistercian self-interpretation. But we must also consider to what extent such myths can become self-justifying and self-delusory. Precisely because myths have power to influence human behaviour, they can become twisted out of shape and be used to justify actions that are totally out of step with the intent of the original myth itself. In considering cistercian origins, I will deal with the realities that myths create in new surroundings. We will leave Bernard for moments but frequently return to him, even as we move from cistercian to american origins. I hope to leave the reader with the realization that myths are necessary in modern as in medieval life, but myths must be in harmony with past experience and present needs.

A Cistercian Myth: The Valley of Fruitfulness

When Abbot Robert and twenty-one monks came from the burgundian house of Molesme in 1098 and found what they prosaically called the new monastery, *novum monasterium*, they were looking for a more literal realization of the Rule of Saint Benedict than the life they until then had lived. This intention is clear from the later accounts we have of the move. Historians of early Cîteaux still debate the origins of these documents and their dating.[4] It is difficult, if not impossible, to approach the 'moment of creation' at Cîteaux. Our

---

the phrase *Quomodo apud extraneos militant* and translates it 'how they observe their Rule' because the language is derivative of the Rule's military imagery. According to Leclercq-Rochais, the letter was written soon after 1135 when the monastery was founded in the diocese of Saintes as a daughter of Clairvaux.

[4] For the early sources of Cîteaux, I have drawn on the texts and datings available in Jean de la Croix Bouton and Jean Baptiste Van Damme, *Les plus anciens textes de Cîteaux*, Cîteaux: Studia et Documenta 2 (Achel, 1974).

earliest records come from a time about twenty years after the events themselves. In spite of the lack of contemporary eyewitness accounts, we are still relatively close to the break with Molesme. Whoever chronicled the first years must have been in touch with monks who had participated in the original move.

But by 1120, the events of 1098 had already taken on a new perspective. For the earliest chroniclers, it was already a well-known 'fact' that the move to what they now called Cîteaux was decisive not just in founding a new monastery but also in creating the first integrated monastic Order. This new Order was set up according to a structure that went beyond anything prescribed in the Rule of Saint Benedict. The first cistercian chroniclers saw in the origins of Cîteaux a turning point in monastic life and history.

When the young noble Bernard and a crowd of his relatives and friends arrived at Cîteaux in 1113, the monastery had already sent out a group of men to found its first daughter house.[5] Contrary to later accounts, the arrival of Bernard did not 'save' the monastery from failure, but his presence undoubtedly was a shot in the arm for the new foundation.[6] Bernard assured that Cîteaux became the centre for a thriving

---

English translations are those of Bede Lackner in Louis J. Lekai, *The Cistercians: Ideals and Reality* (Kent State University Press, 1977). The central work on which I have drawn for the language of Bernard and William of Saint Thierry in terms of images of valley, fruitfulness and growth is that of Jean Baptiste Auberger, *L'unanimité cistercienne primitive: mythe ou realité*, Cîteaux: Studia et Documenta 3 (Achel, 1986). I do not agree with all Auberger's conclusions, for I find some of his distinctions between Stephen Harding's and Bernard's policies too sharp. But the book is a welcome and necessary contribution to a continuing debate about the early years of the Cistercian Order and its self-definition.

[5] Lekai, p 19, presents some of the newer results of recent research on the subject. See also Chrysogonus Waddell, 'The *Exordium Cistercii* and the *Summa Cartae Caritatis*: A Discussion Continued', *Cistercian Ideals and Reality*, ed. John R. Sommerfeldt, CS 60 (1978) 30–61.

[6] Even so outstanding a scholar as Jean-Berthold Mahn in his *L'Ordre cistercien et son gouvernement des origines au milieu du xiiie siècle* (Paris, 1951) p 60, accepted the *Exordium parvum*'s assertion that Bernard's entrance provided the manpower for new foundations.

experiment which transformed the cultural and religious face of Western Europe.

Bernard is sometimes seen as the 'real' founder of Cîteaux,[7] but in his actions he betrays his connection to the abbot of Cîteaux, Stephen Harding. Bernard's own monastery of Clairvaux became, after its foundation in 1115, the most dynamic house in the Order, but Bernard so far as we know remained submissive to the abbot of Cîteaux.[8] There may, however, have been a difference of approach between Bernard and Stephen. According to the most careful and thorough recent review of the evidence, Bernard asked for greater asceticism than Stephen had required.[9] He intended to live the life of perfection, and as his model he took the desert fathers of the fourth and fifth centuries. Bernard wanted to make his home in a spiritual desert, and for him the physical geography of the monasteries became a reflection of this image.

For Bernard, the very landscape expressed the content of this new spiritual regime. His was the first foundation to introduce what became the 'typically cistercian' practice of adapting local place names for monasteries and turning them into semi-equivalent latin forms in order to capture the spiritual quality of the place.[10] What had been called the Valley of Wormwood now became the Valley of Light: Clairvaux (*Claravallis*). Here God's light came down upon the monks and brought them illumination.[11] While Cîteaux was set on a marshy plain, Clairvaux and many of her daughters rejoiced

[7] As Lekai, p 34: 'The often voiced notion that he was the true founder of the Order is a pardonable exaggeration, but the fact that for centuries Cistercians were widely known as 'Bernardines' was not without justification.'

[8] The evidence, however, is very sparse. We have no letter from Bernard to Stephen Harding, and we know practically nothing about the participation of Bernard in the General Chapter.

[9] Auberger (note 4 above) speaks of 'de conceptions différents' (p 84). See especially his 'Synthèse générale' pp 317–24.

[10] See Marie-Anselme Dimier, *Clarté, Paix et Joie: Les beaux noms des monastères de Cîteaux en France*, La Clarté-Dieu 15 (Lyon 1944).

[11] Auberger, pp 127–33.

in being set in valleys where God was thought of as coming down from the heavens by embracing hills and bringing his light to the monks. The valley was also a place of humility. Its lowness betokened a receptivity to higher powers. The valley could be filled with what God offered it. Here could be heard the sound of trickling water coming down from the heights, another sign of the gifts that come from above and are transmitted downwards to men who must be willing to receive them.

At various points in Bernard's writings, we find indications of how he took spiritual truths from physical images. His friend William of Saint Thierry, who idealized Clairvaux in the first book of the *Vita Prima*, went even further in seeing the new monasteries as places of light and beauty.[12] Physical beauty went together with physical activity. The bustle of building and expansion confirmed the spiritual fertility of the place.

Together with waxing lyrical about the valley, Bernard and William praised men who had gone into the desert and made it bloom.[13] Ultimately going back to the Old Testament image of the chosen people taking over a new land and cultivating it, the cistercian image became so strong in the new literature as to create the impression that the monks really had come to a physical desert, or at least to a wild and uninhabited stretch of territory that no one else wanted. This transformation was seen in terms of the language of the Psalms, where God is said to be the one who 'changes thirsty ground into springs of water. There he settled the hungry and they build a city to dwell in. They sow fields and plant their vines: these yield crops for the harvest. He blessed them: they grow in numbers . . .' (Ps 106).

In the *Exordium Cistercii*, one of the earliest descriptions of this process, the compiler used a quotation from the Book of

---

[12] See VP I, ch. 33; PL 185:247–48. Also Auberger pp 129–30.

[13] For what follows, I am indebted to Auberger's section, 'Signification historique et mystique des choix cisterciens', pp 109–27.

Deuteronomy to describe what Cîteaux had been when the first monks arrived, 'a place of horror, a vast wilderness' (*locum tunc scilicet horroris et vastae solitudinis*, Dt 32:10).[14] In another account, the *Exordium Parvum*, it is claimed that the place 'was inhabited only by wild beasts, since it was at that time unusual for men to enter there because of the density of the woods and thorny thickets'.[15] As a note in the critical edition of the text points out, such language must be looked upon as literary rather than literal, for it is well known from the earliest documents that there was already a chapel on the site and that peasants were working the land.[16] There was no desert at early Cîteaux, even if the place was far from towns and sparsely populated.

The earliest cistercian chroniclers did not lie about their origins. They were merely remembering the beginning in terms so couched in biblical language that they left out the realistic details that we in our literal-mindedness would require for the sake of historical accuracy. But the myth of foundation is much more significant than any carping about what really was there. For the cistercian founders, it was important that in cutting down trees, clearing land, and putting up buildings, they were bringing their form of christian life to a countryside they conceived of as devoid of God's light.

Unlike our nineteenth-century romantic ancestors, our medieval forefathers did not look upon natural settings as being close to God. In the rugged and untamed landscape of their origins, they saw a desert that needed to be converted from the province of the devil (unfruitfulness, sterility, wildness) to the realm of the Lord (fruitfulness, fertility, orderliness). In making a valley of fruitfulness, the early Cistercians believed

---

[14] See Lackner's translation in Lekai, p 443.

[15] Lackner's translation in Lekai, pp 451–52.

[16] See the Bouton-Van Damme edition, p 61: '*accessui hominum . . . feris.* Figure littéraire qui devient inexacte si on l'entend au pied de la lettre, car d'après les documents contemporains il y avait sur place un modeste oratoire et quelques serfs qui travaillaient les champs.'

that they witnessed God's blessing on them as they brought God to their new surroundings.

For the Cistercians, as for many other christian reform groups in history, material fruits indicated spiritual blessings. Guided by the Holy Spirit, the monks made a new paradise in a place that had ostensibly been undesirable to anyone else. In the words of the *Exordium Parvum*:

> Arriving at this place the men of God found it all the more suitable for the religious life which they had already formulated in their minds and for which they had come here, the more despicable and inaccessible they realized it to be for seculars.[17]

But was the land really all that despicable and inaccessible? What of the peasants who were living on the land and had to be displaced?

Recent research on the Cistercians in England by the eminent agricultural historian R. A. Donkin reinforces the impression that the Cistercians often came to land already under the plow.[18] The role the monks used to be assigned in medieval histories as frontiersmen who cleared land and pushed back the wilderness has to be modified.[19] My favourite story to illustrate this point comes from the early days of the monastery of Øm (*Cara Insula*) in Denmark. The monks who wanted to found a house in the 1170s had been wandering for almost a decade from one unsuitable location to another. When they finally located a spot where they could

[17] Translated by Lackner in Lekai, p 452.

[18] *The Cistercians: Studies in the Geography of Medieval England and Wales*, Studies and Texts 38 (Toronto: Pontifical Institute of Mediaeval Studies, 1978), esp. the section 'Depopulation', pp 39–44. For 'donations' by peasants to new cistercian houses, see Constance Hoffman Berman's excellent *Medieval Agriculture, the Southern French Countryside, and the Early Cistercians: A Study of Forty-three Monasteries*, Transactions of the American Philosophical Society 76 (Philadelphia, 1986) pp 17–24.

[19] Even in C.H. Lawrence's invaluable and well-written, *Medieval Monasticism* (London and New York: Longman, 1984), we are told that 'the sites they (the Cistercians) accepted were generally on deserted and uncultivated lands, far removed from inhabited settlements' (p 148).

build canals between two lakes and thus take care of water supply and drainage, the monks had to convince resident local peasants to sell or exchange their holdings. One of the holdouts was a rich landowner named Api. One night he had a dream in which an angry woman, assumedly Saint Mary, appeared atop a church tower and threatened that if he did not sell, he would suffer terrible consequences. The next morning, when Api told his wife of the dream, she laughed at it; but he went right over to the monks and sold his land.[20]

The monks saw Api's decision as God's will, but we cannot help looking upon his dream as an expression of the social and psychological pressure these eager young monks could exercise on their contemporaries. We know from papal bulls concerning Esrum abbey, north of Copenhagen, that whole villages of peasants existing in the mid-twelfth century must have been cleared out and placed under the plow within a few years of the Cistercians' arrival in this idyllic valley along the edge of a lake.[21] Danish historians of a materialist bias, who otherwise had no great appreciation for monasticism, were still as late as the 1920s praising the monks for setting up 'agricultural academies' that made the best farming methods available to their neighbours.[22] The medieval monks would not have appreciated such praise, for they would have insisted that they were not interested in communicating their knowledge to seculars. The myth of the 1920s concerning clever monastic cultivators is but a development of the myth of the 1120s concerning dedicated monastic pioneers.

One of the problems with monastic history is that its most visible remnants in the historical record often express its most secondary concerns. Monks existed in order to pray,

[20] *Scriptores Minores Historiae Danicae Medii Aevi*, ed. M. Cl. Gertz, (Copenhagen, 1922 and 1970) p 176.

[21] See my 'Property and Politics at Esrum Abbey 1151–1251', *Mediaeval Scandinavia* 6 (1973) 122–150, esp. 133–34.

[22] Erik Arup, *Danmarks Historie* 1 (Copenhagen, 1926, reprinted 1961) p 224.

not to cultivate the land. The witness of their prayers is forever lost to us, except in little-known liturgical documents, while the land they used is still with us, often in places that to this day are isolated and relatively unspoiled. Here it is easy to imagine the monks arriving in places of solitude and transforming them into centres of purposeful activity.

Medieval Cistercians wanted to emphasize their origins, as well as their success. The transformation of the physical landscape, however, could well mean driving old settlers off the land, or at least convincing them to leave. Cistercian resourcefulness and material success created many resentments and much counter-propaganda, so that by the end of the twelfth century the Order was being attacked not only by articulate clerical pundits but also by popes. Alexander III, for example, pointed to the Order's original ideals and asked what had happened.[23]

In cistercian myths about founding houses in places of desolation and making wild valleys fruitful, I detect a fear of losing the material gains the monks had made. The monks realized that they could be challenged. Cistercians were not so much worried by peasants as by other monks, who in solid foundations dating back centuries might look on the Cistercians as upstarts and newcomers. Cîteaux, after all, had been founded as a breakaway house, and its new abbot had been sent back to Molesme by the pope himself. Robert remained a source of embarrassment to the Cistercians until his canonization in 1222. After that time, chroniclers could call him the 'first abbot of Cîteaux', a status that had been denied him in the *Exordium Magnum Cisterciense* dating from the early years of the thirteenth century.[24]

The trauma of Robert's departure from Molesme and his abandonment of Cîteaux were still much in evidence when Conrad of Eberbach composed the *Exordium Magnum*. He

[23] Jean Leclercq, 'Passage supprimé dans une épître d'Alexandre III', *Revue Bénédictine* 62 (1952) 149–51.

[24] EM pp 10–11.

referred to attacks on the legitimacy of the Order, especially by german Benedictines.[25] Insisting on the holiness of Cîteaux's founders, Conrad added that recent abbots, such as those he had experienced at Clairvaux in the 1170s and 1180s, had maintained the original standard. Conrad saw the foundation of Cîteaux and its growth as part of an unfolding history of christian monasticism which he traced back to Christ and his apostles. He had a sense of historical development. Without denying Cluny's contribution to the monastic order, he saw Cîteaux and especially Clairvaux as embodiments of the true original spirit of monastic life. For Conrad the various foundation myths of Cîteaux were necessary to legitimize the historical success of the Order.

The *Exordium Magnum Cisterciense* is but one, even if the most complete and detailed, of a succession of narratives and documents composed for the purpose of asserting the legitimacy of the cistercian foundation. The *Carta Caritatis Posterior* from the later twelfth century is another such formulation.[26] If we look approvingly at its title and expect to find in it an expression of the affectionate bonds that characterized twelfth-century Cistercians, we will be disappointed. The writer says he wanted to make clear 'by what bond, in what way, and most importantly by what charity' ⟨*caritate*⟩ the monks were 'joined together in spirit.' The decree was called a Charter of Charity, not because it told of brotherly love but because it laid out clear rules and a consistent administration. Within this framework, the monks believed, love among their houses would prevail. In the cistercian view, love and law had to meet and marry if the early spirit of the foundation were to be maintained.

There is nothing sentimental here. Indeed the danger is not emotionalism but legalism. The Cistercians were so

---

[25] EM I.10, p 61. See my 'Structure and Consciousness in the *Exordium Magnum Cisterciense*: The Clairvaux Cistercians after Bernard', *Cahiers de l'Institut du Moyen Age Grec et Latin* 30 (1979) 33–90, esp. 40–41.

[26] Bouton and Van Damme, pp 132–42. Translated by Lackner in Lekai, pp 461–66.

concerned with legitimizing their origins and maintaining a viable administrative structure that they chose to push affective bonds among monks into the background. To a certain extent, this is what seems to have happened in the decades after Bernard's death. His leadership had made the Order concentrate on affectivity as a matter of course, a foundation for spiritual growth within monastic life. But his successors became so caught up in questions of property and privileges that the Order lost its early direction.

Yet Cîteaux had to maintain its uniqueness to justify its origins. Instead of affective bonds, the leaders of the Order turned to the maintenance of asceticism as a guarantee of quality. Appeals for the observance of ascetic practices found in the statutes of the Order at the end of the twelfth century express the fear of abbots that if they relax discipline, they would lose an essential element that made them cistercian and not benedictine.[27] In what can be called a flowering of historical narrative by Cistercians at the end of the twelfth and the beginning of the thirteenth centuries, several houses reviewed the evidence for their foundations to show that everything had been done properly.[28] This conscious and careful return to the past was intended for both internal and external use. The secular church had to be shown that the cistercian foundation, as the danish *Exordium Carae Insulae* put it, was legitimate: '. . . if by chance at some time any person, lay or clerical, should try to disturb this ⟨monastery⟩ or plunder its possessions, once the veracity of its origins and devoutness of its founders are known, they will abandon the evil work begun by them and love and protect ⟨the monastery⟩. . . '.[29]

[27] See Robert D. Taylor-Vaisey, 'The First Century of Cistercian Legislation: Some Preliminary Investigation', *Cîteaux* 27 (1976) 203–18, and especially the tables 219–25, as for the 1190s, 220–21.

[28] As was the case at Fountains Abbey in Yorkshire. See L. G. D. Baker, 'The Genesis of English Cistercian Chronicles. The Foundation History of Fountains Abbey', AC 25 (1969) 14–41.

[29] *Scriptores Minores Historiae Danicae* II, p 158: '. . . si forte aliquando per-

At the same time as the outside world had to be encouraged and warned to show respect to the cistercian foundation, a new generation of cistercian monks had to be made aware of who they were and whence they came. The memory of holy founders and the legal assurances behind the foundation had to ensure that the spirit of monastic life would be maintained. By the end of the twelfth century abbots in Denmark, for example, were no longer foreigners but were native Danes and so did not have family links back to the members of french houses.[30] This new distance meant that traditions concerning origins became more important than ever in monasteries on the fringes of Europe, from Fountains in Yorkshire to Øm in Denmark.

The myth of cistercian arrival in a desert place inhabited by wild animals frequently had little to do with physical realities but was useful in heroizing founders and in providing an ideal for maintaining ascetic standards. This description also gave monks a legitimate excuse for having left existing foundations in order to become Cistercians. It exonerated them of the charge that they had abrogated all-important benedictine *stabilitas*. The monks had gone to a stricter life and so justified themselves even in the narrowest canonical terms. Bernard himself had fought hard for the right of Cluniacs to become Cistercians, while he opposed with every means at his disposal the right of Cistercians to become Cluniacs.[31]

Bernard at every turn did his best to reassure his monks that they were something special, even unique, in the history of the monastic order. They were living up to the Rule of Saint Benedict in the most literal way possible and so provided an ever-present challenge to the monasteries that chose to make compromises for human frailty. Bernard did not want

---

sona aliqua secularis seu ecclesiastica illud perturbare et possessiones eius diripere temptaverit, cognita veritate fundationis et reverentia fundatorum ab incepto malo opere quiescat et illud diligat atque tueatur. . . .'

[30] See my *Cistercians in Denmark*, CS 35 (1982) 106–7.

[31] As in Bernard's famed letter to his nephew Robert (SBOp 7:1–11), traditionally placed first in his letter collection (trans. James pp 1–10).

everyone to join his monastery or his Order, but he certainly wanted to attract the brightest and best young men of his day.

This emphasis on a spiritual elite has been one strand in cistercian monasticism. Another has been a broad acceptance of human differences and a willingness to compromise. This gentler approach, steeped in conviction yet more flexible than Bernard's, is perhaps linked to the initial reform of Stephen Harding before Bernard got to Cîteaux. The Rule of Saint Benedict had been the standard and measure of this reform, while the return to the desert, the emphasis on solitude and apartness from the world, have been secondary.

Already in its first years the Cistercian Order showed a division between those who wanted a 'common observance' and those who insisted on a stricter one. In the course of cistercian history Bernard has been appropriated to both sides, and today his sayings and ideas are more important than ever in the ongoing debate about the content of monastic life and the renewal of the Cistercian Order.

A central problem for Cistercians since the death of Saint Bernard has been to convince themselves and the world that new generations of monks could maintain their original ascetic standard in the wilderness. This very austerity, with its combination of hard work and a simple life, led quickly to the creation of cistercian valleys of fruitfulness. The medieval Cistercians were determined to point to their fruitfulness as evidence of the rightness of their original foundation. Their modern successors can be tempted to do the same. The interpretation of foundation myths has thus been an essential part of the cistercian experience ever since the first years of the twelfth century, a process that continues to this day.

An American Myth: The City on the Hill

Like twelfth-century Cistercians, seventeenth-century Americans wanted to think that they had come to a wilderness. They enjoyed writing about their land as having been virgin and untouched. They described how they transformed the face of the land and made it inhabitable and fruitful. Today it is clear what this colonization of the Americas actually meant: the gradual takeover and ruination of forests and plains that for centuries had been living space and hunting ground for the Indians. Just as Cistercians cleared off peasants, apparently without worrying about what happened to these people, so too early american settlers in one way or another cleared out Indians. The methods were not always cruel or selfish, but the result was the near-annihilation of the first Americans and a termination of their unimpeded way of life. Before the new Americans even got to their chosen land, they had to legitimize their choice of a new place to live. Those who were not poor and who had enjoyed some social position could find it painful to justify the decision to leave behind the world that had made them. This difficult choice needed a defence that would assuage individual consciences and impress a sceptical world.

One of the founders of Massachusetts, John Winthrop, spent 1629 making his decision.[32] He had built up a good law practice at the Inns of Court in London. He came from a newly-established gentry family with lands in Suffolk and could look forward to a comfortable and relatively leisured existence. But Winthrop felt hindered in practising the type of Protestantism to which he clung, and he was convinced that the royal court was becoming all too 'popish' in its ways. So he and like-minded 'puritans' decided to emigrate to a new England in America and there to build a community that would embody their religious ideals.

This story of puritan settlement has been told so many times that it has become embedded deep within the mythic consciousness of almost every American. Here it is appropriate to consider the myth in its own language, to see how

---

[32] Darrett B. Rutman, *John Winthrop's Decision for America: 1629* (Philadelphia: J.B. Lippincott Co., 1975). I am also indebted to Edmund Morgan, *The Puritan Dilemma. The Story of John Winthrop* (Boston: Little, Brown and Co., 1958).

Winthrop could justify leaving behind, at least temporarily, wife and children, in order to take risks in what he thought of as a wilderness. To defend his choice, he wrote in 1629 what we can call the *Carta Caritatis* of the Puritans, *A Modell of Christian Charity*.[33] Here Winthrop described in simple language how the new community would be blessed by God because it would recreate the intimacy and love found in the first christian community described in the Acts of the Apostles (4:32):

> . . .we must entertain each other in brotherly affection. We must be willing to abridge ourselves of our super-fluities, for the supply of others' necessities. We must uphold a familiar commerce together in all meekness, gentleness, patience and liberality. We must delight in each other, make others' conditions our own, rejoice together, mourn together, labour and suffer together, always having before our eyes our commission and community in the work, our community as members of the same body.

Winthrop was not a starry-eyed idealist who could consider only the potential beauties of such a community. He saw that the experiment could fail. In starting such a 'plantation', the settlers risked becoming contemptible in the eyes of others if they did not live up to their plans. When Winthrop used the phrase 'a city upon a hill', he, as a good biblical scholar, was remembering that the phrase is found in the Sermon on the Mount next to a warning that like the salt of the earth, we are blessed but also endangered (Mt 5:13–14). If we lose our strength, then who will salt us? If the city fails, then all will show their scorn. As Winthrop warned, blessings could easily be turned into curses:

> . . .The Lord will be our God and delight to dwell among us, as his own people, and will command a blessing upon us in all our ways, so that we shall see much

[33] Contained in Rutman, pp 100–101. I have modernized the spelling.

more of his wisdom, power, goodness and truth than formerly we have been acquainted with...that men shall say of succeeding plantations: the Lord make it like that of New England, for we must consider that *we shall be as a city upon a hill*, the eyes of all people are upon us, so that if we shall deal falsely with our God in this work we have undertaken and so cause him to withdraw his present help from us, we shall be made a story and a by-word through the world. We shall open the mouths of enemies to speak evil of the ways of God and all professors for God's sake. We shall shame the faces of many of God's worthy servants, and cause their prayers to be turned into curses upon us till we be consumed out of the good land whether we are going.

Puritan Massachusetts would remind itself regularly of its origins, mission, and status. Its first settlers and leaders felt that because they had broken away from the *stabilitas* of life in England, they had to justify their choice by showing the fruits of their new existence. Their charter of love was a challenge not only to their contemporaries but also to themselves and their successors. One false move and they would be the laughing stock of their world.

The image of the city on the hill has lived on in american history far beyond the Puritans. Especially since the Second World War, when the United States became the world's most powerful nation in economic and military terms, its leaders have tried to legitimize this power by looking upon themselves as dispensers of a political and social covenant that could provide a model for all nations. I will not touch here upon the rightness or wrongness of this model, but only point out that in the 1980s, after a period when Americans were in doubt about their place in the world, the myth of America as the city upon the hill of the world had a big comeback. In many respects it was Ronald Reagan and his one-man television revolution that brought this idea out of political mothballs. He gave middle-class Americans a sense that they had little to feel guilty about and much in which they could rejoice.

When Ronald Reagan, leaving office in early 1989, made his last television speech, he used the image of the city on a hill and tried to define it. Even though we have to acknowledge that modern political leaders, like medieval kings, rarely compose the documents attributed to them, there is no doubt that this speech, perhaps more than any other, sums up the Reagan message. He spoke, as it were, intimately and personally, concerning his musings as he looked out the upstairs window of the White House across the mall to the Washington Monument:

> The past few days when I've been at the window upstairs, I've thought a bit of the shining 'city upon a hill'. The phrase comes from John Winthrop, who wrote it to describe the America he imagined. What he imagined was important, because he was an early Pilgrim, an early 'Freedom Man'. He journeyed here on what today we'd call a little wooden boat; and like the other pilgrims, he was looking for a home that would be free.

> I've spoken of the shining city all my political life, but I don't know if I ever quite communicated what I saw when I said it. But in my mind, it was a tall proud city built on rocks stronger than oceans, wind-swept, God-blessed, and teeming with people of all kinds living in harmony and peace—a city with free ports that hummed with commerce and creativity, and if there had to be city walls, the walls had doors, and *the doors were open to anyone with the will and the heart to get here.*

> And how stands the city, on this winter night? More prosperous,more secure and happier than it was eight years ago. But more than that: after two hundred years, two centuries, she still stands strong and true on the granite ridge, and her glow has held steady no matter what storm.

> And she's still a beacon, still a magnet for all who must have freedom, for all the Pilgrims from all the lost

places who are hurtling through the darkness, toward home.[34]

Reagan's words are hard to reconcile with the policy of his administration in making sure that political refugees from El Salvador and Guatemala were not allowed to become modern pilgrims to a new home in America. But if we look at the phrase 'city on a hill' in an historical context, we will notice that his use of the image does not contain the undertone of criticism and danger found in John Winthrop's original statement of the concept. While Winthrop was afraid that a failure to live up to the image would create shame and grief, Reagan left the challenge out of the image. He chose instead to praise himself and his fellow Americans for a city that was prosperous, secure, and still standing strong and true.

A close comparison of Reagan's words with Winthrop's has increased my respect for John Winthrop. He honestly faced the fear that he might fail, while Reagan was self-congratulatory. One has only to return to the original passage in Matthew to realize that Reagan managed in his political magic to defuse an image which kept Winthrop awake sweating in the night: 'You are the salt of the earth. If the salt loses its savour, how shall it be salted? It is then good for nothing but to be cast out and to be trodden under foot by men. You are the light of the world. A city that is set on a hill cannot be hidden.'

The Use and Abuse of History

The Cistercians' self-defence in order partly to obscure the facts of their first years (the breakaway from Molesme and their clearing out of peasants) seems almost innocent in comparison to some of the recent events in american history. For both Cistercians and Americans, however, changed circumstances brought changing views of themselves and their

---

[34] The text of Ronald Reagan's Farewell Address of 11 January 1989 is taken from *The New York Times*, 12 January 1989. Italics are mine.

history. In the cistercian case there was an ongoing attempt in the period from about 1150 to 1250 to defend the legitimacy of their foundation and to remind contemporary monks of what they had to live up to. In this sense every cistercian foundation account, even if it distorted historical realities, still tried to assert basic truths about the identity of the Order. Here the memory of Bernard provided a constant reminder of involvement in the affairs of the church and the world, but also a certain distance from everything except the life of the monastery. In the bernardian interpretation, as given most completely in the *Exordium Magnum Cisterciense*, the valley of fruitfulness had always to remain apart from the rest of the world so that the monks could pursue their community and contemplative life.

The cistercian myth of foundation contains within it a certain integrity, arising from a desire to secure a simple life close to God in the life of the monastery. Here any actual differences between Stephen Harding's and Bernard's views are secondary compared to the fact that the two great abbots managed to live together and to form one Order which met regularly to discuss ideals and practices. In the very cistercian anxiousness about understanding the purposes and intentions of the founders, a concern that continues to this day, I find myth being used to strengthen the life of the individual and of the community.

I do not see the same integrity in the american experience. Here myth in the 1980s became the object of television manipulation and media propaganda that had no interest in any genuine return to early fundamental american values. However much Ronald Reagan may have believed in his own make-believe universe of old-fashioned patriotism, he enabled millions of Americans to deny the social ills of their country and its contribution to tensions in the world.

As an American who chose to leave his country because of the trauma of Vietnam and its aftermath, I have no right to preach to my former countrymen. As a citizen now of a country which prides itself on its international role yet actually mistreats many of the refugees who come to it for protection, I have no illusions about any nation in terms of the myths it creates about itself—whether for domestic or external consumption. Every people seems to need to believe in its own basic goodness, and such a desire enables one government after another to deceive its citizens.

Perhaps this development only shows that our situation on the threshold of a new millennium is much more desperate than it was in the twelfth century, for our most venerable myths have been devalued into empty propaganda. And yet some aspects of the cistercian experience are still parallel with our own. The monks felt that they were God's chosen people and so had the right to disregard or remove the obstacles in their way. When we today watch soldiers, subsidized by american funds, shooting at rock-throwing palestinian youths or when we remember the horrors of american massacres of civilians in Vietnam, we can recall Cistercians and their determination to impose their valleys of fruitfulness.

In such cases we come up against stories that justify behaviour which we may consider unjustifiable. Myths emerge in both medieval and modern societies as powerful, even dangerous, stories that exaggerate some details in order to obscure or ignore others. It is because of the role and power of myths in our lives that it is as important today as ever to deal with history and to dig back into past experience.

A Myth for One World

When Robert and his friends set out from Molesme, they could look upon themselves as an elite and isolated band of men. Their myth of foundation in the wilderness was essential for themselves. Thanks to Bernard and his friends, however, the Cistercians became an order stretching 'from sea to sea' and in the vanguard of the reform of the church as a whole. Within a few decades, the Cistercians had to relate their myth to the rest of the church: to monks and nuns of more traditional observance, to secular clerics, and to people in the world. The Cistercians came to see themselves as an integral part of christian community. Conrad of Eberbach in the early thirteenth century provided a historical framework for this vision in the *Exordium Magnum Cisterciense*. Content and context in the cistercian myth grew as the order grew.

I do not see any parallel growth of the myth of the city on the hill from John Winthrop to Ronald Reagan. In fact I see a distortion of the original puritan myth of America in all its reverence and humility into a defence of selfishness and self-satisfaction. The myth of the city on the hill must now either be discarded or revised. In the light of recent historical events, as well as in the global threat to the environment, the only myth in which I can believe is that of the earth as a pilgrim, a wanderer in a mostly empty universe. Here we have sweetness and light, but also the possibility of instant self-destruction—or the gradual ruination of the environment in which our offspring come to live.

We are a city on the hill in the universe. We are a valley of fruitfulness. Because we now realize that our earth and its human race are small and fragile, we have to admit that no nation, no people, no creed or ideology can any longer afford to assert its superiority. No one person or nation is intrinsically better than any other. We are all children of God who need each other and must make a new charter of charity that does not leave out segments of humanity. We are citizens of the one and only place we have got to live in, the earth, in our pilgrimage through time.

What would Bernard have said to such a vision? It is difficult to say, for his vocabulary and his myths were very different from our own. I can only think of his childhood vision of the Christ child being born again into the world.[35]

---

[35] VP I.4; PL 185:229: 'Apparuit ei quasi iterum ante oculos suos nascens ex utero matris Virginis verbum infans, speciosus forma prae filiis hominum . . .'

This vision of an approachable God-with-us emphasizes the fragility of human life and our need for more than ourselves. Bernard's successors in cistercian houses all over the world today are aware of his vision of a human, accessible Jesus. Monks and nuns in their own quiet ways share at the same time in the modern vision of one world for us all. Their prayers and community continue a life important for Bernard. Monastic networks of administration, dialogue and friendship make the Cistercians one of the few extended families in modern world society that functions on the basis not of economic interests but within a pact of charity. Here as in other families where love finds structure, the myth of the valley of fruitfulness lives on and renews itself in a world seeking a usable past and a viable future.

Index

NOTE. *Names from before 1500 are indicated by first names first, as with Peter Abelard. This index covers only names in the text, not in the footnotes or bibliographical notes.*

CISTERCIAN PUBLICATIONS INC.
Kalamazoo, Michigan

TITLES LISTING

CISTERCIAN TEXTS

THE WORKS OF BERNARD OF CLAIRVAUX

Apologia to Abbot William
Five Books on Consideration: Advice to a Pope
Grace and Free Choice
Homilies in Praise of the Blessed Virgin Mary
The Life and Death of Saint Malachy the Irishman
Parables
Sermons on the Song of Songs I-IV
Steps of Humility and Pride

THE WORKS OF WILLIAM OF SAINT THIERRY

The Enigma of Faith
Exposition on the Epistle to the Romans
The Golden Epistle
The Mirror of Faith
The Nature and Dignity of Love

THE WORKS OF AELRED OF RIEVAULX

Dialogue on the Soul
The Mirror of Charity
Spiritual Friendship
Treatises I: On Jesus at the Age of Twelve, Rule for a Recluse, The Pastoral Prayer

THE WORKS OF JOHN OF FORD

Sermons on the Final Verses of the Song of Songs I-VII

THE WORKS OF GILBERT OF HOYLAND

Sermons on the Songs of Songs I, II, III
Treatises, Sermons and Epistles

OTHER EARLY CISTERCIAN WRITERS

The Letters of Adam of Perseigne I
Baldwin of Ford: Spiritual Tractates
Guerric of Igny: Liturgical Sermons I-II
Idung of Prüfening: Cistercians and Cluniacs: The Case for Citeaux
Isaac of Stella: Sermons on the Christian Year
Serlo of Wilton & Serlo of Savigny
Stephen of Lexington: Letters from Ireland
Stephen of Sawley: Treatises

MONASTIC TEXTS

EASTERN CHRISTIAN TRADITION

Besa: The Life of Shenoute
Cyril of Scythopolis: Lives of the Monks of Palestine
Dorotheos of Gaza: Discourses
Evagrius Ponticus: Praktikos and Chapters on Prayer
The Harlots of the Desert
Iosif Volotsky: Monastic Rule
The Lives of the Desert Fathers
Menas of Nikiou: Isaac of Alexandra & St Macrobius
Pachomian Koinonia I-III
The Sayings of the Desert Fathers
Spiritual Direction in the Early Christian East (I. Hausherr)
The Syriac Fathers on Prayer and the Spiritual Life

WESTERN CHRISTIAN TRADITION

Anselm of Canterbury: Letters I-[III]
Bede: Commentary on the even Catholic Epistles
Bede: Commentary on Acts
Bede: Gospel Homilies
Gregory the Great: Forty Gospel Homilies
Guigo II the Carthusian: Ladder of Monks and Twelve Meditations
Peter of Celle: Selected Works
The Letters of Armand-Jean de Rance I-II
The Rule of the Master

CHRISTIAN SPIRITUALITY

Abba: Guides to Wholeness and Holiness East and West
Athirst for God: Spiritual Desire in Bernard of Clairvaux's Sermons on the Song of Songs (M. Casey)
Cistercian Way (A. Louf)
Fathers Talking (A. Squire)
Friendship and Community (B. McGuire)
From Cloister to Classroom
Herald of Unity: The Life of Maria Gabrielle Sagheddu (M. Driscoll)
Life of St Mary Magdalene... (D. Mycoff)
Rancé and the Trappist Legacy (A.J. Krailsheimer)
Roots of the Modern Christian Tradition
Russian Mystics (S. Bolshakoff)
Spirituality of Western Christendom
Spirituality of the Christian East (T. Spidlék)

MONASTIC STUDIES

Community and Abbot in the Rule of St Benedict I-II (Adalbert De Vogüé)
Consider Your Call: A Theology of the Monastic Life (Daniel Rees et al.)
The Finances of the Cistercian Order in the Fourteenth Century (Peter King)

Fountains Abbey and Its Benefactors
(Joan Wardrop)
The Hermit Monks of Grandmont
(Carole A. Hutchison)
In the Unity of the Holy Spirit
(Sighard Kleiner)
Monastic Practices (Charles Cummings)
The Occuptation of Celtic Sites in Ireland by
the Canons Regular of St Augustine and the
Cistercians (Geraldine Carville)
The Rule of St Benedict: A Doctrinal and
Spiritual Commentary (Adalbert de Vogüé)
The Rule of St Benedict (Br. Pinocchio)
St Hugh of Lincoln (D. H. Farmer)
Serving God First (Sighard Kleiner)

CISTERCIAN STUDIES

A Second Look at Saint Bernard (Jean Leclercq)
Bernard of Clairvaux and the Cistercian
Spirit (Jean Leclercq)
Bernard of Clairvaux: Studies Presented to
Dom Jean Leclercq
Christ the Way: The Christology of Guerric
of Igny (John Morson)
Cistercian Sign Language
The Cistercian Spirit
The Cistercians in Denmark (Brian McGuire)
Eleventh-century Background of Citeaux
(Bede K. Lackner)
The Golden Chain: Theological Anthropology of
Isaac of Stella (Bernard McGinn)
Image and Likeness: The Augustinian
Spirituality of William of St Thierry   (David
N. Bell)
The Mystical Theology of St Bernard
(Étienne Gilson)
Nicholas Cotheret's Annals of Citeaux
(Louis J. Lekai)
William, Abbot of St Thierry
Women and St Bernard of Clairvaux
(Jean Leclercq)

MEDIEVAL RELIGIOUS WOMEN

Distant Echoes (Shank-Nichols)
Gertrud the Great of Helfta: Spiritual Exercises
(Gertrud J. Lewis-Jack Lewis)
Peace Weavers (Nichols-Shank)

STUDIES IN CISTERCIAN ART AND ARCHITECTURE
Meredith Parsons Lillich, editor

Studies I, II, III now available
Studies IV scheduled for 1991

THOMAS MERTON

The Climate of Monastic Prayer (T. Merton)
The Legacy of Thomas Merton (Patrick Hart)
The Message of Thomas Merton (Patrick Hart)
Solitude in the Writings of Thomas Merton
(Richard Cashen)
Thomas Merton Monk (Patrick Hart)
Thomas Merton Monk and Artist
(Victor Kramer)
Thomas Merton on St Bernard
Toward an Integrated Humanity
(M.Basil Pennington et al.)

CISTERCIAN LITURGICAL DOCUMENTS SERIES
Chrysogonus Waddell, ocso, editor

Cistercian Hymnal: Text & Commentary
(2 volumes)
Hymn Collection of the Abbey of the Paraclete
Molesme Summer-Season Breviary
(4 volumes)
Institutiones nostrae: The Paraclete Statutes
Old French Ordinary and Breviary of the
Abbey of the Paraclete: Text and
Commentary (5 volumes)

STUDIA PATRISTICA

*Papers of the 1983 Oxford Patristics Conference
Edited by Elizabeth A. Livingstone*

XVIII/1 Historica-Gnostica-Biblica
XVIII/2 Critica-Classica-Ascetica-Liturgica
XVIII/3 Second Century-Clement & Origen-
Cappodician Fathers
XVIII/4 *available from Peeters, Leuven*

TEXTS AND STUDIES
IN THE
MONASTIC TRADITION

*North American customers may order these books
through booksellers or directly from the warehouse:*

Cistercian Publications
St Joseph's Abbey
Spencer, Massachusetts 01562
(508) 885-7011

*Editorial queries and advance book information
should be directed to the Editorial Offices:*

Cistercian Publications
Institute of Cistercian Studies
Western Michigan University
Kalamazoo, Michigan 49008
(616) 387-5090

*A complete catalogue of texts in translation and
studies on early, medieval, and modern monasticism
is available at no cost from Cistercian Publications.*

DATE DUE

JAN 05 1995			
SEP 14			